GOD'S

GLORY

MY STORY

BRIAN KOTLER

Hardcover ISBN: 979-8-9887091-0-7
Paperback ISBN: 979-8-9887091-1-4
eBook ISBN: 979-8-9887091-2-1
Audiobook ISBN: 979-8-9887091-3-8

Library of Congress Control Number: 2024916026

Special First Edition April 2025

Published in Hagerstown, Maryland USA, Brian Kotler, LLC

www.briankotler.com

Thank God

CONTENTS

Sen. Tillis,

Two decades ago, North Carolina fixed a ton of judicial corruption then broke it. Please help repair it there and across the U.S. by spreading word of this book. Thank you.

1

TWO EMPTY BEDROOMS

T WO EMPTY BEDROOMS ARE WAITING for my kids to come back. Lucy's bed, chest and nightstand are still there, matching mahogany-stained pine passed along from my childhood. But they sit empty, like everywhere else in her room.

Colored pencils and anime drawings that she stored in her nightstand vanished. Lucy's *Fairy Tail* anime books, wall hanging, and Funko Pop! figurines disappeared. Her *This is Pusheen* cat book that sat atop her dresser is long gone, along with the dresser itself. So is her smiley face poster and Lalaloopsy doll collection.

The desk we assembled together was thrown away. So was the rug that she accidentally stained making slime with her friend. Her wooden jewelry box with rotating necklace holder and drawers for her earrings and hair clips is gone, as is everything that was inside it.

The wall my daughter and I painted pink melted behind a fresh coat of lifeless beige.

One of the boys' beds remains. So does their desk, a mass-produced black workspace my daughter also helped build. But their *Disney Infinity* and *Skylanders* figures and video games no longer exist here. Ethan and Colin's Beyblades battle-spinner tops and arenas are lost. All their games, clothing, and wall decorations, like my daughter's, are missing.

Scuff marks on the wall where Colin and Ethan played ball have retreated behind the same barren color that destroyed my daughter's room.

It's been seven years since they've been here. Few traces of them survive, but their spirits live within if I play pretend well enough.

Two of them still don't know why they no longer live here. There's no reason we should've stopped playing their favorite Jumping Pillow Game.

Ethan, my oldest son and the most athletic, was its official founder. While all three kids bounced on the bed, they had to either jump, duck, or avoid falling daddy. I said, "Jump!" as I swung the pillow low, "Duck!" as the pillow went high, and "Falling daddy!" as I turned around, held the pillow behind me and fell backwards. Their riled-up laughter and delight were infectious. I miss it.

The screechy sounds of kids learning to play violin, trumpet, and bells echoed throughout the hall as they practiced for the school band. They loved watching the milkshake maker turn a solid block of ice into a smooth, frosty treat. And they latched onto the craze that found Pokémon hiding in the most absurd places around town.

We traveled to music concerts, festivals, and amusement parks. At Hersheypark, as feint chocolate scents wafted through the trees, we rode the train and gondola over the river again and again.

Six Flags was closer to home. With a season pass, Colin, my youngest, loved going on his favorite ride with me. The Dragon Wing was a giant swing that cranked us 150 feet high in the air. Harnessed flat on our bellies as we dangled in mid-air, it plunged with the pull of a ripcord toward the ground like a pendulum. Lucy, my second-born, enjoyed seeing him soar through the air like a superhero, afraid to try it herself.

After enough park visits, she was game to give it a go. Strapped in, the crane hoisted us high above a waving grandpa. During our ascent, I said, "Colin, I know you like pulling the cord. But we'll let Lucy do it if she wants."

"I don't know, dad," she said through giggling fright.

We reached the top and heard the signal.

"Lucy, the cord's right there. If you don't want to pull it, you don't—" Wind blasted our faces before I finished my sentence. Side-splitting laughter ensued as we raced back and forth through the air, our arms stretched forward like humans in flight. When the ride ended, we got back on and Lucy pulled the cord again. That time, I was ready.

The kids always loved swings, but our favorite trip entailed riding granite slides in New York's Central Park with their New Jersey cousins. That weekend, they gave Colin a fuzzy purple-and-blue backpack for his stuffed caterpillar, whom he chauffeured all around the city.

The kids loved *YouTube*, and Lucy became a popular YouTuber. When she was 11, she may have had one friend following her one video when she called me into her room.

"Dad, look at my *YouTube* account. I have 40 followers!" She clicked refresh. "50 followers!" For ten minutes, we watched her subscriber count skyrocket.

"Did you post a new video?"

"No," she said as her following surpassed 200.

"How'd you get all the subscribers?"

"I bought them."

"How much did you pay?"

"A couple dollars."

"Are they real people?"

"I don't know," she said as she refreshed and saw the number jump to 350. "Isn't it great?"

Her following exceeded 500 by night's end. The next day, I asked how her channel was doing.

"I still have 550 subscribers."

One day after that, we watched them all evaporate. Her cheery, "Look what I did," smile turned into her classic, "Oh well, that didn't work," frown.

That summer, Ethan and I toured Philadelphia before attending a U.S.A. soccer game. For dinner, we stopped for Philly cheesesteaks.

"Dad, let's try them both," he said, as inviting lines down the sidewalks manifested from two caddy-corner, rival cheesesteak joints that each consider themselves the best in the country. So, we did. Then we decided which was better.

The Verdict: They're both sending us straight through hell because Jews aren't supposed to mix meat and milk.

All three kids played plenty of soccer in Maryland, our home state. Hagerstown's Fairgrounds Park, replete with a dog park, skate park, BMX track, and softball fields, hosts thousands each year for our city's Fourth of July fireworks. And it holds six soccer fields on which my kids played for five seasons.

Each year had spring and fall seasons, which they played in from 2014-16. I was extremely lucky to coach over ten of their teams. They relished arriving early to set up the field and announce the post-game snack menu as they greeted teammates one by one.

When the kids were younger, we hiked across a field to the gymnastics center visible from the front door of our old Frederick home. The open gym was most fun because they could do a bit of everything. The balance beam, jumping pit, and giant trampoline were their favorites. A rope dangled from the ceiling 20 feet high. Ethan, 14 when I lost custody in 2017 but nine at the time, was quick scaling to the top to ring that bell. Sometimes I could play with them. The most precious video I have is their gymnastics warmup. Colin, at just four years old, followed the stretching routine's directions best.

God blessed me with three very healthy, very smart children. They excelled in magnet schools and were often on the honor roll.

Ethan paved the magnet path, but after moving to his mom full-time, he began failing classes and barely graduated on time. He didn't attend his high school graduation ceremony.

Lucy, who treasured dress shopping for our annual Daddy Daughter Dance, averaged an 87 in her Arts and Academic Excellence program in 2017, our last year together. She was 12 years old.

The very next year, after the court flattened our relationship, she failed three of her six classes. She failed multiple subjects every year since and scraped by to graduate high school in 2023.

Then there's Colin, whose beaming smile surpassed his intelligence. Ethan tested 99th percentile in math, Lucy scored 99th percentile in reading, and Colin was 99th in both.

One of Maryland's exams focuses on reading comprehension. Colin took it in 8th grade. An advanced 8th grader scores 1190 and an advanced 12th grader scores 1390. He scored 1550!

But the kid failed five of his seven classes in 2023 during his last quarter as a high school freshman and had to attend summer school. He had course grades as low as 0, 3, and 12. His zero was in Parent/Family Dynamics. Because of the way the court's treated him and his family, I'd expect nothing more.

Colin was only ten when he lost his daddy and best friend. And he doesn't really smile anymore.

Where are the adults?

My kids are now two of them. Ethan's 22 and Lucy just turned 20. Colin becomes 18 this October.

My ex-wife, a former Miss Tiny Tot and later Mrs. Tidy Not, and I tied the knot in 2002, when I was 24 and she was 22. We divorced in 2009 after almost seven years of marriage, and though there were issues, things went well enough. Because they've only known divorce, the kids were accustomed to sharing equal time in our two homes when a 2016 incident caused custody to be reevaluated, opening a case that sat dormant for years.

When examining child custody cases, the court appoints a lawyer to represent the children. Courts label this person differently in each state. Many states call these lawyers Attorney for the Child, Amicus Attorney, Minor's Counsel, or Guardian ad Litem. In Maryland, they are called Best Interest Attorney (BIA). As the title suggests, the BIA is supposed to act for the sake of the kids' "best interest".

At the start of the case, my ex-wife's counsel asked for a specific BIA, and the court obliged. Unfortunately, the judge rejected my lawyer's request. That's the moment I lost my case.

The BIA sided with my ex-wife's lawyer about everything. She had a clear motive—to help the guy who provided the $70,000 job. The BIA wanted the kids with his client, my ex-wife, no matter the cost to the children. Because I challenged the BIA's decisions and questioned her ethics, she hated me.

As a result, this seasoned professional forced 14-year-old Ethan to lie in court to protect herself. It netted my ex-wife full custody in November 2017 and stuck me with one hourlong supervised visit per week. Sadly, not much has changed in the seven years since.

Meanwhile, my mom and dad, two wonderful people with whom the kids and I lived since 2012, knew the court wronged me and my children. They understood there were dozens of witnesses to back me, and they read letters from some. But the moment I sent my story and evidence to The Washington Post a month after losing custody, they thought I was nuts.

My parents, a couple of New Yorkers transplanted to Maryland with Alabama beliefs, rely on different news sources than me. When mine was investigating on behalf of me and my kids in the days that followed, theirs persuaded them I was mentally ill.

"You should be proud of me for what I've done," I said, harping on the fact that I compiled buckets of evidence over many months and shared it with a trustworthy investigative source. But my then-70-year-old dad replied with his involuntary head shake of objection that I've grown to detest unless we're sitting at a *Scrabble* board.

Equally frustrating, it became impossible talking to my same-aged mom. "You weren't at my supervised visit," I said, after sharing the incident that marked The Post's arrival. "How are you positive The Post didn't come?"

"I'm going to do what you did to me as a teenager," she said as she pressed her hands over her ears. "Whatever! Na na na na na! I can't hear you! Na na na na na!"

Beginning December 18, 2017, The Post contacted me innumerable times at a vast variety of places, but my mom and dad never accepted that the newspaper would investigate. My parents believed I hallucinated everything—never while they were around, but always when they weren't.

Six weeks after I contacted The Post, repeated arguments led to them calling the police on me and I mistakenly shared my involvement in an investigation, setting off an unreal chain of events.

During my monthslong disappearance afterward, my parents trashed all my kids' belongings. Their childhood lies buried somewhere in the landfill.

My parents gave up hope, but I never have.

Then, as the years progressed, the BIA watched my kids lose friendships, drop activities, and fail school year after year, despite remaining on the case as their Best Interest Attorney. The extent of her interest was passing my concerns about school grades to their mom's lawyer and billing me to read them.

Eventually, in 2022, an emergency hearing was issued because of the kids' atrocious school performance. But it didn't trigger a change. The BIA told the court it was their mom's wake-up call, and she deemed no modification in custody was necessary. Colin's awful start to high school has kept the case open, but she continued advocating for the same thing.

The BIA knows I never should have lost custody of those kids because she read letters from families freeing me of guilt and said she accepted them as true. The woman knows two of her three child clients wouldn't corroborate the lie that cost these kids their dad.

Because of her, Ethan and I became estranged several months before his false testimony rescinded my custody on November 14, 2017. If it weren't for her, we'd still have the same fun-loving relationship we always had.

Fortunately, my connection with Colin and Lucy stayed fairly strong—for a little while.

Like their mother and me, the kids have brown hair, though the shades lightened with each child until Lucy began highlighting hers. Ethan, whose dark chocolate eyes matched the ultra-straight bangs covering his forehead, was a gifted son who was attached to me until the BIA appeared in late 2016.

We horsed around, literally. Ethan liked to "hop on pop" and ride me around like a cowboy on his trusty steed, while Lucy and Colin awaited their turns.

Ethan and I watched hockey, built Legos, and lived on Xbox's *FIFA* soccer video game. I remember his call to action. "Hey dad, *FIFA*." Equally enthusiastic about outdoor soccer, he practiced longer and competed on more teams than his younger brother and sister.

In 2009, months after my ex-wife left me, he sent me emails. He was only six years old.

One about hockey, titled "i love my dad", said:
> "daddy did you see the caps game last night.we were playing the toronto maple leafs we won 6 to 4.i miss you see you on every friday."

A few months later, he sent another that said:

> "i love you daddy. i am really sad. i was crying in the car on wednesday december the 23rd. i can not have a better daddy."

Though he still didn't capitalize letters, at least he learned to space after punctuation.

Thanks to years of shared custody through 2016, Ethan, Colin, and Lucy were satisfied floating back and forth between me and my ex-wife. The judge even said so. Then a new guy surfaced living with them. My ex-wife found him in November 2015 on a dating website using a profile that outwardly advertised she had four kids. This included her oldest son, whom I've known since he was one. Soon after, Colin began refusing to go back there.

I first met my ex-wife's new boyfriend in August 2016, a few months after he moved in, despite them living five miles across town. That day, I drove to my ex-wife's trailer home to pick up the kids, and he was standing alone outside doing lawn work. Within seconds of meeting him, an argument ensued.

Minutes passed before my ex-wife ushered the kids past us, out to my van. When they were situated, she joined the argument before darting inside to grab her cellphone to record. The moment she was indoors, he lifted a weed whacker to my face.

Ethan saw it, he said he saw it, and he wrote he saw it. That night, I pressed charges against the boyfriend for assault. Days later, he did the same to me.

The State's Attorney for those criminal charges testified a year later at our 2017 custody trial. She told the court she dismissed the weed whacker case without speaking to any of the parties. She added that she was aware my son was a witness, but said they never talked. "I believe Ethan was 13 at the time and did not want to have him testify." (Later that day, the judge said the State's Attorney never testified to that.) Without investigating a thing, the State's Attorney dismissed the case. Based on her testimony, that negligence is a pattern for her.

"Typically, I found when I have situations where I have two individuals giving conflicting stories about what happened regarding the same incident, many times my decision is to just *nolle pros* both, not to prosecute either charge."

Apparently, when one commits a crime, counter-alleging something deems that person innocent with this woman.

The BIA rationalized letting the boyfriend care for my kids when she repeatedly said, "It was never prosecuted, so it didn't happen."

Though the State's Attorney said she was uncomfortable having 13-year-old Ethan testify, the BIA considered him plenty old enough to lie in court about his father months later.

Ethan, whose button nose is more reminiscent of my ex-wife's than mine, began acting like her, too. They alleged the same thing that cost me custody, but he's the one who would have experienced it because we lived together. And unlike his mother, he elaborated on the lie, claiming I told countless people around town.

During my ex-wife's testimony, her lawyer said, "Let's move to [one of the two younger children]. Do you have concerns about that child being at home with Mr. Kotler?"

"Yes," my ex-wife said.

"And can you please tell the court what those concerns are."

"That child is almost constantly subjected to hearing about supposed abuse that had taken place when the child was too young to even remember." She avoided detail, unlike Ethan, whose dramatic depiction broadened the number of witnesses far beyond that child.

Ethan testified behind closed doors two months later, on October 10, 2017, the last day of a four-day trial that began in August. The judge summarized his testimony.

"Ethan expressed concern of dad frequently reporting that [abuse occurred to one of Ethan's siblings]. He reports this is brought up all the time. That he tells this to everyone, including that child, the other children, people he's Skyping with, friends he's talking to. This is a frequent topic of conversation to and in front of the children."

For those unfamiliar, *Skype* is a program that lets people chat to friends online, similar to *Zoom*. Not one word is true. Nobody questioned Colin or Lucy. Not the judge. Not even their own attorney.

"You have discussed the alleged abuse of your child with or around that child several times. Is that true?" the BIA asked me during the hearing.

"That is not true," I said.

"You never talked about the abuse around that child?"

"Correct."

"And that's another issue that Ethan is lying about?"

"Yes."

"Okay," she said. She never asked if I believed Colin or Lucy were lying—because they never said it happened. And one of them is alleged to be the main target.

The BIA suggested Ethan is the only one of her three child clients who ever claimed this occurred.

It's a concocted story that the BIA and my ex-wife pushed. And the judge, a good friend of the BIA, accepted it. On November 14, 2017, the judge ruled I lose custody and must entertain my kids under a stranger's watch in a cold, unfamiliar mental health facility 30 minutes from our homes.

"I'm going to order supervised visitation at the Mental Health Association for six months," she said. "During that period, there will be no communication with the children regarding any allegations of prior abuse. The purpose of this is to enable the children to disengage from father's perception and influence regarding alleged abuse."

Those six months have become seven years. She stated the purpose of visitation and ordered it based on something that wasn't true. The judge further explained that Ethan's allegation was just cause for taking my kids from me. Referring to Ethan's sibling, the judge, whose oversized ego complemented her physique, dealt me the blow of my existence.

"To tell this child this repeatedly with no evidence of it—if it is not true—it is so, from the court's perspective, potentially damaging to the child. I can't overlook this. *So based on that,* I am going to award primary physical custody of the three children to mother."

Nobody asked that child if it was true. Not the judge; not the BIA.

Because Ethan was young, had lied about other things, and told the judge he harbored a grudge against me, this should have discredited his testimony. Instead, he acted as star witness for the BIA.

The BIA visited our home a year earlier in November 2016—a few weeks after she forced the kids back with the boyfriend, and a few weeks before Ethan and I became estranged. With her spiky blond hair and voice that sounds like a woman impersonating a boy, she plodded into my house like a very tall Bart Simpson in heels.

My parents and I spoke to her for hours around the same wood dining room table that hosted Passover Seders of my childhood and piles of ungraded papers from my mom's time teaching. I showed her a short letter signed by Ethan. Dated two months prior, her eyes bugged out when she read it. Ethan had written a statement to the State's Attorney saying he saw my ex-wife's new live-in boyfriend hold the weed whacker to me the first time we met.

"[The boyfriend] had rose the weed whacker about at my dad's chest…it looked like it was 6 inches or closer."

Stuttering, she said, "Yes, that, that is a concern." But ultimately, she dismissed it.

Soon after, I called Ethan downstairs to speak to her face to face. After all, she is his lawyer. I asked him two or three spontaneous questions, to which he offered equally spontaneous, truthful answers. He expressed worry that something could happen again.

How much did I inspire him to be honest? After she left, Ethan said, "It's so easy just to tell the truth." It's like he wasn't used to that.

The BIA rejected it, explaining she didn't think Ethan said what he believed, insinuating he lied on my behalf. "That was a lot of pressure you put on him," she said. "You shouldn't have asked him those questions." A few minutes of questions by his dad at his kitchen table were deemed wrong. Yet, months later, she forced him into a courthouse for days, waiting to respond to a judge's questioning.

Though the BIA would never admit it, that must've been excruciating for Ethan, because he didn't get to tell the truth.

It seemed the BIA was out to get me, no matter what.

Ethan wrote he saw me threatened, then later said it never happened. He either lied to help me early on or he lied to his mom later. Either way, he was untrustworthy.

The judge wanted to know how I asked Ethan for his letter, so I relayed the conversation I had.

"Ethan, you're dealing with the court, and unfortunately, if you're not honest, you could end up getting in trouble. If you saw something, you have to write that you saw it. And if you didn't see anything, you have to write that you didn't see anything. You just have to be honest. That's all I ever told all my kids with everything involved in this case. Please be honest. Just be honest. Just be honest."

After becoming estranged, Ethan visited my house one time several months later. That night, he slapped me in front of my parents and Lucy, and got in legal trouble for assault. He later told the judge he was mad that he got punished, and I didn't.

Throughout the three long August hearing days, Ethan waited outside the courtroom to testify. But because his criminal case for slapping me was still open, the judge refused to allow it. By the October add-on date, he had written his essay to close the case.

During August hearing recesses, Ethan could be found just outside the courtroom, whittling away those many hours on his cellphone. My ex-wife and her lawyer accompanied him, alongside her parents and that weed-whacker-wielding boyfriend. The BIA grabbed a seat with them, joking around like a longtime companion of theirs. Should that be concerning?

Meanwhile, I sat with my parents and my lawyer across the building. Busy chumming around with the lawyer who requested her, the BIA never spoke to us.

By trial's end, the BIA, my ex-wife, and Ethan got what they wanted, but the two younger kids don't know why their relationship with me ended in a flash.

Along with plummeting grades, they've stopped playing sports, dropped their old friends, and have become shells of their former selves. They no longer have any outside activities or interests. Lucy recently blamed her failing grades on depression and stress and said she and Colin became introverts after the custody change.

In April 2022, the court awarded an emergency hearing because their grades were so poor. The BIA remained on the case while becoming Chair of the Maryland State Bar Association's Family Law Section. She spoke to a magistrate, newly added to our case, who is one of its 16 statewide members:

"And Your Honor," the BIA said, "I will just share that I had a lot of frustration about their grades. And they're much more capable than what they're doing... I don't think [Lucy] needs to be honor roll, and she's not interested in college."

"Ooh. Sad," said the magistrate. "Because they're both so capable."

"Oh they are. They really are. And in particular Colin, I think. And dad did put them on notice because he would send me emails the last couple of years and I would send them on to [mom's attorney] who sent them to mom. And it's very frustrating she didn't follow up on that, but I think this certainly has brought it to her attention. And I can't say that anything should change at this point."

Nothing changed, as the BIA recommended, and their grades continued to decline.

When custody was shared, the kids were content, well adjusted, and thriving in school. Then the BIA pushed for them to lose their dad, the judge agreed, and they now have "sad" futures according to a magistrate. But none of it matters. Courts don't acknowledge their mistakes and the statute of limitations expired to bring forth the witnesses I allegedly targeted.

"You can't re-litigate after two years." Many attorneys reiterated that devastating news.

The court broke these children. They don't care that they caused it, and the law protects them from ever having to hear it. Meanwhile, my kids' lives go on.

I feared losing custody during the 2017 ruling the moment the judge said, "I have serious concerns regarding father's fitness as a parent."

She highlighted a few minor things that would never cost a parent their custody. She voiced concern with the kids missing school, but they've been absent twice as often since her ruling than before. And she blamed me alone for the slapping incident she called "chaos". But it's hardly my fault Ethan tried forcing Lucy out her second-story window at night, smacked me when she refused to go, and got in trouble because he called the cops and told them. She spoke for all of 70 seconds on these types of matters.

Then she focused on the false allegations.

"This is the thing that has given me the greatest pause… I'm very concerned that this allegation of abuse is repeatedly raised to the children, and what that does to all of them, but particularly the child involved."

The child involved would have said it never happened, but that voice was silenced.

Why didn't the judge ask the BIA, "What did Lucy and Colin say about this?"

That never came up, yet she ruled I lose custody for something "that shouldn't be talked about all the time in front of [one of them]," the judge said. "It shouldn't be a topic of discussion so frequently."

The judge was new, having been appointed by our governor less than a year earlier. She and the BIA had concerning connections, having both worked as clerk for the county's long-serving chief judge.

My case's judge served him in the '90s. The BIA was his clerk a decade earlier. They worked together for almost 30 years, in the same foreboding red-brick-and-brown Frederick County courthouse that rises in stark contrast to the neighboring idyllic stretch of downtown parkland along Caroll Creek.

A stroll through the covered bridge that passes over the tree-lined creek and the rhythmic splash of fountains amidst the pond's cattails feel a million worlds away.

But the courthouse is its own little world, and it has all the power. The judge, like the BIA, was a local lawyer. Most concerning of all, the judge and her three family members have shared the same office suite with the BIA for years, directly across the street from the courthouse.

Upon her appointment to the bench in December 2016, she passed three open cases on which she worked as an attorney directly to the BIA. At the time, they worked together on four more. Profiting from her close connection to the judges, the BIA was President of the Bar Association of Frederick County at the time of my trial.

That's what one of my lawyers was referring to when she said, "The BIA is too connected to the courts. You can't fight her."

From the moment the court appointed her, the BIA seemed most interested in helping my ex-wife because her lawyer requested her services as BIA in this case, which should never be allowed. The BIA said she never even met him before his solicitation. That meant he wanted her solely because he heard something about her reputation. I know why; she sided with him on everything, including against active court orders. If it benefited him and hurt me, she did it.

The problem with everything was the three young children involved. The BIA acts as their voice, their only voice. It turned out she was on this job to help an attorney, not her vulnerable clients. Had she asked Colin and Lucy about the abuse allegation that cost me custody, she'd have known it was a lie. She never did, or if she did, she concealed what they said. They were never called to testify. Only my oldest.

Two days after losing custody, I flew alone to Colorado to decompress for over a week. Soon after I returned home, my nephew visited me and my parents. He's a good kid who loves family. He's taken to the Orthodox Jewish lifestyle in recent years and is excited about starting his own. But before he was dancing the *hora* to Benny Friedman and Avraham Fried in New York and studying in a Jerusalem yeshiva, he was a mild-mannered Reform kid from Maryland staying up too late, shaking it off with Taylor Swift. He lived minutes from me. It was back then, mere days after he turned 18, that I explained in our living room why his cousins were absent.

"They're not living here anymore because somebody claimed I'm constantly saying something to them and their friends that I shouldn't be."

Without hesitation, he said the most important words of my life. "I'll be a witness."

That's when everything clicked. I could get witnesses.

Nobody asked Colin and Lucy. Who else wasn't asked? The friends they talked to, the people they Skyped with, and whoever "the other children" are. It was alleged I told the kids in my community about something horrible happening to one of my own.

I know lots of folks where I live and many of them are children and their families. Hagerstown is a conservative city near the eastern gateway to Maryland's panhandle and the Appalachian Mountains.

Known as the Hub City for its central location on several railroads including half of those found on a *Monopoly* board, over 40,000 people call it home. Half an hour beyond Frederick—the location of our old marriage home and custody case—and an hour from Washington, D.C., it's minutes from both Pennsylvania and West Virginia. Many of these people are alleged victims, meaning they're witnesses.

Because I coached ten soccer teams and assisted at several schools, I had contact with hundreds of children. That's a lot of youngsters to target. My kids spent over a thousand hours Skyping with classmates online. Plus, they had loads of friends to our home, and they were close companions with our neighbors' children.

Kids were constantly coming and going. Our next-door neighbors own a giant trampoline that my kids and others from the neighborhood frequented most days. Their kids were here almost as much. They were Colin's best friends from school before he switched to magnet school in the next town over.

Lucy's best friend from her separate magnet school and her brother lived less than half a block down. There were overnights at my house and theirs. Our other next-door neighbors liked Ethan. Fifteen different kids from the block were in and out of my home, and no one ever heard what I'm accused of.

These children and their families make impressive witnesses, but without financial resources or further backing from my parents, I proceeded alone.

I needed help from my kids' friends, but I didn't want to ask Ethan's buddies. Ethan was against me, and one peep from his pals could sabotage everything. Lucy's friends also weren't ideal. I figured teenage girls gossip, and I didn't want my kids to know what was happening.

Colin's two closest chums from magnet school were young, not from the neighborhood, and alleged to be primary targets. So, I reached out to their families during the December holiday season. Those warmhearted people were a gift from God.

Jews love Hanukkah, which celebrates the wondrous moment God gifted us a great miracle. Because oil represents divine holiness, when one day's worth of our temple's oil burned eight—long enough to prepare a new batch—we knew God was fighting for us. God battled for me and my kids that Hanukkah just the same.

The eight-day Festival of Lights was in full swing—though the mood was quite somber—while I contacted those families. When they emailed me their letters, two of the most blessed Hanukkah presents I ever received, God worked a major miracle. But miracles can be small, too. I soon witnessed one of God's littlest, and it turned out to be the greatest I ever experienced.

One family's letter contained two sentences that were hard to understand, plus one word was missing a suffix. I requested rewritten sentences but didn't mention that single word. The reader could comprehend it, and I was already asking a lot with those two sentences—bugging her during her holiday season in the process. She agreed to change them.

Late that night, I received one more email from her. It was December 14, 2017, exactly one month after the court ruling. Little did I know these words would change my life forever:

"I just reread the letter and if you're still able to edit the letter, change the word 'consider' to 'consideration.'"

That was the entire email.

Because I left that word intact, she told me she reread the letter. She still seemed concerned, so I wrote back, explaining in detail what happened. I thought, from her perspective, the situation had to be confusing. Because Colin and her child spent hours upon hours every other week Skyping, she knew us well. For years, they were classmates and she knew us from field trips.

That afternoon, I typed. Before her one-sentence email, it never crossed my mind to put on paper my story to share with anyone. It wound up being five pages long. In hindsight, it was quick to write, but without a feel-good reason, it felt far too daunting to write about the hell I endured.

In the span of four days, the miracle of one missing suffix led me from nowhere to contacting The Washington Post with a written story and piles of evidence. "Thank you" to her.

The day after I typed the story, Friday, December 15th, I gave both families' letters to Colin's school and to the Mental Health Association in Frederick, where I had my supervised visits. I provided them with my nephew's letter five days later.

On Saturday the 16th, I wrote the following email to my cousin, who, along with her kids, would've been great witnesses too:

"We'll see what happens, but I'm definitely more optimistic than I thought I would be by this point. I sent a couple letters from the families of Colin's best friends vouching for me to both mental health and the school.

"I explained to the school there are allegations that I am targeting children at the school, and here are letters from the families of my alleged primary targets. The school has to investigate. Do you know what this may end up being? It could be the school district and mental health facility against the court.

"The media may get hold, and if that happens, who knows where this could go? It's definitely far from typical."

On Sunday the 17th, I was dazed in a fog. Because those last two sentences to my cousin resonated with me, I paced back and forth, hoping the family with my story would pass it on to the news. I was afraid to send it myself, worried I might face problems with the court if they learned I intentionally outed them.

On Monday, December 18th, I took to the internet on The Washington Post website and read their investigations page. "Are you aware of corruption or abuse of power? We want to know. If you have evidence, documents, or other information, send it to us."

Because the family didn't possess hundreds of emails and other pertinent info like me, I had to be the one to send it. "I can risk myself against the court," I thought, "because The Post will shield me."

Since my parents made abundantly clear they had no money to continue to fight in court, this felt like my only option. Otherwise, those excellent witnesses would be wasted, and my kids could be gone forever. I figured The Post would provide the help I needed.

After mulling it over for half an hour, that afternoon I sent the five-page story to the second family as a courtesy, then passed it to The Post along with a short message:

"This is the story of my 14-month custody case, the ruling of which came a month ago. I originally wrote the attached story to the two parents whose children, along with my own, would have been my alleged primary targets. I have not changed any of what I sent them. I think this case may come down to the School District and Mental Health vs. the Court. And the parents are on the side with me, the school district, and mental health."

That Monday night, as I laid in bed, I shut my eyes and envisioned papers shuffling through a machine and flying hot off the press. I hoped, but I didn't truly know, The Post was already busy on my case. By Thursday, I was certain.

In a Christmas Day letter I sent to The Post the following week, I explained how, in 2008, I wanted to be a hockey reporter. Covering the Washington Capitals for The Post would've been my dream job. Back then, I worked in sales and was in college, writing and editing the school paper. On the side, I ran a website where I blogged about Capitals hockey. The team's site linked to mine. Even a sportswriter from The Post trusted me enough to send his readers my way.

But that June, I got hurt by an irascible doctor during a routine medical procedure. My marriage ended 11 months later. School, work, and website went by the wayside.

After letting the domain name expire, my site reached its highwater mark. Because very reputable websites linked to it, my little site had a high value to *Google*. Someone bought the domain name and listed it for $10,000. To my knowledge, they didn't collect a penny. My hard work cost both me and somebody else time and money.

When my marriage dissolved around Mother's Day in 2009, my kids no longer saw their daddy each day. We spent every other week together for a while. But within months, because of another bogus reason, it dropped to a handful of days per month. That lasted a few miserable years, but our 50/50 time resumed in 2013, and the kids never spent more than a few days without me.

The 2017 court ruling ended four years of that constant presence overnight, inexplicably for Colin and Lucy. They didn't know their mom and brother accused me of repeating something inappropriate to them and their friends. Because it never happened before, I wasn't about to inform them.

When I returned home from court the evening I lost custody, Lucy and Colin were waiting for me. I had the impossible task of explaining it was our last night together.

Colin struggled to find breaths between his tears as he leaped into my arms. "Are you serious, dad?"

Unfortunately, I was. We were inseparable. Not anymore.

We said our final farewells the next morning when I dropped them off at school. I stressed to the kids how important the truth was. If someone spoke to them, I imagined, their honesty would exonerate me and we could restore our relationship.

Lucy said, "I love you," one final time, and that was it. She was gone. Then it was Colin's turn. We drove the two blocks to his school and shared a heartbreaking goodbye. Colin wiped his tears as I watched him slowly drift away, sulking into the front entrance of his school.

The next time I saw them was a couple of weeks later, in late-November 2017, for one hour at our first supervised visit. To enter the building, they had to walk under a giant sign that said, "MENTAL HEALTH Association".

The first person I met at the facility was my case supervisor. She performed my intake a week earlier and supervised several visits, including the first. After summarizing the events during my intake, I tripled down on honesty.

"If I'm making any of this up," I said, "I want you to give it to me. I want you to really stick it to me."

"You know," she said, "your case is really unique. Well, every case is unique, but yours is *very* unique."

A few weeks later, the Thursday after I sent my story to The Washington Post, I saw her in the hallway and said, "Hi."

She turned, bolted around the corner, and resurfaced in the most mind-blowing form I'd ever seen, conveying she was off limits.

My parents weren't there, however they were certain it never happened.

After a month, my supervisor and I could make small talk but kept it minimal. Because I slept only four hours a night, elated that the news was investigating, I appeared exhausted as she poked her head in the door before the kids' arrival.

"What's wrong?" she asked.

"I'm tired from being up all night. With all that's happening, it's hard to sleep."

"I'm sorry," she said as she looked down. "I hope everything works out exactly how you hope—as soon as possible."

Good to know it's not just my wishes that don't come true.

2

WINNING THE JACKPOT

THIRTY-FOUR DAYS AFTER I left that Frederick County courthouse a father no more, I sent the five-page story to The Post. That was Monday, December 18th, 2017. By Thursday, I hadn't heard a thing. Then came my visit with my kids Thursday evening.

I knocked on the Mental Health Association's side door as always to be let in. "Brian's here!" A different site supervisor shouted, announcing my arrival throughout the building, which never happened before or again with anyone.

While killing time prior to my kids' showing, I bumped into my case supervisor in the hallway on the way to the bathroom.

I smiled and said, "Hi."

Without a word, she darted backwards around the corner, out of sight. I froze.

Two seconds later, she reappeared flanked by two men wearing bright royal blue suits. They almost ran into me as they blitzed past and stopped outside our visitation room's door.

The two men divided me from my supervisor, who was pressed against the far wall. One guy stood beside her while the other stared in her face from three feet away as she gazed in wide-eyed fear at a blank spot high on the wall. They stayed silent and motionless.

When I emerged from the bathroom a few minutes later, the three of them hadn't moved. I scurried past, afraid to say anything.

For the entire hour I played with the kids, my supervisor's back remained visible outside the door. She never moved. As I said goodbye to my kids, the three of them disappeared.

The Post made their point clear without saying a word to me. They met one of my prime witnesses, and for whatever reason, they didn't want us speaking anymore.

Her bizarre behavior across the hour taught me the seriousness of what's going on, but it's nothing compared to what they had me doing later.

To my parents, however, this incident never happened. Without being present, they insisted the men in blue suits were a delusion. I hallucinated their existence with my supervisor in the hallway. They ignored the fact that someone observed me every second for my hourlong supervised visit without noting a word about me behaving oddly. My parents weren't there, but they insisted The Washington Post would do nothing because they were not legitimate news.

I brought up Watergate and asked if The Post was involved in ending the Richard Nixon presidency.

"Do you believe The Post investigated Watergate?"

"Yes," my dad said.

"Do you think their reporting was accurate?"

"I do."

"So, do you believe The Post would investigate the judge and BIA wrecking my family?"

"No. The news doesn't do that anymore. They're rat-like sycophants with agendas. They're fake news and they investigate nothing."

The news channel he watches on TV that he's been addicted to since the 1990s has warped his opinion of the media. My mom had free time to join his bandwagon after retiring from teaching school due to declining health the following decade. They teamed up against me, insisting they knew how the world works.

I supposed my luck changed when the Steven Spielberg movie, *The Post,* was released amid all this. It hit theaters in mid-January, three weeks after The Washington Post first appeared at my visit. My dad and I went the day it arrived. He likes Spielberg and Tom Hanks and thought it was a good movie. He also thought it was as factual as *The Wizard of Oz.*

I've often said, "Without politics, my relationship with my parents would be too perfect." After suffering on disability from a doctor's malpractice for a decade, I owned nothing. Suddenly my generous parents, who were my only support, saw me as insane. After watching the movie, we continued to argue almost every hour for the next two weeks. I saw and heard from The Post nearly every time I left the house, but as I relayed these encounters to my parents, I received head shakes and eye rolls.

Around the time we watched the movie, I ate alone at a local seafood restaurant. The table of three beside me was loud. "Did you see Brian today?" one asked.

"I did. He has a beard," said another, referring to my scruffy appearance back when I refused to shave to the skin. "He looks younger than 39."

"I know! And he has blue eyes like his daughter." These random ladies nailed my name, age, and facial features, and they knew about Lucy too. My parents didn't witness that, but I told them about it. My dad's I-don't-even-realize-I'm-doing-it headshake of disbelief reinforced that he regarded me as nuts.

I continued experiencing the most unusual occurrences every day while I was alone. I encountered them with my dad too, but he always wrote off the improbable or impossible and said, "It's just a coincidence."

My dad witnessed a bizarre event outside a Chinese takeout, but he chalked up a massive display of emergency vehicles as a routine false alarm.

As we were out shopping, we discussed ordering Chinese food. Sometime later, we drove to the far end of the shopping center and placed our order in the restaurant. While awaiting our food by our car in the parking lot, an extensive line of 15 or 20 fire trucks and ambulances turned into the shopping center and crept past us with flashing emergency lights on full display, but no sirens. They traveled in formation, slow and steady, like a meandering funeral procession that was in no rush to an unfolding crisis worthy of that sizable response.

The moment they passed us one by one, each emergency vehicle cut their whirring strobe lights off, made an immediate U-turn, and drove out the way they came. My dad acknowledged he saw nothing like that before, but insisted it was normal.

How big of an emergency would trigger so many emergency vehicles? Do fire trucks, ambulances, and fire-chief pickups travel close together at leisurely speeds to a massive emergency? Why didn't a single vehicle continue into the small neighborhood to ensure all was well?

He was there for this, but he still considered me crazy.

Every day was surreal. That's a word I'd never associated with my life's events, but I repeated it so often throughout this period.

My early century blue Dodge Grand Caravan that once comfortably housed my children was no longer in the greatest shape. Its brakes scraped and smelled like roasted metal. The stopping mechanism worked as well as it sounded. One day, I was discussing the repairs it needed with my dad, but he refused to help because money was tight after spending thousands on custody litigation.

As he downplayed the severity of the issue in his downstairs office, I popped my head into the hallway and said, "Hey, Washington Post, if you're listening and you want to get me a gift, I need a new car. And if you want to make it nice, I would love a red Range Rover."

Hours later, I left the house. At the nearest major intersection, a typical yellow school bus was in the furthest left turn lane. On its side were oversized bold, italicized letters that spelled **G I F T** instead of Washington County Schools. That was the exact font. In the turn lane beside it, a line of five different red vehicles accompanied the bus. Red vehicles comprise 10% of all colors on the road. The chances of seeing five in a row are one in 100,000. Has anyone ever seen a bus with GIFT on the side? Toss that in. I told my parents about the bus and cars, but they didn't buy it.

A year later, my dad and I waited at a red light in those same turn lanes. His eyes bulged as if a ghost scooted by when eight red vehicles passed through, one after the other. "Did you see that, dad?"

"All the red vehicles? Yeah." How he minimized that, I'll never know.

I've seen a few GIFT buses, the last of which was this past year. The afternoon I told a close friend about the bus story, we went on an errand. Because I became so conditioned to keep my mouth shut as I experienced unusual things, I said nothing as a GIFT bus rolled past an hour after sharing the story.

Around the time those eight vehicles failed to persuade him, I unexpectedly bumped into my ex-wife working at a sporting goods store. I passed the store twice more the following week. Both times, six red vehicles were parked out front in a cluster. Both times, all six vehicles were different. It's a one-in-a-million chance to see an unbroken group of six red vehicles once. This was two consecutive incidents, and those are one-in-a-trillion odds. That's like I won the Powerball jackpot 3,422 times.

Because my parents never believed what I told them, I snapped photos and showed them the separate groups of cars outside my ex-wife's work. "That's amazing," my dad said, but he gave it no further consideration. Days later, he was astounded to see my car parked in front of a restaurant amid nothing but red cars—five of them.

"That's incredible!" he said.

"Now, do you believe me?"

"Well, I believe *you* believe it." That's been his common refrain.

My parents, whose feint New York accent is detectable by most people other than me because my New York relatives really sound like New Yorkers, would sooner accept their son lost his mind than The Washington Post would seek the truth.

Beneficent, hard-working people, my dad performed magic shows at schools to coax families to invite him into their homes, where he sold encyclopedias and phonics programs to help their kids. My mom taught foreign languages in middle and high school. They cared about other people's kids, and they cared about their own.

Unfortunately, my mom's been in poor health for the past ten years, so she's homebound. My dad and I have taken care of her, preparing all her meals and helping with her life's necessities. She was the one tending to the family when I was growing up; now it's our turn to do the same for her. The nurturing nature they possess made it even more frustrating that they didn't trust a word I was telling them. Throughout my life, I long held they had a firm grip on reality, but after years of their news' persuasion, now I'm not so sure.

Stuck at home, other than seeing photos and videos, my mom didn't experience what my dad did, such as the light display outside the Chinese restaurant. But she, too, insisted I was delusional. The time she glared at me and said, "And what if I'm right?" still haunts me. She remained in my dad's ear, asserting her rightness that I suffered a mental breakdown from losing my kids.

Beginning with The Post's first appearance at my supervised visit on December 21, 2017, I spent three months fighting with my parents, who couldn't fathom The Washington Post would investigate. To them, they're fake news, something frequently repeated to them by their TVs.

My dad knew the significance of my ordeal and he envisaged it as a movie.

"This is a great human-interest story," he said. "You should write a screenplay." Why would he conclude the newspaper was disinterested? He refused to accept that The Post agreed with him, and was already looking into the story.

Exasperation reached many boiling points. The bickering continued day in and day out.

His solution, rather than to believe his son or his own eyes, was to sell the house. "The real estate agent is coming," he said. "Clean up so people can walk through."

"What?" I was incredulous. "Why are you letting strangers pass through our house weeks after I attacked the court? I've just made more enemies than I've ever made in my life, and you want to let them into our house?!"

Days later, he canceled the real estate idea, but not because he believed any of this.

In 1968, my dad Harvey, who could've been described as tall, dark, and handsome if he weren't 5-foot-10, worked at a shoe store while majoring in history at Queens College in New York. A snowier female version of equally average height Jewry needed shoes. My dad saw a Queens College notebook in her hand and made his move.

Days later, he bumped into his friend walking out of a campus building.

"Hey Harvey," said his buddy.

As my dad responded, the QC cutie from the shoe store strolled from the opposite direction. My dad's friend, a classmate of hers, stopped her in the breezeway.

"Maxine, I want you to meet my friend Harvey."

That was my dad's move.

Months before they graduated, they planned their first date: Italian food and the movie *The Graduate*.

The first time my dad visited her at her parents' house, a passenger jet rumbled its approach just feet overhead.

"Aahhh!!! Maxine!!! A plane's going to crash!"

"Oh, no. We live under one of JFK Airport's runways."

By the fall of 1969, after cheering on the Amazin' New York Mets to a very unexpected World Series baseball championship, they married.

The secret to their successful wedlock, they say, was a second TV, because my mom couldn't handle watching constant sports. Now they agree on the news channel, but my mom complains my dad can't stay awake for anything else, not even Mrs. Robinson. "I ask you to watch a movie with me, and five minutes later you're sleeping."

My somewhat active 77-year-old dad falls asleep like it's breathing. You can find him awake or asleep at any hour of the day or night. Nine in the morning or nine at night? Sound asleep. Three in the afternoon or three in the morning? Wide awake. Or vice versa.

My disabled mom is now sufficiently hunched to a less-than-average height. She spends almost every second in her lift-chair under an old, framed photo of her mother, binge watching classic movies, old-time TV shows, and one news channel. It is the only source of information she receives about the outside world. That news channel often criticizes The Washington Post and every similar newspaper in the country.

After stepping away from his TV, my dad complained about Democrats hiking taxes on the middle class like him. A moment later, he said, "My taxes improved under Barack Obama."

"You're joking," I said, shocked that he'd reverse his stance and actually say something nice about our "worst president in history."

"No, it's true." With a bit of a smile, he said, "I got thousands more each year." But to this day, he still thinks Democrats are bad for his taxes.

It's not just cluelessness that he learns from his news channel. There's virulent hatred, too. After another "worst president in history," Joe Biden, disappointed in the 2024 presidential debate, he said to my mom, "Good. Now the Democrats have a problem. That's what they deserve for the shit they are."

After reading his quote, he said, "Oh. I didn't know you heard me say that."

As I've become a devout Jew the past five years, I've discovered perhaps the hardest Commandment to observe is the Fifth. Revering one's father and mother is one I struggle to wrap my head around. Why don't they have to honor their kids? It feels like a one-way street and I'm wrong far too often. Thankfully, God is abounding in forgiveness. I suppose God knows it's inherently easier to love your kids, probably the simplest thing I've ever done.

But before my sincere devotion to God, our arguing reached the point where my parents, with whom the kids and I lived in harmony for over five years, called the police. When cops came and interrogated me, I mistakenly blurted out that I was involved in an investigation. Whoops!

It ignited a yearslong succession of events that the greatest fiction writers would struggle to produce, a story only God can conjure.

3

THE COVER-UP

THE POLICE WERE QUESTIONING ME at our house.

"Why are you fighting with your parents?"

"I'm trying to explain something to them."

"What are you explaining?"

"I can't say."

"You need to say."

"I really shouldn't."

"We're not leaving until you tell us."

"I'm trying to explain an investigation to them. It's not an investigation into us. It's against someone else, but I'm involved."

I feel like an idiot every time I read that conversation. In hindsight, I should've lied, but my crusade of honesty got the better of me. After disclosing too much secret info, I told the cops I'd leave for a few days. Everyone agreed.

Over the days and weeks that I argued with my mom and dad, I spoke a few times to my New Jersey cousin and my Manhattan aunt. So, naturally, I assumed they could clue my parents in.

After agreeing to leave about 11 PM on January 26, 2018, I began the five-hour drive from Maryland to the New York area. My cousin, who lived in a nearby suburb of New York City, didn't answer the phone or respond to texts for hours. Eventually, she wrote she wanted nothing to do with helping. It seemed she accepted what my parents had been telling her, not me.

Beforehand, I shared with her some emails and documents that I sent to The Post. They supported what I told her, but she either didn't read them, or it didn't sink in because she trusted my parents for so many years, and with good reason. My cousin, the one person I confided in since losing custody, figured I was as crazy as my cop-calling parents did. I let some frustration fly in text messages that night, which I'm certain angered her.

My aunt wasn't sure what to believe. She might understand me, or she might not. As a result, I'd have to explain The Post's involvement and show her confidential documents to find out. We arranged for me to come by in the morning, so, short on funds, I asked my parents to book a hotel in Allentown, Pennsylvania, about two-thirds toward my Manhattan destination. As always, they helped with just enough. I arrived at the highway-side hotel about 2 AM and laid in bed processing what happened that evening.

My favorite cousin presumed I lost my mind. I was furious with her and I'm sure she was mad at me. Like my cousin, my aunt was conferring with my mom and dad for the past month, so I wasn't confident she'd trust me either. I'd been fighting with my parents every day for over a month, and they phoned the police for the first time. Plus, I told the police I was involved in an investigation. Wait, back up. I told the police about an investigation? Cops work closely with the court, and the investigation targets the court. They shouldn't know.

At four in the morning, without a wink of shut-eye, I shot off a brief email to The Post telling them I messed up and more details would follow. An hour later, I explained everything in a more specific email:

"Honestly, I'm so tight on money right now and the people closest to me have no clue what I'm talking about, so they won't help me. It's creating a ton of friction. I was just trying to explain to my parents that they're about to be in the middle of a media frenzy, and they don't believe a word of it thanks to Fox News.

"My mom ended up calling the police because she doesn't have a clue what's going on. I can't lie to the police, so when I mentioned a situation, he asked to be more specific. I couldn't think of anything else to say, so I just said that I'm trying to explain an investigation to my parents. So, the police know my name is involved in an investigation.

"My cousin has a couple emails. I will forward them. Nobody else as of now has emails, but I'm kind of stuck at a hotel without money. The only alternative is for me to go to my aunt in New York City in the morning (it's already set up) and explain what's going on so she can help me. That would entail having to show her the emails, too.

"I'm so worn out. I've been fighting with my parents since I sent you the first email to try to get them to understand what the heck is about to happen.

"This whole thing is unraveling because of my own parents. You guys need to come get me and stick me somewhere or this thing is totally finished.

"I'm stuck in Allentown, Pennsylvania, without money or support unless I reveal all the evidence to another person. I thought my luck changed. I'm at Wingate by Wyndham Allentown, Room 339.

"If you're coming for me, please wait until checkout time. I want to eat breakfast and enjoy this bed for as long as possible before I disappear.

"I'm so sorry. I've been doing my best."

By 9 or 10 AM, I opened the door and stepped out for breakfast. A man wearing sunglasses indoors exited an adjacent room one second after me. He followed me through the winding hallways to the breakfast room.

Standing by the cereals, a guy wearing a bright, reflective construction shirt stopped filling his bowl and whirled around to stare at me. Another construction guy near the coffee station observed my every move. Two women seated at a table were interested in me, not their food. And that never happens.

The whole thing was such an uncomfortable experience. Tears welled in my eyes as I fled the dining room to avoid eating breakfast under so many prying eyes. Thirsty, I wandered to the vending machine at the base of a stairwell to buy bottled water. As I reached into my pocket for money, I sensed I was still being watched. When I glanced over my shoulder, the glasses guy who followed me from my room was peeking around the corner with a smirk. He oversaw my water purchase and disappeared.

I hurried back to my third-floor room, but realized I forgot to take the key. Back downstairs, the front desk made me a new one. When I returned to my room a few minutes later and opened the door, I couldn't believe my eyes. Two cameras with red blinking lights were affixed to the sprinkler heads jutting from the walls. The Post responded to my plea for help, and they did it in as weird a way as they announced their arrival at the Mental Health Association.

I didn't know the plan, but I was on board, so I called my aunt to cancel my visit. The exact moment I told her I wouldn't be coming, those red camera lights turned green, and the blinking slowed. I thought, "They're listening, and they approve of me not going there."

Leg cramps from dehydration kicked in as the stress of fighting with my parents caught up with me. After downing both bottles of water, my muscles still hurt. So, I sent The Post an email letting them know, hoping they'd bring more water to the room. The moment I clicked send from the bed, instantly, those cameras flipped toward the ceiling. They gave me privacy. These people seemed to be my friends, but they left me thirsty.

After asking them to come stick me somewhere, I knew they were there. I expected they'd hide me in a secluded house or hotel because separation from my parents was my priority, and that would've done the trick. Plus, I hoped it would encourage a swifter buildup of communication. I discovered, however, they had a much different scheme.

Checkout time arrived. A parked car sat outside the main entrance at the curb with its engine running. Like the cameras and glasses guy inside, I figured it was for me, so I popped open the door and hopped in the passenger side.

"Oh, I'm not an Uber driver or anything, sorry."

Surprised, I got out and shuffled across the lot to my van. Another car was waiting, stopped right behind mine. I assumed that was the one I was looking for. When I jumped in my van and switched on the ignition, the car coasted off, so I followed it.

The vehicle traveled a roundabout way to the empty end of an extensive park & ride lot near the hotel. It stopped next to the only vehicle around, a ridiculously conspicuous work truck, complete with its bumper falling off and a severely damaged cherry picker. I parked next to the truck, slid the back door open, and hustled inside. The engine was running, but the driver behind the wheel said nothing. Then the back door slid open and calm as could be, a second guy questioned me.

"What are you doing getting in our truck?"

Oh no, how was I botching this? I needed to flee that truck fast and vanish out of sight. The car that led me there hadn't moved, but the moment I leaped back into my van, the car cruised off again. I'm supposed to follow it, right?

We reached a narrow, two-lane road where a parked car sat at the edge of the street in a house's driveway. Like coordinated clockwork, the guy I followed stopped in the street just beyond the driveway and the second car rolled to the bottom. I turned into the driveway, parked next to the car, opened his passenger door, and sat inside. Finally, this must be the guy, right? Nobody else was around the private property, so it felt right. Unnerved, he sounded like the last guy.

"What are you doing getting in my car?"

"Oh, I'm sorry." I climbed back into my van and reversed out of his driveway when I saw the person I'd been following still camped in the street. He pulled off the moment I did, so I continued behind him. Half an hour after it all began, the car led me to a chain restaurant five minutes away from where we started. Nothing was normal about that food establishment.

I parked my van and walked inside, where the host nodded and motioned his head toward the bar. He didn't say a word. The guy never welcomed me or asked how many people needed seats. Instead, body language said, "You're in the right spot, now go there."

I perched myself at the end of the bar for a minute, where a half-dozen servers gathered in the corner, chatting eight feet from my stool. They were very loud and spoke simultaneously over top of each other, so I couldn't understand a word they were saying. There was nothing natural about it.

Another server acknowledged me as he drifted past, so I followed him into the dining area. As he began chatting with a table, in the opposite corner, a middle-aged woman motioned toward me as if I was her server. Are they the ones bringing me into hiding? I sat at the table's empty chair and the woman looked at me.

"Why are you sitting at our table?"

Perplexed, I stood and swiveled to find a man with four others at his table motioning me. The empty sixth seat held someone's coat. I pulled out the chair and settled in on the soft fleece when he offered a familiar phrase.

"Why are you sitting at our table?"

Thoroughly confused, I ventured outside to the parking lot. As I strayed toward the edge of the lot, a delivery truck at the loading dock began beeping. A man stood on the truck's lift operating it, causing it to ping like a truck backing up. The guy stared my way as he activated the bare shelf up and down. Scanning the lot, I noticed nothing else unusual, so I walked away again. Beep, beep, beep. I backed up. Every time I tried to leave the lot, he timed the empty shelf to beep me in reverse.

Then, two women exited the restaurant, waved my way, and strolled to their car. "God, please let this be it," I mumbled to myself. As they climbed in the front, I sat in the back. They greeted me with the customary, composed response.

"Why are you getting in our car?"

Since leaving the hotel, six people spoke as I encroached on their worlds. Each said practically the same thing, and I startled none of them. It felt highly organized.

As I left their car mentally drained, a woman with curly brown hair strolled from the restaurant and approached me.

"Do you need help?" she asked gently.

"Yeah, I could use some."

"Come inside and sit down."

We returned to the restaurant's lobby, where weird got weirder.

The woman brought me a glass of water and stood nearby as I rested on the bench in the waiting area. Customers and employees milled around, at least 15 of them. The woman asked me basic questions like my name and where I'm from. Everything I answered, she repeated loud enough that those onlookers got wind of every word. The questions grew more personal, and she yelled out every one of my responses.

"You're 39 years old!"

"You're from Hagerstown, Maryland!"

"You were going to your cousin!"

"Your cousin lives in New Jersey!"

"You had nerve damage from a vasectomy!"

She ensured everyone in the place knew my name, where I was from, where I was going, and my distinguishing characteristics.

An ambulance transported me to the hospital, where a nurse wheeled in a monitor displaying a counselor on video chat. As I explained my story, her voice shook as her face turned the color of the Range Rover I never got.

"I think it's a good idea for you to stay a few days," she said. "Will you voluntarily check into the mental health ward?"

It wasn't the accommodation I was expecting when I emailed The Post, but it would suffice. So, I signed myself in. I was unsuspecting that I would spend the next eight days there, stuck ordering copious amounts of food from a vast hospital menu that I'd soon be longing for.

When I first entered my psych ward room, I donned the hospital gown from the ER. The street clothes I arrived in rested on my bed, so I got dressed and left the room.

The woman in charge stopped me in the hall. Puzzled, she asked, "How did you get your clothes?"

"They were on my bed."

"That's weird. That's never happened before. You're not supposed to have those."

Every day since I sent my story to The Post, I lived the unimaginable. And it just occurred again inside the secure mental health ward of a hospital. I knew I wasn't alone in this place either.

4

OUR LAST GOODBYE

WEEKS BEFORE THAT MID-NOVEMBER 2017 day when the court made its ruling, I told my parents I wanted to go to Colorado if I lost custody of the kids. They agreed it was a good idea because I love mountains but had never seen mountains like that. It would be the perfect escape if the unthinkable were to happen. Losing custody remained in the back of my mind ever since an attorney warned me early on about the BIA.

"She's too connected to the courts," she said. "You can't fight her. You're in line to keep the 50/50 custody you have. But if you oppose her, you can lose it."

Neither her legal secretary, the kids' therapist, nor the mediator could understand why the BIA insisted on allowing the boyfriend around my children after such a dangerous threat. There were other concerns, and the kids barely knew him, but she enforced it. That was disturbing.

November 14, 2017, arrived when the judge dictated my fate with my kids. I fired that attorney in May 2017, three months before the August trial began, because she avoided conflict with the BIA. Outside the courtroom, her replacement, who saw me through the trial, expressed high hopes.

"I think you might get the kids," he said. "The judge presided over another case of mine earlier this month, and she treated me better than ever. She was far friendlier and ruled in my favor on an appeal, which I win only five percent of the time."

It appeared the judge took a liking to him during my trial, so he assumed it had something to do with me.

When I learned half an hour later that my worst fears came true, disbelief pinned me to the chair behind the table. The decision was so harsh, as the judge criticized me, the bailiff approached me from the back of the courtroom and hovered over my shoulder until she was finished. When it ended, I didn't want to move. I assumed everyone else would clear out of the courtroom and I could have some peace. Imagine that—I expected peace inside a courtroom.

My lawyer motioned for me to step outside, but I refused twice. When I glanced across the courtroom at the BIA, she was hugging a swath of people I didn't recognize; so many, it looked like it would last for ages. Because I was a headache for her, I presume this was a meaningful case to close. Rather than wait that out, I rose from the chair, watched the bailiff flinch, and zipped out of that building as fast as I'd ever moved without running.

Outside, I was fuming. I was angrier at the BIA than the judge, my ex-wife, or anyone else—though I was mad at them all. The BIA met all my children enough times to have detected Ethan's story to be false. She was the person who advocated for my 14-year-old son to testify, even risking his wellbeing by insisting he do so with an outstanding criminal charge. Ethan committed perjury on her behalf, and she must have known his statement wasn't true.

There was nothing left to do except figure out how to say goodbye to Colin and Lucy waiting at home with my mom. I reached home after sunset to begin my last night with them.

We played games. I wish I remember what, but those final hours were far too fleeting. The night was a blur. But I'm sure I kept them up late.

When I arose the next morning, I started readying them for our last day of school together. The depths of my soul never experienced such a gutting, helpless, and empty feeling as getting Colin and Lucy cleaned and dressed to leave and packing one last lunch. What sticks out most is saying goodbye at school.

Outside Lucy's school, she stepped from the van and listened. Colin heard too.

"Lucy, I've loved having you. You're a truthful kid. Please stay honest. You're a wonderful person."

"Okay."

Tears forced their way out. "I'm going to miss you, Lucy. I love you."

"I love you too, dad." The door slid shut, and she disappeared into school.

Next, I dropped off Colin at his school one minute away. Hugs and sobbing filled those final few moments together. Wiping tears off his cheeks with his shirt sleeve, he slinked into school without looking back. He and I were inseverable and spent so much time together. That morning, we each lost our best friend.

My parents bought a house in Hagerstown in 2012 with the intention of us living together. A different lawyer back then (I've had eight) claimed that arrangement would make it easier for me to regain shared custody. She was right; they were back in no time. My mom's deteriorating health made that move even more sensible.

They lived in an in-law suite downstairs, while the kids and I occupied the four rooms upstairs. Their two now-vacant bedrooms are on the front of the house. Lucy had her own room, while Ethan and Colin shared the other. Ethan wanted the bottom bunk bed; Colin loved the top, where he played hide-and-seek buried under scores of stuffed animals—better known to Colin as his stuffies. His upper bed is gone, leaving very distant memories of finally finding an ensconced Colin thanks to his giggling.

A loft lies at the top of the stairs where we watched family movies, played video games, and built the best forts out of couch cushions, sheets, and giant stuffies. The loft separates the kids' rooms from my master bedroom, where Colin played online with his friends.

Lucy used the computer in her room, and Ethan played on one in his. Since Colin loved the desktop in my room, we naturally shared the most time together. According to the allegations, that's where I would have been inappropriate with Colin's friends.

Colin's *Skype* friend had an older sibling who often occupied the same room and also would've overheard improper comments. Now an adult, that person and their mother corroborated in their letter that I never once said what cost me custody. I figured it wouldn't take long for The Post to meet with them and shed light on the truth.

Unfortunately, I relied too much on The Post to swiftly mete out justice when they planned on a deeper probe. Unable to afford an attorney, I assumed they would connect me with free legal help. However, I've since learned massive investigations can take a decade to bear fruits.

In a hurry to get my kids back, I expected the news to bring public opinion on my side, giving me leverage against the court. The Post took interest off the bat but I discovered the hard way, there were loads to investigate. They had to sift through a quarter century of the BIA's and judge's cases and courthouse connections, along with vetting scores of potential witnesses—only to learn they're not the lone guilty courthouse.

When The Post first got involved, I figured it would take six months before everything would become public. My visitation supervisor's comment wishing everything would work out for me ASAP always gave me belief I would speedily reunite with the kids. After all, she met investigators and minded their presence. What they discussed, I don't know. But surely her shared sentiment should bring my kids home sooner than later. Because of that, every week that passed felt like the week I might regain my kids.

But weeks became months, which turned into years because my case was emblematic of an immense national problem. However, that was unknown when I continued fighting my parents into the mental hospital and more.

The Washington Post was sly those first weeks. They routinely interrupted my everyday life and shared more than enough to keep me going. They hacked my cellphone, through which an unanticipated voice or message often encouraged me to visit a park, store, or even a house, where surprises often awaited me. My car radio played what they wanted me to hear, including the directions to a used auto auction that landed me in hot water, and not the kind I was expecting.

In public places, I'd see written signs or listen to folks mimicking something said in the privacy of my house earlier that day. People approached me wearing shirts that said things like "We are watching," "We care about you," "You are not alone," and "We're on your side". The Post was exploring things, learning about me and my family, and shrewdly letting me know.

They knew I was aware because I often spoke aloud to them in my car or my house in an ongoing, one-sided conversation of sorts. Being surveilled can make one chatty. "I talk to myself because I need to hear an expert opinion."

I'm still waiting for one.

Peculiar phenomena were happening every day, and knowing I was no longer alone in my world, I set off on frequent excursions. One evening after my stay at the hospital in Allentown, I walked from my house around town a bit, including through the soccer fields where I once coached my kids.

I stumbled into the adjacent ice rink, where kids were practicing inside, close to middle-school-aged. I approached the glass where the goalie stood along the boards, mere feet from me. After offering a glance and a smile, he fell flat on his face.

Over a month earlier in that Christmas letter to The Post thanking them for their help, I told some stories about myself. One of them was about me falling flat on mine:

> "As goalie, everyone notices you; I guess I enjoy being noticed. You often either win games or lose them for everyone on the team, and the pressure of the position drives you to be better. As a goalie, year after year, I was my team's representative in the annual shootout tournament. They held it between the first and second periods of Caps games at the old Capital Centre.
>
> "Every year, my coach paired me with a different skater. Being the team's only goalie, I never missed a tournament. Two years in a row, I won the entire tournament, attending more Caps games with each victory along the way. A third year, I lost in the finals because of a bad ref call. Don't worry, I let him have it out on the ice, giving the fans a bit more for their money.
>
> "Another time, I stepped on the ice in front of 10,000 fans still in their seats between periods. One glide out, I was flat on my face, staring at the ice an inch from my eyes—hearing thousands of people laughing at me. Hockey tape stuck to my skate was the culprit, but I shut them out that day, so I had the last laugh—and a great story."

The next day, after my walk about town, while reminiscing over reliving one of my childhood's great memories over a Chipotle burrito, I began crying. While sitting at the table in the near-empty restaurant during an off hour, I sent a brief email to The Post. Titled, "That's the first time I ever cried from happiness," it said:

"Thanks for the trip down memory lane—especially the goalie falling."

Upon sending that email, I paused, set my phone on the table, and looked up. Ten people rushed through the door and scurried into line. Four others wearing hats and dark sunglasses, dressed in plumber uniforms, darted out of a box truck into the burger place next door. Right behind the folks who dashed into line in Chipotle was a lone woman. She took one step through the double glass doors and stopped. Standing with her arms crossed, she stood just inside, blocking exit or entry to the restaurant, and stared right at me with a smile across her face.

Within a few seconds of clicking send on that email, that sleepy restaurant was bustling with actors. I wasn't sure of its meaning, but it felt like they were there to keep me safe. Outing the court carries risk.

In the same email that stirred up the falling goalie scenario, I shared the deciding factor that spawned my complete trust in The Post. I contacted them one month after they broke a major national story— and they targeted a judge.

Alabama's chief justice, Roy Moore, was running for the United States Senate as a conservative from the reddest state in the country. He was a lock to win. The news broke on November 9, 2017, five days before I lost my kids. Several women accused Moore of sexual assault decades earlier, but because of his power as the head of Alabama's justice system, the women were afraid to come forward. I was too. The judges I was attacking have the power to imprison me for life.

Like the Roy Moore scandal, my case also involved a chief judge, just one of lesser standing. I was uncovering the shady acts perpetrated by a BIA and judge who both had deep-rooted relationships with the county's chief judge for the past quarter century. What might happen if they learn I'm after them?

For that reason, I hesitated before sending my ordeal to the news. But I sent it anyway, thinking, "By the time these court officials become aware, the news would already be entrenched in the story and could go public so the judges can't lock me up." That's why it was best that I didn't tell the police about it, and thankfully, The Post covered my behind.

In my 2017 Christmas letter to The Post, I said I trusted them because of the Roy Moore story. A news report said they kept over 40 witnesses silent without the judge's knowledge until the story broke nationally. Even more witnesses needed concealment as I went after a pair of judges, but 40+ seemed trustworthy enough.

The Post let my existence play out longer than I expected. Sadly, my kids' troubled childhood inspires greater change and urgency. The system devastated my children and has done worse to others. Had I won back custody within those first few months, we'd have been on our merry way. My story would've made news, but I'd have been the fortunate one with salvaged kids. The public never would have identified the systematic harm our country's courts repeatedly cause to innocent children.

Imagine if Emmett Till was briefly kidnapped and slapped once or twice. Would the outcry have been enough to initiate nationwide protests and the upheaval of a system ingrained for centuries? I think we all know the answer. Because the boy was brutally tortured and killed for being black, he evoked enough compassion and support to become the catalyst for the civil rights movement.

So, too, by allowing my kids' struggles to evolve for years, the damage done to children when fit parents are wrongly removed from their lives is examinable. Their grades instantly collapsed, and they've never recovered. They've reported depression and personality changes, leading to minimal life interests and limited career plans.

Before the custody change, my kids had every chance to become pillars of their generation. My daughter's English teacher said she tested the highest among all his classes her senior year. Yet she had to retake 9th grade English in 12th grade just to graduate. Colin's freshman math teacher claimed he's given up.

According to the finest experts in the field, my kids now face increased struggles with grades, self-esteem, trust, relationships, anger, fear, anxiety, depression, memory loss, and drug and alcohol dependence thanks to our massively flawed justice system.

When courts exceed their authority, they forget their goal—a better, fairer world.

For centuries, American law has provided judges the power to misuse their domination for evil. A couple North Carolina cases illustrate this.

In the 1839 case of Cunningham v. Dillard, the court ruled, "The law is clear, that in general no action can be supported against a judge or justice of the peace, acting judicially and within the sphere of his jurisdiction, however erroneous his decision, or malicious the motive imputed to him."

This was further bolstered 140 years later in the 1978 case of Jacobs v. Sherard. "Judges and judicial officers have always been awarded 'absolute' immunity for their judicial acts. Absolute immunity covers even conduct which is corrupt, malicious, or intended to do injury."

Even the United States Supreme Court has weighed in. The nation's highest court stated during the 1871 case of Bradley v. Fisher, "Judges of courts of record of superior or general jurisdiction are not liable to civil actions for their judicial acts, even when such acts are in excess of their jurisdiction and are alleged to have been done maliciously or corruptly."

For 200 years, judges have ruled that judges may do as they please. It's time for a change.

The judge, in my case, used her power and immunity to ignore my 25 pieces of evidence and rule for the side that presented zero, without fear of repercussions. That's what her longtime friend and law partner, the BIA, wanted. To this day, she's gotten away with it and there's nothing I can do but shed God's light of truth.

Albert Einstein said, "The world will not be destroyed by those who do evil, but by those who watch them without doing anything." I've got enough to worry about on my path to Heaven. Don't add "destroyer of the world" to my list.

The first chapter of the Book of Isaiah, which prophecies the Messiah's arrival, depicts the proper course.

"Learn to do good. Devote yourselves to justice; Aid the wrong. I will restore your magistrates as of old, and your counselors as of yore. After that you shall be called City of Righteousness, Faithful City."

5

WITHOUT MY KIDS

THE SUPERVISOR AT FREDERICK COUNTY'S Mental Health Association oversaw my first Hanukkah apart from the kids in 2017. It was my last visit before contacting The Post.

She placed us in the little-kids room, which was quite nice. The toys, even though they targeted kids a third of my children's age, blessed us with an exuberant, bright, and colorful atmosphere. We played dreidel to win tasty chocolate gold coins and ate our traditional treat of latkes, potato pancakes deep fried in oil.

Hanukkah blessings over the menorah were a special time. Colin feared the fire, so he recited the Hebrew blessings while Lucy lit the candles one by one. The experience mystified and freed us from our forced predicament, if ever so briefly.

Back home before the ruling, unlike me as a kid, they never requested all their gifts on the first night. Hanukkah began with 24 presents by the fireplace, enough for each of the eight nights for all three kids. On night one, they chose which present to open. As soon as the gift wrap was shredded, I said, "You know, that present over there goes well with the one you picked. Open that too." I spent the rest of Hanukkah shopping to replace the gifts that I forced them to open early.

Hanukkah's expansive eight nights felt extra special. Not so at the mental health facility, where it was one and done.

Gifts couldn't be wrapped so the security officer could rifle through them, ensuring I wasn't concealing contraband. The kids loved pulling their gifts from blue-and-silver, Star of David-crested gift bags, but we all longed for wrapped presents at the fireplace.

After the allotted hour passed, our visit continued. A few minutes later, another woman whispered to the supervisor, "It's past an hour." She shushed her away and gave us 20 unexpected minutes.

When the kids and their gifts were gone, the supervisor choked back emotions. "I've never experienced that before," she said. "That was amazing." This hour and 20 minutes was the best eight nights of Hanukkah I've had with my kids since they've been gone.

My ex-wife isn't Jewish, so I've been the one teaching them Jewish values and traditions. Perhaps if Ethan had a Bar Mitzvah, the start-behaving-like-an-adult ceremony held for 13-year-old Jewish kids, he'd have learned virtues of truth and integrity. But because religion became a sticky topic late in our marriage and throughout the divorce, I aimed for a mostly secular approach to parenting, with a few interspersed Jewish holidays. As a result, none of the kids had a Bar or Bat Mitzvah and Ethan thought it was fine to lie in court.

Before the court's decision, the High Holy Days of Rosh Hashanah (the Jewish New Year) and Yom Kippur (the Day of Atonement) brought us to synagogue. As did game-filled Purim carnivals in costumes, which became an early spring highlight. And of course, who can forget seeing eight nights of Hanukkah presents piled by the fireplace? The kids lost all that with the custody change. In their absence, I yearned for it again.

There's one synagogue in town, a three-story reform temple that dates back to 1892. The High Holy Days just passed without my attendance. I felt bad, and I'm sure God felt angry, so I visited a Friday night service on Shabbat (Hebrew for Sabbath) and nestled in the same spot where I used to sit with my kids near the back of the sanctuary. My heart splintered as I tried to sense their spirit from prior years.

But it was Simchat Torah! Meaning "Joy of Torah", the holiday celebrates our yearly completion of reading the whole Torah, the first five books of the Bible which Jews hold most sacred.

The congregation gathered in a circle as the rabbi unfurled the entire Torah scroll over 100 feet around the sanctuary. We each held a section as the rabbi visited us with explanations of our portion. He pointed out highlights like the Ten Commandments and waves of text forming Moses' *Song of the Sea* after God freed us from bondage in Egypt. After reading the end of the Torah, then the beginning, we closed the scroll and danced it around the temple.

When I stumbled in, I fought back tears. By the end of the evening, I was smiling and laughing with a bunch of people I just met. We only had Judaism in common, but they felt like instant family. One thing I learned about religion that night is when we're feeling down, it'll lift you up. And within a year, the rabbi will become my best friend.

Everyone has a Covid story. He's mine.

It was March 9, 2020. Four months after I began attending synagogue every Friday night for Shabbat, Purim arrived. The holiday celebrates the courage of Queen Esther, who saved the Jews from genocide by the evil Haman. It's often referred to as a mix between Halloween and Mardi Gras, and both kids and adults are equally involved.

Everyone dresses in costumes ranging from superheroes to mermaids to Queen Esther herself. The adults prepare a carnival of games, treats, and prizes for the kids, then perform a play retelling the story of Purim. And we bake and eat Hamantaschen, triangular cookies with sweet fillings shaped like evil Haman's hat.

Days after our Purim festival, NBA basketball shuttered its doors when several players contracted the coronavirus. The Washington Capitals hockey game I had a ticket for was the first NHL game canceled when the league followed suit.

At the temple, we worried kids might have become sick during our Purim carnival. Thank God no one did. But like everything else, the synagogue shut down.

The rabbi knew my name and nothing more. I'd been coming for a few months but only volunteered a few times. I served soup at the Potters Bowl, where pottery was auctioned off for a good cause. Someone posted me at Alien Pinball during the Purim carnival. And dozens of poor souls donated to charity for me to wrap their gifts at the mall on Christmas Eve.

I've since discovered a gift with ugly wrapping leads to a better surprise inside. Too bad the Uggs guy didn't care because he stopped me halfway since, apparently, I can't wrap a shoe box. But I disappointed, and somewhat angered, the woman wanting the curled ribbon the most. Now you can properly imagine our Hanukkah fireplace scene.

Every week, I attended Shabbat services, but I had done little to help the community and nothing for the rabbi. With my variety of suddenly in-demand skills, that was about to change.

In the past, I'd done everything from managing large teams of people to home theater installation, computer editing, graphics, and web design. The synagogue needed to reach everyone quarantining at home, so I offered to be the guy to do it.

Three people showed at the temple each week wearing masks: the rabbi, the musician, and me. We had a fraying sound system, my cellphone, and my computer. So, I signed up for *Zoom*, rigged the sound into my computer, and used my phone for video. Sure, their lips and audio didn't sync that first night, or the third night, or the seventh, or inexplicably, the 15th, 16th, and 17th. But everyone partook, and we were off and running.

The production grew as we took advantage of all our sanctuary offered. I provided upgraded mics and a soundboard, then wired everything up to the choir loft, which originally hosted seating for women and children many decades earlier when the temple served an Orthodox congregation.

While working alone into the wee hours trying to perfect the set-up, the haunting noise of creaking floors and doors accompanied me. The crashing sound of a dropped book by the spirits of Jews past occasionally split through the late-evening silence.

I snapped close-ups of our floor-to-ceiling stained glass windows and the blue-and-gold rendition of the burning bush high above the Holy Ark housing our Torah scrolls. As time passed, I added video editing to our live online service, incorporating those photos with on-screen prayer liturgy. The dozens of Hebrew blessings I typed and the opportunity to work side-by-side with the rabbi each day, gave me a splendid crash course in Judaism—all thanks to the pandemic.

Still quarantining for the High Holy Days that September, I merged prerecorded videos and sound of the musician with each individual choir member so we didn't have to miss out on the full musical experience.

With holidays every month, I stayed busy assembling fun events like our *Zoom*-based Hanukkah performance. It was a wonderful diversion from missing out on the holiday with my kids while visitations were shut down thanks to the virus.

The rabbi adored the Broadway play *Hamilton*, so I rewrote many of its songs using Hanukkah-themed lyrics for our online holiday play. Being the one Jew who could rap, I played three or four characters.

When I was married, I mentioned to my wife that I should wear a fake beard and top hat to audition for *American Idol* as Abraham Lincoln, The Rapping Jew. She didn't think I could beat Carrie Underwood, but I insisted I could also attract the religious crowd. In all seriousness, I wasn't that good, but I figured I could be the next "She Bangs" guy.

At the synagogue, my competition was a bunch of Jewish *bubbes*, so compared to those grandmas, I was a shoo-in. But they got everything that sounded remotely like singing. Though the girl whom I tutored for her Bat Mitzvah said, "Your singing's not that bad," it is. If you're listening to the audiobook, you'll know.

All this one-on-one time with the rabbi provided me a unique perspective on a rabbi's life. For example, I learned he's always busy caring for others. Above all, I was making a best friend. It's not common to meet someone who discusses politics and refers to his relationship with mayors, senators, and governors. He helped me through the stress of losing my beloved children, and I did something similar for him.

His dad had fallen ill and spent many months in the hospital. As his health worsened pre-pandemic, he ended up on a ventilator, the machine most in demand during the Covid crisis. Upon witnessing the ventilator's effectiveness for his father, the rabbi worked tirelessly to secure hundreds of ventilators for our state when Covid reached its peak.

His dad spent the last year of his life in the hospital before passing away days before the following Purim. I remember sitting next to my rabbi as I videotaped him dressed as Super Mario, joking around and making silly faces for the kids as he avoided being hit by the loud, oversized twirling noise-maker used to drown out evil Haman's name.

When the camera stopped rolling, he turned to me. "You have no idea how hard this is for me. My dad just died."

The rabbi's father lived a long, happy life and had a wonderful family. He left behind his wife, his son, and his car.

The rabbi's college-aged son drove the car, and all was good. I didn't know the mid-90s station wagon even existed. But longtime congregants did. The car was 20 years old when it started showing up eight years earlier, when he first became our rabbi.

I'll never forget the emotional day he met me outside the temple to explain he'd be leaving that summer for a synagogue in south Florida. He also told me he wanted to sell the car.

Because I was always willing to help, I said, "Don't worry about paying to transfer the tags and title to Florida. I'll sell it in Maryland."

After he left town, I ventured out for some September photos in the fall foliage. The car was green, so those bright yellows, oranges, and reds made it pop and reflected beautifully in the paint. Never mind hundreds of minor scratches and the slightly lifted hood.

While out snapping away, the power steering broke. The rabbi decided to fix it, so I bought steering fluid, poured it into the desperately dry car, and drove an hour south to his dad's old mechanic. They don't perform same-day fixes there, so I bussed home and back days later once fixed. With the repaired car, I exited the interstate near my house to discover the power steering broke again.

Rinse and repeat everything I just did.

The car made it home the second time, but couldn't last overnight. So, I made a third trip to the mechanic. Halfway home, after getting the car back, I found a two-lane road lined with vibrant autumn-colored trees and whipped out my phone for photos. As I made an illegal U-turn on the mostly empty road, the steering went out, this time with a check engine light to boot.

Since it was late in the day, I finished the drive home before making the return trip the following day. The rabbi apologized for all this, but I assured him it was fine. A block from the Metro train station, the shop's convenient location gave me an excuse to spend each day touring D.C. before grabbing the bus back home.

On the way down, I grabbed lunch. Forgetting I wasn't opening my new car with a touch sensor, I yanked on the door handle. It snapped in half. But before fixing the handle, we needed to fix the steering. So, I continued the drive down and later found a replacement handle online, which I tried to install myself, landing the car in a body shop for two weeks.

I arrived at the mechanic to learn the car needed a steering pump, instead of the fluid lines we kept repairing. Why? "Because someone drove it without steering fluid."

We put one in; it went out. Back home with the car, I was tired of calling them. Upon revealing my identity, they said, "You still have that thing?!" "You haven't gotten rid of that car yet?!" or my favorite, "Hold on," followed by minutes of silence.

I brought the car in a fifth time, then received good news. "We're certain we fixed it."

On the highway home with the ready-to-list station wagon, rush-hour traffic came to a standstill, but the car thought it had some place it had to be. It crashed into the back of an SUV. Serves me right for thinking I could go a day without coffee.

I'd planned to add full insurance coverage when I got back home because this was my last time behind its wheel. God taught me that was wrong. So did the rabbi.

"How did you wreck the car?" he asked.

"On the highway changing lanes behind another guy, he slammed on his brakes and so did I. My car would've stopped in time, but not yours."

"Did you give him your info?"

"No," I said. "We both stared at his crumpled rear hatch, but he said, 'I'm prepared to drive off.'"

"That's weird."

"I agree. He said that twice, then left. For all I know, he could've been a news investigator following me around, so he let me go. My life's been crazy for a long time."

The car's valued at less than $3,000. Many sedans of that model are listed in that price range, but this was a station wagon. "It's a uni-corn," the rabbi often repeated. "We can get five to seven thousand for it." Unfortunately, there aren't too many unicorns shopping for dec-ades-old station wagons. A rare car means a rare buyer.

Without insurance, rather than taking a complete loss, we set out to fix it. Nice guy that he is, the rabbi insisted on paying for the repairs to the damage I caused.

Despite hearing the car should be totaled, we found a good deal. It cost less than $1,500 to fix.

When the rebuilt car appeared with its glossy new hood and one shiny new headlight, everything else in bad shape stood out. So, we replaced the original dull headlight, fixed thick scratches on the back, repaired the taped-on side mirror, and fixed the center armrest that was suffering a massive laceration.

As I cleaned under the hood and made the engine sparkle, I feared I'd finagle something loose, and we'd be dealing with another costly fix. So, I stopped midway. The glistening engine and hoses contrasted the corroded fluid lines and rusted clamps nicely. Then I steam cleaned the seats, only to find that I sucked years of grime to the upholstery's surface. After a half-year of headaches and a lot of seat scrubbing, the car was ready to sell by spring.

Those fall foliage photos no longer seemed suitable, so I photographed the car amongst the bright spring blossoms—about five times. The photos were never good enough because they always highlighted the car's worst features, like the closeups of the wheels and tires. I don't know how it drove so straight, as many curbs as it plowed into in its lifetime, but the wheel covers recorded each one of them.

I put new wheel covers on and showed the rabbi. He said, "I don't like the wheel covers." I said, "I don't care."

An auction rejected us before we listed it on a few websites, pricing it to move at a cool $6K. Somebody offered that, then three hours later, pulled the offer and disappeared. Someone else did that too. A few different people arranged test drives that showed our meeting in Pacific Standard Time. But I live in the East, so I drove to the appointments twice apiece—once at Eastern Time and again three hours later at Pacific Time. They never showed up. I guess they lived in Chicago or Cheyenne.

I threw "For Sale" signs in the windows and parked the car in the same busy shopping center as my ex-wife's sporting goods store, and where my dad and I witnessed the procession of emergency vehicles outside the Chinese restaurant.

A few people called. One lady was interested. She phoned on a Friday and I asked to meet her on Sunday. She said, "Do you mind if I ask you a question? Why do you want to meet on Sunday? Everyone else would meet on Saturday."

"I don't like to do business on Saturdays," I said.

"Oh, you observe the Sabbath on Saturday. So do I."

Happily surprised, we arranged to meet on Sunday. The rabbi and I thought it was *beshert*, Hebrew for destiny. But it wasn't because she canceled.

Meanwhile, at the rabbi's temple, they were preparing to celebrate Passover with a community Seder. With the guy who would typically organize such major events out of town, he asked me to arrange everything in south Florida from my home in Maryland. Almost 150 guests later, I wasn't one of them because I had to stay behind to sell the car.

After dropping the price twice, we heard nothing for weeks. We thought we'd be lucky to get half our asking price when the interested lady from the shopping center called back.

She wanted to arrange an inspection of the car with the notion of buying it for $6,000. Terrified she'd cancel again, I offered it to her for $4,500. Her mechanic loved the car, so she agreed. We were both happy.

Though I missed out on a Passover visit, fortunately, I could see him before the whole car fiasco. The centerpiece of a 16-day Southeast road trip, I stayed with him and his family for four days. My last night visiting was the cat's first night in the guest room.

"Snoopy needs to sleep in the room," the rabbi said. "If he scratches, just tell him to settle down."

By 1 AM, I got to sleep. By 2 AM, the cat wanted out.

"Settle down, Snoopy."

Scratch. Scratch. Scratch.

"Settle down."

"Meow!" Scratch. Scratch.

The cat scratched and meowed for half an hour.

"C'mon. I have to be up early. Please stop."

"Meow!" Scratch. Scratch.

"Quiet Snoopy! I mean, settle down."

"Meow! Meow! Meow!"

Two hours of scratching later.

"Settle down, Snoopy."

Scratch. Scratch. Claw. Claw. "Meow!"

"Would you be quiet already?"

"Meow! Meow! Meow!"

"Snoopy, I'm trying to sleep. I've got over ten hours to drive to-day." The cat just didn't seem to care.

By seven in the morning, I hadn't slept since two.

Bleary-eyed, I hit the road so I could run around Providence Canyon, Georgia and jump back-and-forth between time zones before spending the night in Montgomery, Alabama. Then the rabbi called halfway up the Florida Turnpike.

"How was Snoopy?" he asked.

"He clawed and meowed all night. I haven't slept since two."

"Oh. You should've just let him out."

6

I'M BLESSED

H E WAS HAGERSTOWN'S FRONT PAGE story when he left for Florida. The rabbi's new synagogue shares the same name as my childhood synagogue in Bowie, Maryland. There's only a handful with that uncommon name meaning trailblazer, a distinction I'm proud of. Many of my fondest childhood memories took place there.

I remember all the friends I spent years learning to read, write, and speak Hebrew with, kids whose Bar and Bat Mitzvahs I attended. I remember my teachers, who I'm sure would remember me perfecting my skills as a class clown. I remember showing up late for Sunday school, sweaty from having just played hockey games. I remember the delicious foods and festive holidays. I remember the sobering moment I watched Holocaust atrocities on TV for the first time, searing images of emaciated ancestors into my soul. And more vividly than everything else, I remember receiving my Hebrew name.

There were a dozen of us in my grade's class. The teacher went around the room, assigning our names one by one. Most kids had English equivalents of Hebrew names, but a few did not, and I was one of them.

"You're not even close to having a Hebrew name," my teacher said, referring to the 10th century Irish kingly origin of Brian. "Baruch is similar, so that's your Hebrew name."

I couldn't have been happier. The word Baruch means blessed, which begins most of our Hebrew prayers: "Baruch Atah Adonai Eloheinu" meaning "Blessed are You, Adonai, our God."

If God wants to be called blessed, I do too.

I later learned it's also a college in Manhattan with notable alumni like Ralph Lauren and Jennifer Lopez, though she spent about as much time there as I did the day I used their bookstore's bathroom.

Despite all the glorious memories of attending the synagogue, perhaps my favorite wasn't very Jewish. In 1989, my best friend from elementary school brought in a *Bowie Blade-News* ad. Our temple would host its first baseball card show. "Wow!" I thought, "My temple's done nothing this cool before!" I've since learned that hosting God every week is much cooler.

Never having been to a card show before, we went. Rows of tables filled our sanctuary, the same spacious room my Bar Mitzvah would be held in two years later. We wandered around and scoped out everyone's supply before I settled on buying several packs of unopened cards, and may or may not have been blessed by God.

Inside the sanctuary, I opened them and pulled two of the most sought-after cards on the market: An off-center, smudged Ken Griffey, Jr. rookie and a high-dollar error card, Billy Ripken with his "Fuck Face" bat, pristine. What was God trying to tell me?

A few years down the road, VHS tapes of my Bar Mitzvah, the only known videos of me as a kid, disappeared. That's too bad, because I'd love to hear my sermon regarding Moses' last speech before his death, considering I have trouble with those sorts of sad endings. My *Diary of Anne Frank* rests in my bedside nightstand, but I haven't read past June 12, 1944. The British, Canadians, and Americans just landed in Normandy on D-Day six days earlier, and it was Anne's birthday. Things looked up, so I ended right there.

I spent most of my Bar Mitzvah money on a 1983 Topps baseball card set, whose value fell to one-tenth what I paid within a few years. But thanks to today's massive inflation, it's now worth what I spent 30 years ago. With the crappy luck I later had in the stock market, that's been my most formidable investment.

My parents were in the synagogue scene strictly for the Bar Mitzvah. I attended Hebrew school for four years before my Bar Mitzvah, and none afterward.

When I revisited the synagogue a few years ago, they provided the grand tour. The picture-lined wall outside the classrooms featuring each year's confirmands included everyone from my class, except me. Because I'm not a morning person, I was fine skipping Sunday school.

Tired of early morning hockey too, I quit playing about that time and opted instead for a life of underage cigarettes and drinking. I managed that well because it led to of-age cigarettes and drinking.

My smoking even inspired my dad to write a financial book. One day, my mom found a pack of cigarettes in my backpack and told my dad. When he found weed and water bongs, he kept it silent from her—but not my mom, the snitch. He ran with the idea and published a book the following year.

I learned to do a better job of hiding my cigarettes, and according to my dad's book, at $2 apiece, they cost me $100 a pack out of my retirement.

I hate termites.

My dad spoke to the termite guy.

"Do you ever hear this?" my dad asked. "What do you think hon?" He elaborated. "When you explain the extermination cost, has one person asked another, 'What do you think hon?'"

"I think so," said the termite guy.

"Here's what you do. I sold books and this worked for me almost 90% of the time."

Like it was a pack of cigarettes, my dad wrote another book. This time, though, he was elderly and got scammed by foreigners.

Almost $60,000 later, credit card companies helped him get every penny back. But the ride from the start was its own book.

I've seen too many others his age endure similar circumstances and its affecting generations of people. My dad is the extremely lucky one who recovered his money, but we'd have been in a lot of trouble if he didn't.

New York City gave birth to both my parents in 1947. My mom grew up in Far Rockaway in Brooklyn near the ocean and dad hailed from Jamaica, Queens, by the turnpike. They hate their names, Maxine and Harvey. My dad prefers his middle name Stuart, while my mom's just happy to have ditched her maiden name. She thought Maxine Moskowitz was the worst.

In 1960, Hurricane Donna swept up the eastern seaboard, and took aim at New York neighborhoods by the ocean. Water poured into my mom's childhood home. She shut her shutters as stormwater surged inside. "God, please make it stop," she said. The moment she appealed to God for mercy, the floodwater subsided. "I felt like Moses parting the sea," she later said.

Whenever we visited New York, we almost always stayed a little further inland on Long Island with her brother, his wife, and their two kids. That's how I became so close to my cousin, who since moved to New Jersey and in whom I confided about losing Ethan, Lucy, and Colin.

Papa Sol, my mom's dad who spent the last days of his life living with us in Bowie around my Bar Mitzvah, got the Hungry Man TV dinners when I only got the regular. But I made up for it at the Bob's Big Boy buffet. He was a house painter by trade, while Grandma Beulah cared for the family until her passing in 1975.

I'm blessed to be named for my grandmother, because my mom still glows about her every day. In Judaism, we often name children using the first letter of a deceased relative's name. So, American-born Grandma Beulah cleared the way for me to be named either Beth Ann if I was a girl or Brian Ames if born a boy. They changed my name to Brian when I was five days old.

All joking aside, my newborn birth certificate says Brian and my Papa Sol's says he was born in Poland in 1910. He spent his childhood there, but moved to America before Hitler took power and decimated the country's Jewish population. Papa Sol recalled fighting in his hometown during the First World War, one reason they emigrated.

Late one night during a battle, his family heard urgent banging on their front door amidst the gunfire. They were terrified to open it. The next morning, they pulled open the door and found a dead Polish soldier resting on their doorstep with blood smears blanketing their door.

To survive, he and his family combed potato fields searching for their next meal. That menial existence convinced him to flee to America. "The day I arrived in New York," he said, "was like I went to Heaven."

Thankfully, life treated him harshly in his native land, so he escaped. Otherwise, the Nazis would've moved in, and I never would've come into this Earth. Sadly, like many Jews' families, not many of his relatives survived.

My dad grew up with an older brother and two sisters, including my Manhattan aunt who lives a few blocks from Monica and Rachel's fictitious *Friends* apartment.

His older brother, who passed away in 1997, prepared for an evening out with friends long ago. My very young dad jumped in the back of his car and hid. Wanting to join the fun, my dad's antics delayed his brother several minutes.

Finally on the road without little brother in tow, a stranded motorist caught my uncle's attention, and he pulled over to help. As he did, a passing car sideswiped him. The collision destroyed one of his legs, and it was removed from the thigh down. "He wouldn't have been there at that time if I didn't stall him," my dad said. To this day, he lives with regret over his brother's lost leg.

In the 1950s streets of Queens, my impish dad played the manhole-cover version of baseball, called stickball, in the street with his neighbors. Mailboxes marked first and third bases while the manhole covers sufficed for second base and home. And anything other than a baseball bat served as the stick.

His biggest accomplishment of the day was being neighborhood punchball champ. "I could punch the ball clear across the blacktop."

He grew up a massive Brooklyn Dodgers fan and idolized pitcher Sandy Koufax. My dad was a left-handed Jewish kid, and so was Sandy. At ten years old, my dad cursed the day the Dodgers moved to Los Angeles. Since they won World Championships in three of the next eight years, my dad's curse wasn't nearly as powerful as Babe Ruth's on the Boston Red Sox or the Billy Goat's on the Chicago Cubs. They lasted 86 and 71 years, respectively.

Because his parents owned a successful department store in New York, they were more financially secure than my mom's, a source of conflict early in their relationship. His dad, my Papa Al, was born about the same time as Papa Sol, also in Poland. His mom, my Grandma Gertrude, was born and raised in New York like Beulah.

Of all my grandparents, Grandma Gertie was the only one who lived to meet any of my children when Ethan, my parents, and I visited her in Queens shortly before her passing.

Several family members eulogized her four months before my marriage ended. While hurting from the vasectomy pain, thoughts of my children moved me to make an unanticipated trip to the mic. "Grandma, thank you for teaching your son to be such a wonderful dad to me. Because of you, I learned to be an excellent father to my own kids. Your legacy will live on for generations."

Huge gatherings welcomed our New York arrivals. No matter whose house we visited, ten other family members popped in. Between my numerous Jewish relatives, the overload of Jewish delis and bagel shops, and the synagogues on seemingly every street, it's easy to sense that Jews are everywhere in New York.

Not so in Maryland. Sure, there are pockets here and there, but it's commonplace for Jews to be outsiders, especially in the rural country-side where I live now. In hopes of locating a decent gathering of Jews, a local friend and I heard about an outdoor Rosh Hashanah service at a park outside Baltimore.

Neither of us had ever been surrounded by so many fellow Jews. Over 10,000 attended the stirring High Holy Day service on a perfect cloud-free evening. "We found our new tradition," we said on our way back to my car. I never imagined being around so many Jews in one place. Little did I know, two months later I'd be amassed with over a quarter million others at the March for Israel in D.C. with my Florida rabbi and his temple's president.

I donned the president's Israeli flag as a cape, like thousands of other Super Jews in attendance, and applauded our people in the midst of the impassioned rally, a few shoulders away from CNN's David Gregory.

A year later, as the one-year anniversary approached, I visited my nephew in Israel. After a few days in Jerusalem, I drove alone to an isolated desert town in south-central Israel where I toured the beautiful, barren crater around Mitzpe Ramon.

Then I went back to town for dinner. Halfway through my fish and olives, I heard a short buzzing alert on someone's phone. He stood and motioned for his family to follow him toward the door. The next five seconds saw everyone else in the restaurant do the same, staff included. I thought to myself, "We must be headed for a bomb shelter."

A hundred feet outside the restaurant, I followed everyone down some steps into a shelter filled with bright, cheerful murals. A couple hatch doors were sealed and I began taking selfies and trying to translate the murals' Hebrew writing (that didn't go well).

With 40 kids, adults, and dogs jovially joking around, it felt like a routine drill. I assumed the Houthis fired a few rockets from the south that were passing overhead toward the bigger cities and we'd be out in no time.

Without an internet signal or the ability to understand a word from anyone, I was mesmerized by the experience. If only I brought the rest of my beer like some other guy did.

Thirty minutes later, my dad sent a text: "I'm hearing it's a heavy attack by Iran in waves trying to overwhelm the defenses." People were still joking and laughing.

Almost an hour after it began, I kibitzed with a few delightful Israelis while leaving the shelter, marking the first time I insisted walking out before a lady.

Back in the restaurant, people were more friendly and talkative than before. "That's the first time we've been to a bunker in forever," my server said. Even my hotel's owner contacted me a few times.

It had been several years since that small, wilderness town had to go underground, but I never would've guessed it. Israelis really are resilient.

Thanks to the court, I don't think my kids are even aware they should be supporting Israel. They've drifted so far from Judaism. Our lengthy ancestry and the passing on of traditions define what it means to be Jewish. But the kids, and particularly Ethan, have been estranged from the religion since 2017.

Ethan, who liked electronics so much I became one, joined me on one father-son trip. It was one of the greatest days of his dadPad's life—memorable for all the right reasons. But the revolting gift of parental alienation transfigured that day into a major cause of our estrangement.

The United States men's soccer team had a game scheduled for the summer of 2016 in Philadelphia. Ethan and his newly spiked hair wanted to see his first pro game, so I explored getting tickets. But he was due to be with my ex-wife on game day. I'd never requested to take a kid on her day, but I figured she'd be fine with us going.

I texted her, apologizing that the game took place during her week. Because it was a night game, I asked to take Ethan sightseeing to places like Independence Hall and the Liberty Bell beforehand. She texted me back. "Sure. Sounds fun :)"

This was June 2016, two months before her boyfriend held the weed whacker to my face. And the BIA was on the case by September.

Soon after the BIA's involvement, I entered Ethan's room discussing our fun Philly trip filled with our Founding Fathers, cheesesteak subs, and a 1-0 American win over Paraguay. He lambasted me for taking him. "According to the custody agreement, you broke the law when you took me to Philly without mom's permission. You never should've taken me out of state."

What 13-year-old knows the words "custody agreement"?

His comment wasn't even true. The agreement said nothing about out-of-state travel, and she never once asked me before taking the kids beyond Maryland's narrow borders—because she didn't have to. This time, I needed her approval since it was her scheduled day, and I got it. I even had to pick him up from her house.

Ethan read the text exchange but brushed it aside as meaningless. I stopped short of showing him the custody agreement that made no mention of needing permission, though perhaps I should have.

His mom turned our magical trip into an outlawed day where his father committed a crime by taking him to see our country's birthplace and a soccer game. After this, our relationship soured, and the BIA seized on it. She never cared that my ex-wife lied to him about the trip, only that we had a fracture she determined didn't need a bandage.

During an early-December meeting in her office, I showed the BIA a chart. It displayed Ethan, Lucy, and Colin's ages, the years I had shared custody versus the years I barely saw them thanks to my vasectomy, when my ex-wife baselessly claimed I was misusing my pain meds. Ethan was aged 6-10 when my ex-wife had primary custody. Lucy was 4-8 and Colin was 1-5.

"When Ethan rarely saw me," I said, "he was at an age where everything his mom said seemed true. Before age six, kids have little memory, and after age ten, they begin to think they're right about everything. But between those ages, kids trust what their parents tell them. That's why he believes I'm bad, and not Lucy or Colin. Because they spent those critical ages from six to ten with me, they trusted my parenting skills and the relationship we developed, not my ex-wife's negative portrayal of me."

Like everything else I presented, she dismissed it.

Two weeks later, just before Hanukkah, Ethan left for his mom and never returned.

We tried therapy. Less than two months after he ceased coming here, my dad and I picked him up from school and drove him to a therapist near my lawyer, 45 minutes toward D.C. That's where my ex-wife's lawyer was too. Ethan, my dad, and I joked on the way down and we caught up on the past two months.

Then Ethan and I met together with the therapist. After discussing that we both wanted to repair our relationship, Ethan and I left the building that February, hugging each other. We said, "I love you," and resumed bantering with my goofy dad on the return drive home. Another therapy appointment was scheduled for the following week.

However, the BIA crashed the party. "That's too far away," she said, unenthusiastic that therapy proved successful. "You need to take him somewhere locally."

She knew of issues concerning nearby therapists. They either didn't take our insurance, had no upcoming appointments, or their website preached Jesus. After being divorced because Judaism became a primary problem for my ex-wife and her mom, I sought a non-religious approach. The only nondenominational therapist who accepted our insurance had no availability for two months. The BIA was disinterested. That's what she insisted upon.

After two more months of not speaking to Ethan, I drove to get him for our therapy appointment in April 2017, but my ex-wife refused to let me take him. Again, the BIA didn't care. Successful therapy was problematic to her, but she deemed my ex-wife's therapy refusal okay. She never requested we seek therapy again.

By that August, Ethan sat in the Frederick County courthouse day after day, waiting to badmouth me to the judge. It's not his fault; he's a good kid who was caught in the middle.

The same little boy I watched captain a tourist-filled duck boat through the bridges of Pittsburgh as his baby sister slept on my lap wants nothing to do with me now. And after seven years of off-and-on supervised visitation, Colin and Lucy have fallen away too.

Our first supervised visit was ridiculously upsetting.

About two weeks after I lost custody, I arrived at the Mental Health Association's side entrance, where they forced us untrustworthy parents to enter 15 minutes before our children and their good parent. Outside the side door was a small, fenced playground where we later planted seeds for flowers that never grew. Inside stood a security guard beside a table. After emptying my pockets, being wanded for weapons, and having our dinner searched, he led me into our visitation room.

The kids passed through the front main entrance, under the massive "Mental Health" sign, that the quality parent used.

A basic wooden table and four gray chairs greeted us. There we ate dinners and played games. The additional luxuries of a bookcase, TV, small sofa, soft chair and ottoman rounded out the room. A few old games, books for preschoolers, and some little dinosaurs and army figures were the offered entertainment. Every week, I purchased different board games so that we'd have something age-appropriate to play.

I didn't know what to expect when supervision started, but seeing Ethan wasn't on the list. I assumed I'd spend the hour with Colin and Lucy, not my estranged son whose lie put us there.

Ethan strutted into the room, followed by his brother and sister. He seemed excited to witness me at my lowest, as three strangers peered over us, clipboards in hand, in a room no bigger than a bedroom. He sat on the sofa smirking and leaned forward, pressing his elbows into his knees as he clasped his hands. He gazed around and nodded his head, approving of the excruciating conditions under which I had to see his siblings.

After five minutes, I mouthed to the supervisor to remove him from the room. She did, but she approached me afterward. "We like to have all the children visit with their parents," she said. "Why don't you want him here?"

I explained my unease, his smug expression, and my concern that his lie forced this situation. "I'm not comfortable having him here right now. Can we arrange something?"

"What?"

"I want you to determine if he's telling the truth. When you know one way or the other, you can invite him back."

"Okay, that's reasonable. I agree."

Within two weeks, she possessed three letters from my witnesses and The Washington Post made their presence known. Ethan never returned.

The supervisor loved us. Everyone at the mental health center was kind. I liked the security guard whom my poor kids had to watch mosey about wearing his SECURITY hat, ensuring everyone's safety. I even had a favorite observer.

But spending time with my kids was far from a celebratory occasion. Enclosed in a building at the end of a shopping center parking lot, we no longer planned for the future. The common questions ceased because there was no point in asking them.

Where do you want to go? Would you like to sign up for this? Can I help you with that? No, I couldn't.

But because The Post showed up at many early visits, I was excited, wondering what fresh surprises they had in store each week. How long before I win my kids back? I pondered that future, not the old one.

The kids were none the wiser.

Then after divulging the investigation to police, my visits were interrupted as The Post began transforming me into a true mental health nutcase and crazed criminal.

I missed one visit while in the mental health ward in Allentown.

During the following week when I was reintroduced to society, a litany of odd events marked the unmistakable realization that the newspaper was part of my daily life.

The trash truck arrived on trash pickup morning. A garbageman jumped off the truck, strode to our trashcan, looked at me and my dad in our driveway, never lifted the trashcan, hopped back on the truck and drove off without taking our trash. A minute or two later, that identical garbage truck rolled back around. The same guy hopped off and looked at us. He touched our trashcan's handle again, left it in place, and boarded the truck. It drove off.

"What the heck was that?" I asked my dad.

Always in disbelief, he said, "I think one of them was recycling."

The Post cracked into our computers, tablets, cellphones, and house phone. Our devices slowed and a voice occasionally rattled me as it interrupted through my iPhone and spoke. One day the house phone rang, and someone chatted to my dad about a file on our computer. How could a random caller know that?

Once I asked a question aloud to myself while musing in my daughter's empty, darkened room. Moments later, the answer appeared as a notification on my iPad. And no, I didn't ask AusSiri, the Australian-accented Siri that my ears find much more palatable. She doesn't respond in riddle form with emojis.

Another day, while alone in my bedroom watching a *YouTube* video, my iPad went dark and a single tweet flew into view. "I admire your courage and bravery." The message was from an intriguing name. I'd spoken to my parents about the kids earlier that day and referenced a celebrity who recently died. The tweet was from his wife. I doubt she had anything to do with it, but The Post enjoyed name-dropping celebrities to me.

Among those who mentioned the famous to me were the "police", who invariably acted far different than one would expect whenever they arrived. Because our phones were hacked and the officers were too kind and omnipotent, I think phony cops were sent by The Post. I believe the 911 calls from my parents were intercepted, and impersonators appeared in uniform.

Early one day before getting into it with my parents downstairs, I waved a painting of Beasley, my childhood dog, out my bedroom window because I planned to visit the cemetery. I assumed somebody was watching. Hours later, after hours of fighting with my parents, the police entered my bedroom. They immediately pointed to the painting. "Who's that a picture of?"

A minute later, the cop asked, "Have you heard of this singer? She likes you. You should check her out." It sounded like my days in Tulip Grove Elementary School all over again.

Despite witnessing many of the same things I did, my parents maintained I was losing it, and they continued calling police. The cops made a strange demand on their next visit late one evening when they told me to leave.

"Pack your bag," said the smiling cop in my upstairs bedroom.

"How much should I pack?"

"Take enough for a few days," he said. "Put your stuff in your car and drive."

Amidst the packing, I had another abusive message for my parents. The cop laughed and said, "Brian," as if I was his own beloved child.

Moments later, we reached the driveway, where I sat in my car and looked at the cop.

"Drive," he said again, still grinning.

"Where should I go?"

"Just drive." He never asked if I had a place to go or spend the night.

As I pulled out of the driveway on my quiet street, a car rolled past. Two weeks after following that vehicle around Allentown, I was at it again. This time, it misled me to a stone-and-granite warehouse three miles across the state line into Pennsylvania. It was mid-February 2018, three months after losing custody. A light dusting of snow coated the grass.

I followed the vehicle to the warehouse and it disappeared, but I did not. Long story short, I fell two stories into the warehouse, saw nobody, exited from a nearby door, climbed back in the van and circled to the rear of the building.

A thousand feet of wooden pallets, dumpsters, and other assorted behind-the-warehouse wares encompassed the shadowy site. I reached the end, turned around, and started back. Then a bright light flashed on to my right from the overhang above some pallets, disturbing the darkness. As I inched back the way I came, the overhang illuminated one light at a time. Because I rode past from the opposite direction and nothing happened, motion-sensing bulbs weren't being triggered. They seemed human-controlled. I rolled along until the brightest light of all shined on my prize at the end of the overhang—a small below-ground loading dock oddly filled with water beside two dumpsters.

Hearkening back to that GIFT bus and all the staged red cars, I thought if I drowned my rickety van, they'd hook me up with a right-eous replacement. So, I advanced slowly into the waist-deep water be-low the beaming light. Unimpressed, I backed up, floored it, and…SPLASH! My van became an amusement park log flume, which felt far more satisfying.

As I soaked my pants and shoes climbing out of my freshly totaled van's window, an impromptu voice blasted from a nearby speaker. "Start a fire. You've got to stay warm." On this freezing winter night, that voice's idea sounded viable.

"Where?"

"You'll stay warmest inside the dumpster."

There were two to choose from. One said, "waste," while the other said, "scrap metals". The scrap metals dumpster was no ordinary dump-ster and this was no ordinary night.

Moments after I clambered in, I stood on a large piece of hard Styrofoam as I was shifting objects to make room for the fire. The foam whipped round 180 degrees like it was remote-controlled, nearly toss-ing me off. Somehow I stayed planted, but it launched another remark-able experience.

Five tall stacks of wooden pallets stood alongside the dumpster. So, I tossed a few in and ignited my personal fireplace. I placed a bag of fried chicken on a discarded metal shelving unit near the fire, then climbed out. Several feet away from the dumpster, I was airing out my wet clothes when…BOOM! An enormous explosion sent me ducking for cover. The flames dwindled within seconds.

Figuring that whatever was flammable dissipated, I climbed back in to find my food scorched from the blaze. Verbally upset that I lost my chicken, they later taunted me in a local newspaper article by saying a food place was visible from the scene. Long afterward, I drove back to check and it wasn't true. It was on the opposite side of the building, so I didn't feel so stupid.

Throughout the night, I added pallets to stay warm, but sleep eluded me. For the next dozen hours, I kept toasty listening to music. A strange metal box whose sides heated and cooled independent of the fire, provided a bit more cozy shelter from the chilly evening breeze.

The pallet stacks that acted as firewood behaved oddly. As I climbed the stacks barefoot to heave pallets into the fire, they sometimes wobbled intensely. Then the next time I scaled the same stack, the pallets were inexplicably still as a stone.

When the sun rose over the snow-dusted scene, that voice reemerged. "Get that fire roaring," he said. So, I did.

As I ascended the palette stacks, I experienced something new. The wood became almost too hot to stand on, despite them being outdoors on a snowy night far from the fire. How could that happen? Like the wobbling wood, that self-heating metal box, the well-timed explosion, and the spinning Styrofoam, they seemed human-authored. Something unique was taking place.

I tossed pallets into the dumpster until the fire grew so fierce that a sprinkler system triggered from above. I sped into higher gear, throwing pallets in that were getting heavier by the second from being doused by water. After dumping dozens into the dumpster, I stepped away to catch my breath, soaking wet and cold.

A mocking voice from the speaker began ridiculing me. "Why are you walking away? Come on! Why can't you do them all?" I ignored it and took a few deep inhales. The moment I turned around to throw the last 30 in, several fire trucks and an ambulance rounded the corner.

They had me sit on the ground about 100 feet from the dumpster. Firefighters reeled out a hose and dropped it on the ground, then slung a couple of axes on the lip of the dumpster. Next, they did nothing.

Minutes passed while two firefighters stood motionless near the blazing dumpster. Their stillness was abnormally reminiscent of the blue-suited men standing with the supervisor outside my visitation door. A few other firefighters milled about their trucks as the fire raged.

Curious if they were waiting for my help, I stood and stepped toward the dumpster. "Sit down," they said as they sprang into action, quenching the flames within seconds. They did nothing for minutes until the moment I rose and started over there. It was eerie.

When I laid on a stretcher in the back of the ambulance, a short-haired female paramedic leaned over me, two inches from my face. Nose-to-nose like a bully on the playground, she pierced her gaze into mine and asked, "Are you going to tell me the truth?"

"Yes."

She leaped backwards into her seat, grinning ear-to-ear.

"You gotta tell me about driving your van into the water!"

Instantly, her threatening posture succumbed to exuberant glee. She made it sound like dunking my van into the drink was the coolest thing, one of The Post's ways of encouraging me to act crazy.

The paramedic couldn't have been sweeter as she warmed my feet en route to the hospital. When we arrived, she wheeled me in. Just inside the doorway of the ER's ambulance entrance, a man in scrubs leaned into my ear as he strode past and whispered. "Thank you, sir."

Huh? Can it get any weirder?

It does.

In my hospital room, a nurse asked me a lengthy series of questions, some very atypical of an ER visit. She rattled them off one after the next until I lied. She stopped and stared at me for a good 15 seconds before asking any further questions. Nervous and unsettled, I lied again while faking a yawn. "Sorry, I'm tired." She finished her inquiry and left the room.

A minute afterward, I called her back, apologized for lying, and shared the truth. That's how uncomfortable the experience was.

Seconds later, a man wearing street clothes walked into the room. He took a seat beside me, grabbed the TV remote, turned it on, and tuned to the last period of a hockey game between the Pittsburgh Penguins and St. Louis Blues. He moved the volume to 67. I said, "'67, that's the year both teams entered the league." He smiled and nodded. During the next commercial break, he flipped the volume up and down through some players' numbers. How often does someone cycle a TV's volume to 87, then to 9, back to 71, and down to 27 before settling on something appropriate?

When the game returned, 30 fans turned to wave at the camera as if to say hi. I've seen thousands of games, but never that. Maybe one or two fans will do it, but not half a seating section. After the game, I never saw him again.

At least my exploits finally made the news. The headline in the *Chambersburg Public Opinion* said everything: "Man charged with 'risking catastrophe' for setting dumpster on fire, police say."

In the Christmas letter to The Post two months earlier, where I also filled them in about my vasectomy, I wrote:

> "The other day I was curious what you would find, so I Googled myself for the first time in years. The photo that popped up was a closeup of me playing zombie with the kids. Whoever found that pic must have thought, 'Crap, this guy really has had a rough 10 years!' How that ended up on the internet becoming one of your first impressions of me, I have no idea. I gave up after seeing that and figured I'd leave you to it."

Nowadays, the top result is my mugshot. They charged me with felony risking catastrophe, reckless burning or exploding, misdemeanor possession of drug paraphernalia, and criminal mischief. I spent the next 11 days in jail before my parents paid bail. Like my life outside, jail was far from normal—in fact, it grew even stranger. And I was there more than 11 days.

7

INJUSTICE FOR SALE

I WEAR A SILVER NECKLACE featuring a Hebrew word. Its two letters resemble one, look a little bit like Stonehenge, and spell *chai* (sounds like the tea, but gather phlegm to make the "ch" sound.) *Chai* means life, our most precious gift from God. When Jews celebrate, we toast, "L'Chaim!"—"To life!" The Lord has given us many commandments to follow, but we're allowed to break them for one overriding reason—to save a life.

Every Hebrew letter has a number associated with it, and the two letters in *chai* equal 18. Life is considered so valuable and precious, we symbolically wish recipients a good life by giving gifts and donations in multiples of 18.

Lawyers don't donate by 18s. They donate by thousands, and it goes straight to judges for election campaigns and courtroom favors, ravaging the lives of countless innocent people.

Judges are not to be messed with because their immunity allows them to do anything for any reason. Thanks to this, lawyers routinely make financial contributions to judges' election campaigns to sway them to their side in the courtroom. Business isn't good for a law firm that never wins a case.

In states across the country, family law judges have routinely sided with attorney donors while neglecting all facts of the case. There are millions of innocent children involved, and judges don't care. Neither do the lawyers who charge hundreds per hour to win for their client, regardless if they're right or wrong and no matter the cost to the kids. In far too many instances, lawyers and judges exhibit a complete disregard for them. It's not about which home is best for the kids; it's about which parent can hire the most connected lawyer.

Here's a frightening fact: A ruling detrimental to children behooves the court system financially. If judges and lawyers make a mistake, the case winds up back in family court, without juries or oversight, increasing their exorbitant income.

My kids' BIA billed me $9,000 since our case reopened in 2022, solely because her previous handiwork devastated her clients' school grades. My personal lawyers cost almost twice that. Attorneys pocket the cash parents spend in efforts to help, or sometimes hurt their kids. But it doesn't end there.

The court, or court-appointed attorneys like the BIA, often hand-select outside professionals like psychiatrists with whom they've often had prior successful dealings. These outsiders profit repeatedly, as long as they cater to the whims of the court or BIA. To stop this, everybody in mental health and related medical fields should have to work with the court. That way, judges and BIAs don't repeatedly recruit the same few who profit off that close relationship and conceal malfeasance. More eyes will be on the court system.

Currently, as appreciation for a successful outcome and gesture in hopes of future favor, both enlisted medical professionals and lawyers send money back to judges as campaign dollars to keep them positioned to strike again. Judges game the lucrative system because they can, but kids are caught in the crossfire. Children such as my own, who fail school and have limited plans and goals, are destined to become strains on society without intervention.

Moses served as the earliest judge in the Bible. Shortly after God freed the Israelites from Egypt, Moses' father-in-law visited and recognized the high volume of cases was too burdensome for one person, so they established a system for selecting judges. The prerequisites were knowledge of the law and fear of God; the latter, Torah teaches, leads judges to spurn ill-gotten gain. We're taught bribes are forbidden because they blind the eyes of the discerning and upset the plea of the just.

Campaign contributions are modern-day bribes. How are we supposed to pursue justice when we've made it legal to buy off our judges?

Instances have arisen where lawyers complained about opposing counsel giving money to the trial judge. And judges retaliated. They've refused to file cases, innocent people have been carted off to jail, and children have lost loving parents. All because someone confronted injustice.

Judges are often elected to their post or to remain there, and they spend fortunes on their campaigns. As much as two-thirds of that funding comes from law firms. Most money is given by large law firms that represent big companies, who seek to win more cases while corporations they represent are protected from lawsuits by wronged employees. It's a win-win for those with significant money and power. But it's a lose-lose for the rest of us because we're those employees and those same law firms often have family lawyers.

There are plenty of high dollar suits, but by far, the court's most lucrative legal area is family law. Estimates say anywhere from $50-200 billion a year flows through the family law court, more than all other segments of court combined. The high end is more than the GDP of 17 U.S. states. Poor judicial decisions result in continuous re-litigation, which pours more money into the hands of lawyers, judges, and complicit professionals.

Lawyers contribute about half the total campaign dollars judges raise, whereas lawyers account for only five percent of money given to others running for public office. They know who to pay off. Judges rely on the people who bring cases before them to propel them to the bench and entrench them there. Those who stand to benefit most are lawyers who contributed money, making justice a tradable commodity rather than the discernment between right and wrong.

In Texas, a mother lost custody because the father's lawyer and the court-appointed lawyer for the child were both big campaign donors to the judge. A second judge ruled there was no conflict of interest regarding campaign funds.

"This thing about campaign contributions is as uncomfortable for a judge as any topic you can get on," the second judge said during his ruling. "That's because you folks that are non-lawyers don't contribute to judicial campaigns. And the only way that a judge can run for reelection is to raise money for all those things that cost to get your name before the public. And you know who has the most interest in seeing that done? The lawyers."

Conflicts of interest like this frequently arise, and the law requires judges to disqualify themselves from the case. But they usually don't. A petition can be filed requesting the judge to step off the case. However, their cohort judges routinely dismiss these appeals so their buddy can remain in cases, harboring additional grudges against the concerned parties that petitioned.

From 2004 to 2012, North Carolina curtailed private campaign contributions. Instead of receiving large payouts from lawyers and businesses with something to gain, judicial candidates (including those vying for the State Supreme Court) could opt for a public grant that encouraged many smaller donations between $10 and $500. Once they reached a threshold of $80,000, grant money provided a larger sum of double or triple that amount raised.

With no single donor accounting for more than $500, conflicts of interest were decimated, and studies showed judges who chose the public grant route became far more impartial in their rulings. Despite its success, the State House repealed the law in 2013.

Fast forward to 2022. Over $15 million was contributed toward four candidates who vied for two North Carolina Supreme Court seats, with over $8 million coming from two Super PACs alone. How can judges rule impartially when they won their election solely because of a political party's aid?

States that insist on private donations should require anonymity. Lawyers are the people most familiar with a judge's ability, but they also stand to benefit the most from corruption. Quid pro quo would be eliminated if judges don't know who paid money to their campaigns. Additional fundraising events exist, such as dinners that rake in $100 per guest, where all anonymity is lost. They should be abolished.

Issues with campaign dollars are prevalent in all levels of state court, including supreme courts. Without juries, proper supervision, and public awareness, family law judges are exploiting their immunity to the extreme detriment of our family structures. Kids are growing up thinking a good parent is bad and vice versa.

Many judges, like mine, are first appointed by the state governor before ever seeking election by public vote, so politics plays a hefty role in our courts from the start.

Voters, however, face limited options. My judge won her first election in 2018, the year after taking my kids from me and two years after the governor's appointment. The county's voters had two candidates to choose from—both incumbents—and two Circuit Court spots to fill. The only way the sitting judges could've lost was if a write-in candidate took home more votes, but only 0.6% of voters chose that option.

In Maryland that year, 40 Circuit Court positions were up for election; with 45 candidates to fill those 40 spots. Voters from 12 of the state's 16 jurisdictions had no option but to choose an incumbent judge or provide a write-in ballot.

Several states, including Maryland, also feature retention elections for judges. These provide voters a "Yes-No" choice whether to retain judges in their current position another ten years. "Yes" routinely wins about 85% of the vote, despite voters declaring they know little to nothing about the judge.

Voters complain they are unfamiliar with each candidate's judicial track record or whether disciplinary actions have been levied. That info isn't readily available nor presented publicly. Online case searches don't allow us to search by judge. Even if they did, case outcomes are often very difficult to interpret and there's no mention of evidence. Little, if anything, is known of their background, and basic biographies don't suggest conflicts of interest or questionable motives.

The unfortunate reality is that many voters either leave their ballot blank or choose a nominee because they like their name, saw them on TV, or saw signs around town.

That marketing derived from campaign contributions, which prevent outsiders from wasting their time and money running while risking their career and wellbeing in the process.

Without fear of job loss or public awareness, there's no incentive for judges to deal honestly or fairly, only motivation to profit as much as possible for themselves and their friends.

My judge sided against the facts because of friendships dating to the 1990s. Like most judges, she began as a local attorney. In the six months preceding her judicial appointment, she worked ten Frederick County cases as a lawyer. Seven of them involved my BIA. Upon appointment, she passed three of her open cases directly to the BIA, and they were the only two lawyers working on two more. They collaborated closely and there's no oversight.

They both worked as clerk for the county's chief judge, who retired months before my trial after serving 25 years as chief. All three worked alongside his replacement for almost 20 years. These people spend decades backing one another, with complete immunity, at the expense of innocent parents and children.

There is a state commission where I could file a complaint about the BIA. The Attorney Grievance Commission is a group of lawyers that decide whether an action against a lawyer goes to court before a judge. My judge ruled over such a case this year, so it's likely she would preside over this complaint as well. What chance do I have when the target of my complaint shares a law office with the judge?

How absurd can this conflict of interest get? In Brooklyn, New York, the Grievance Commission shares the same office suite as the Office of Attorneys for Children, their version of the BIA.

There's a joke amongst lawyers: What is the difference between a good lawyer and a bad lawyer? A bad lawyer procrastinates and makes a case last forever. A good lawyer makes it take even longer. My BIA is a good lawyer.

The case should have been resolved in months; instead, it's lasting the entire second half of Colin's childhood. As a lawyer, she knows how to make money, but she never had to learn to do her job properly.

Best Interest Attorneys in Maryland are required to have just six hours of training before working cases that decide children's futures. According to *Maryland Standards of Practice for Court-Appointed Lawyers Representing Children in Custody Cases*, they're expected to know and successfully be able to implement the following by the end of that six-hour class:

(a) Representation guidelines and standards,

(b) Children's development, needs, and abilities at different stages,

(c) Effectively communicating with children,

(d) Preparing and presenting a child's viewpoint, including child testimony and alternatives to direct testimony,

(e) Recognizing, evaluating, and understanding evidence of child abuse and neglect,

(f) Family dynamics and dysfunction, domestic violence, and substance abuse,

(g) Recognizing the limitations of attorney expertise and the need for other professional expertise, which may include professionals who can provide information on evaluation, consultation, and testimony on mental health, substance abuse, education, special needs, or other issues,

(h) [Be familiar with] available resources for children and families in child custody and child access disputes.

I spent more time in food safety class learning to refrigerate stuff between 33 and 38 degrees before becoming assistant manager at a pizza place.

Family court judges are similarly undertrained. Because they rotate over more exciting matters like jury trials and serious criminal offenses, most family court judges dislike family law. They're there because they have to be, and they make it worth their while by taking advantage of the court's loopholes.

More money flows through family law than any other entity, and it extends beyond the walls of the courthouse. Complicit doctors, psychologists, and therapists side with court-appointed lawyers to make bank, and to secure future profits as they are reemployed. Easily swayed judges earn their vote and campaign funds. And judges do as they please when slamming the gavel since jury trials are nonexistent in family law courts.

I'm pleased with my current lawyer, especially compared to most of the others I've suffered through. She's the eighth divorce attorney I've had in 15 years.

Upon searching for this latest lawyer, my selection process narrowed my choice between her and one other. The alternative was a partner in a law firm whose lead attorney recently lost a close election to the county's incumbent Circuit Court judge. Who knows what mudslinging transpired?

I assumed the winning judge might frown upon that attorney and would take revenge on the client. So, I opted for someone else.

Because they later docketed us with that judge, I was content with my decision to hire my attorney. We settled in mediation in 2023 so that I could try to mend my relationship with Colin, though Lucy and Ethan were a lost cause since they're now adults. Therefore, we avoided going before the judge, but the political nature of the courts persuaded me to select one attorney over another.

Judges are almost always former lawyers, and that lawyer joke is one of their favorites. A revolving door of discontent families pockets them and their accomplices more and more cash. Many folks, like me, have spent more time in divorce court than in their marriage. I was hitched for seven years but have been mired in the legal system over twice that long. Others spent as many months married as they've spent years in court litigating their divorce.

Many in the field don't find family law fulfilling, so they seize on the immense financial profits. It's ravaging millions and millions of children every year. These innocent victims have no clue they're being preyed upon, and well-intentioned parents are picked apart by vultures who collect their take before they move on to the next unsuspecting victims.

My situation is not rare, and frighteningly the BIA in my case is among thousands who profit at the expense of children. If she was rare, The Post would've published this story years ago somewhere in the depths of their local Metro section. But after five years of investigating, they discovered the problem to be so rampant, they couldn't handle everything themselves.

In June 2022, I passed my story and evidence to many other major news outlets. I made that a 75th birthday present for my dad. Oblivious, he liked his 76th birthday gift better when I cleaned and detailed his SUV.

Over 30 national and local news agencies received everything on June 5th that year. The next morning, a conspicuous work van made an odd U-turn in front of my house the moment I stepped outside. The driver stared at me a few seconds, pulled away, and everything else remained the same. I continued my daily routine, knowing my every move was being observed from the shadows.

Eating lunch four months later in the food court inside CNN Center in Atlanta was an extraordinary experience. What did they think of me sitting alone after downtown museum hopping, munching on my sandwich surrounded by a dozen stories of office windows glaring down on me from their newsrooms above?

8

CROSS-COUNTRY CORRUPTION

WHY COULDN'T THE POST COPE with everything themselves? As they followed the money, they exposed a half-century of family court corruption nationwide, more prevalent today than ever.

Devastated parents have nowhere to turn but the same expensive legal process that callously wrecked them and their children. They're left bankrupt at a dead end, with their kids' entire lives forever upended.

How many sad souls are affected?

Half of American children will witness the end of their parents' marriage. That means one of every two children we encounter has either been preyed on by racketeering family court judges and lawyers or is at high risk of being victimized. If it's not your child, it's their best friend.

Because our courts seem to enjoy breaking apart families for profit, almost a quarter of American kids live in single-parent homes, the highest rate of any country in the world.

Every year in this nation, nearly four million new family court cases are filed. That's four million sets of mothers, fathers, and children signing themselves and their savings over to a corrupt system. Because the flawed court process encourages high conflict divorce, over 22 million American parents report being alienated from their children at varying degrees.

Via taxes, we pay judges to destroy our families. They then appoint lawyers, custody evaluators, psychologists, and other complicit medical professionals to take us for yearslong rides as they profit financially with no surveillance or backlash. Those experts reciprocate for the high-paying job by ignoring facts which conflict with the judges' wishes—such as siding with the parent's attorney who contributed campaign money to the judge.

These professionals often operate with indifference and routinely neglect the true best interests of children. And parents, including those who are railroaded, are forced to pay each of them thousands upon thousands of dollars.

Early in my divorce, a clinical psychologist teamed with a different BIA on behalf of my ex-wife. A week after meeting with her for an hour, the psychologist recommended removing the kids from me, claiming it was because of something I supposedly told her. I forget what her accusation was, but I know I said, "I never told you that."

"Yes, you did," she said.

"I don't remember saying anything like that. That's not how I talk, and I never would've said it."

Her response sealed my fate. "It's common among people who take pain medications like you to not remember what they said." She could've claimed I said anything, and she did.

Judges have gotten away with that too. They've sealed cases so expert witnesses and lawyers can't access records or the judge's findings and opinions to build a defense. Parents have lost their kids, and because of the seal, nobody knows why.

Further, judges across the country presented with documented evidence of child abuse—physical, sexual, or otherwise—have insisted that children be returned to the abuser, under threat of imprisonment of the protective parent.

A New England judge whose catchphrase is, "It's my courtroom and I'll do what I want," gathered lawyers, a BIA, and psychological evaluator to work on behalf of a father. Then she disallowed the mother's witnesses and medical providers, in favor of her own handpicked therapists who further backed the father. As the judge praised the attorneys and court process that removed custody from the mother, she insisted marital assets be sold to pay the attorneys.

But a few other judges from an adjoining district in her state presided over a case that might be the worst I encountered, something detailed in Chapter 33.

Out West, a woman with children from two separate relationships had a different judge in each case. One judge's wife was a friend of the opposing attorney, while the other had no such conflict. Despite presenting the same evidence to each judge, the mother lost custody of her oldest kids before the conflicted judge, but maintained custody of the youngest with the latter.

In Colorado, a custody evaluator received tens of thousands of dollars per case to decide on custody involving parents alleged of abuse. Several plaintiffs sued him upon learning that he himself pleaded guilty to a similar charge. He was on record saying he didn't believe 90% of abuse claims.

In the center of the country, the problem in and around St. Louis, Missouri, has grown so bad, multiple podcasts, news articles, and petitions have arisen to shed light on the corruption rife throughout its family court. Not surprisingly, investigations discovered the situation pervades the entire state.

In one wretched rural Missouri case three hours south of St. Louis, a convicted child sex offender imprisoned for raping his oldest daughter, paid off a Guardian ad Litem to testify at a sentencing hearing for his release from prison. The Guardian ad Litem told a younger daughter that the abusive father would get custody of her if prison sets him free. The next day, tragically, that 14-year-old girl died by suicide.

Teen depression and suicide are up, and as tough as things are for us wronged parents, they're the most affected and vulnerable from corrupt court decisions. How improved will the world's future be if we repair the next generation now?

The America First Policy Institute indicates almost a quarter of American children live without a father at home, but they represent over 70% of youth in jails and substance abuse centers. Fatherless kids are six times more likely to commit criminal acts and live in poverty.

They represent 90% of homeless children and 63% of youth suicides. Over 80% of school shooters were raised in unstable family environments. Of kids exhibiting behavioral disorders, 85% don't have a dad at home. That's 20 times the national average.

Why do so many kids lose their father?

There's a number of reasons, but everything filters from the top. Courts set the standard for society to uphold. When courts don't care about family structure, our communities won't either.

A judge refused to look at a father's evidence upon his asking for the mother to be held in contempt of court for refusing to let him see the kids. The judge denied the contempt, and said regarding the mother, "That's the children's caretaker."

"What am I?" asked the father.

"You're the financial support."

It turned out the mother alienated the child from him so much that upon meeting her father years later, the kid said dad was nothing like what her mom portrayed. By choice, she switched to live with her dad, proving another botched case by the court.

A 2019 study by the Dad's Resource Center reviewed 700 contested custody cases in Pennsylvania and found mothers received full or primary custody at a 5:1 rate of fathers.

Because a major portion of the court's financial profit derives from child support, it incentivizes giving one parent more custody than the other to trigger pricey child support payments. Mothers earn more than fathers in just 17% of households. It's hard not to note the exact same percentage of single parents awarded custody are fathers, thereby leaving the vast majority of dads on the hook for child support. That enriches the court. And if they can't afford the payments, which can be 20-60% of a parent's income for one child, they get locked up.

There's 50,000 people in jail every day that wound up there because of child support. Nationwide just a decade ago, 76% of those incarcerated for not paying earned less than $10,000 per year. How can they make money for child support if they're in jail? Upon release, they racked up interest owed to the state that never sees the other parent so they're further behind. And jobs are lost or future employment opportunities take a nosedive when they're behind bars. It's a vicious cycle.

And because family court doesn't give parents access to a public defender since it's civil, not criminal, a needy parent has no legal representation despite facing incarceration.

An involved father of four was issued an arrest warrant for owing $18,000 in child support, mostly interest to the state. A prior child support arrest cost him his job, so the payments became even more difficult. Stopped by police for a broken taillight, he ran. They shot him to death. Four kids lost their dad over a few thousand dollars.

One of the economic incentives to destroy families derives from the 1975 Social Security Act. States receive federal money from Title IV-D, which reimburses 66¢ for every dollar spent to collect child support.

Though the funds aren't intended to cover judicial salaries and expenses, they encompass practically everyone else, including magistrates, clerk's office staff, courthouse attorneys and their staff. Plus, funding reaches folks who locate parents, establish paternity, and collect and distribute child support. They all get padded paychecks thanks to Title IV-D.

Likewise, Title IV-E repays court officials and foster care agencies involved in removing kids from their parents and placing them in foster care. It's another avenue exploited by these same court-appointed people.

In the family law world free of checks and balances, abuses of these federal programs run rampant.

Kids affected by Title IV-D must live without their paying parent, usually a father. Statistics show they face a future of poverty, addiction, depression, and legal woes.

In contrast, cases where parents receive 50/50 shared time are presumed that each parent covers their own costs of raising the kids. Unless the income disparity between the mother and father is significant, the court will not award either parent child support. Such was the case when I shared 50/50 custody with my ex-wife. Therefore, the court and its actors walked away without a penny.

However, if one parent is granted more time with the children, it opens the door for collecting child support, which enriches those affiliated with the process. That's what's occurred when I haven't shared 50/50 time. Though children suffer, the court makes out—and as case after case reveals, that's what they seem to care about most.

Perhaps the worst element is this: Having winners and losers in court creates unnecessary hostility between the children's parents. Children are shattered by it. Equally shared parenting has proven to deter such conflict and is ideal for kids. But it isn't profitable. Only families thrive, not courts.

Courts have become a financially rewarding system for lawyers and others as custody cases become more involved, keeping them on the payroll for years rather than months. At upwards of $400 an hour, the money parents shell over sends the lawyer's kids to college rather than their own.

Because family courts frequently ignore evidence, parents' lawyers have discovered that concocting false allegations often not only helps their client, it frequently guarantees a one-sided outcome. That opens the door for substantial child support, and means more time lawyers spend on complex cases involving devastated kids resulting in bigger paydays for themselves.

A quickly mediated 50/50 split does no such thing.

There is essentially no penalty if the allegation is proven false, which is often hard to do. Colin and Lucy had their lips sealed by the BIA. Had Ethan not said I targeted the entire community, how could I possibly prove my innocence? The risk is worth the reward, but it can be catastrophic for the wellbeing of children.

False allegations go one of two ways: either the protective parent's fear garners support that is weaponized throughout the process, or they lose the kids because they are assumed to be alienating them. My case had both.

I was initially the protective parent concerned about the new live-in boyfriend, but had my worries reversed when my ex-wife and son claimed that I was verbally abusing my kids and their friends. The court, therefore, perceived me as both alienator and abuser.

The BIA accused me of coaching Ethan to offer concerning statements about witnessing the boyfriend's threat. But she ignored the fact Ethan must have been directed by his mother, the only other person to have made the false allegation. Because she wasn't my biggest fan, the BIA trumpeted the phony charge. And with only the BIA-friendly judge to convince, I lost.

Screwing me meant nothing to them because not only do judges have immunity, the attorneys they appoint on behalf of children do, too.

Judges take this oath: "I do solemnly swear that I will administer justice without respect to persons, and do equal right to the poor and to the rich, and that I will faithfully and impartially discharge and perform all the duties incumbent upon me as Judge under the Constitution and laws of the United States. So help me God."

How much worse would they be if God wasn't helping?

One of *Netflix's* top movies of 2021 is based on a true story out of our country's corrupt family court system.

I Care a Lot follows a nefarious court-appointed guardian whose real-life counterpart from Nevada is serving a 16-40 year prison term for threatening and swindling elders out of money. Elderly individuals and couples were removed from their homes, separated from family members, and bilked of their life savings under the guardian's guardianships.

Guess who else performs guardianships. My kids' BIA. In fact, she's the county's point of contact for all things concerning their Elder, Disability, & Guardianship Law Section.

It's not just kids being destroyed by these people. They prey on everyone who's vulnerable.

They operate with immunity in a world where our general assumption that evidence matters is absent. "Beyond a reasonable doubt" doesn't exist. And there is no right to an attorney, often forcing parents to face criminal allegations without legal counsel.

Without my parents' financial aid, I could never have afforded a lawyer who helped me fend off spurious claims a decade ago. Without that lawyer, I doubt I would've regained 50/50 custody from 2013 to 2017. Then, after losing my kids in 2017, I couldn't afford another attorney's $5,000 to $10,000 retainer fee to re-litigate using witnesses. Money didn't arrive until the statute of limitations expired.

Judges have supreme and absolute authority to determine the fates of divorcing parents and children they never meet and barely know. The system is designed to fail kids, which fails the future of our country.

Judges have no understanding of the long-term repercussions of their decisions. Maybe an electronic system that links school grades to custody change can highlight when mistakes were made and allow judges to correct their rulings. We just need some anti-corruption folks to enforce it.

Though statistics and studies prove the value of 50/50 shared parenting time, only a few states have enacted laws to that effect. A survey revealed 77% of Americans agree that children are better off when both parents focus equally on their careers and home life. That's very much in line with the advantageous 50/50 shared parenting plan that courts so infrequently adhere to. They actually profit if they don't.

An American teenage girl who lost her loving father said, "As far as relationships go, I have a lot of trust issues now."

Contrast that with a teenager from Sweden, a country that has presumed 50/50 custody unlike the United States. Because she split time with both parents, she said, "It's like I have two different lives. You have your life at mom's and your house with mom. Then you've got your life at dad's. I find that really fun."

9

THE FEARLESS GOALIE

U NLIKE MY KIDS, I HAD a pretty easy childhood. Hockey played a major part of it. It began when my dad took me to a Washington Capitals game when I was three years old. I don't remember it, but he says I loved it so much I wanted to play.

My first skating lesson went as well as my first day of preschool, which God knows wasn't good. So did my mom, teachers, and the entire class. "Take me home!"

Though I continued preschool that year, I stopped skating. Two years later, my dad brought me to another Caps game. "Dad, I want to play." That time I fell in love with skating lessons, joined a hockey team, and won the coveted Most Improved Skater Award in my first season. It sucks when the highlight of a hockey career happens so early on.

I played eight years as a kid, letting me experience life at an early age. On our first day of practice, when I was in kindergarten, we were on ice dressed in skater's gear when the coach huddled us together. "We need a goalie," he said. "Does anyone want to play goalie?" My hand flew in the air. No one else's did. As I told The Post, that was my best impulse decision ever.

I was our team's only goalie almost every year I played, which taught me responsibility because I couldn't miss a practice, and certainly not a game. The added pressure was fun, knowing I could either win games or lose them single-handedly for the entire team.

When we won, everyone said, "Great game, goalie!" When we lost, they said, "Great game, goalie!" With such low standards, losses weren't much of a letdown.

Our team often competed in out-of-town tournaments, where we'd play in Philadelphia, Montreal, Toronto, Buffalo, and Boston. Our keisters got handed to us in Canada, but those were entertaining, because it's seldom a goalie faces 60 shots in a 36-minute game.

My greatest hockey experiences were our annual shootout tournaments during intermissions at Capitals games. They were one-on-one competitions where each team brought a skater and a goalie. Each skater had three chances to score goals, like the shootout that decides the end of tied pro games today. Whoever scored more won the shootout and moved on to the next round, earning tickets for another Caps game, and another opportunity to dress in the referees' locker room where Muhammad Ali prepared for his fights a decade earlier.

Our team employed a different skater each year, one of whom became my best friend. Since I was the lone goalie, I was the only kid who participated every year. It was so much fun!

We arrived at games early and walked through the players' entrance, often bumping into some of them. Down many flights of stairs, we passed the Capitals' dressing room and stuck our equipment in our locker room beside the visiting team. I always had a good peek inside the away dressing room, where the obstructing white cinderblock wall was a sight to behold.

From our seats, we watched the first ten minutes of action before heading downstairs to change. Suited up and ready to hit the ice at the end of the first period, the Capitals' opponent passed us as they left the ice. Players, many of whom are Hall of Famers, whacked my pads and wished me luck on the way by.

For whatever reason, I seemed to be my best in these shootouts. I think some kids were nervous playing in front of thousands of fans, but I was stoked.

After winning, we got tickets for another game to compete in the next round. If we lost, I had to wait until next year. To win the whole competition, there were about four rounds to sweep that year. Of all the trophies I ever received, including a team MVP and the Most Improved Skater award, these were the nicest. I won the trophy back-to-back years, and should've won a third.

As I alluded to in my letter to The Post, the lousy ref screwed me. Afterwards, our opponents said we should've won, not them. But it doesn't matter if the ref doesn't understand the rules.

There's a simple shootout policy that as soon as the goalie touches the puck, the skater can't regain control and score, something the ref should have known. The kid skated in on me and I dove out, knocking the puck ten feet away from him. That should have been it. Shootout over, we win the trophy. But it wasn't. I started celebrating, and the kid quit until we realized there was no whistle. We looked at the ref, who said, "Keep going." Because skaters move faster than goalies, he grabbed the puck and scored before I was back in goal.

Man, I let that ref have it. Fans behind the glass laughed as I chewed him out. I couldn't figure out what was so funny.

Sure, I performed these feats on Bowie's B team because I wasn't good enough for the A team, but it was fun to feel like I might have belonged.

When our team played out-of-state, we often made a family trip out of it. Whenever we went to Boston, we visited historical sites like Plymouth Rock, Boston Common, Faneuil Hall, and the Salem Witch Trials. We took in a baseball game at Fenway Park, road-tripped to the end of Cape Cod, and went whale-watching off Nantucket.

My dad used to travel with his parents to New Hampshire to ease summer hay fever attacks, so we made it a point to spend the week at Lake Winnipesaukee and North Conway in the White Mountains a few times. I loved the local card shop, where I always failed to coax my parents into buying an early 20th century Christy Mathewson baseball card. Rather than spend a small fortune on one card that also advertised tobacco, they settled on two boxes of modern hockey cards, filled with sticks of crunchy, waxy gum. There's nothing like chilling poolside with my dad at six years old, opening 72 packs of cards and shoving 72 sticks of brittle gum into our mouths.

One of the most sobering moments of my life occurred during a trip to Buffalo. I always wanted true Buffalo wings, but my dad doesn't like chicken and my mom doesn't like spice, so it never happened. Instead, my dad preferred the hotel restaurant. It was 1989. I was ten years old when the world's most gruesome sports injury occurred in that city the week before I arrived.

The Capitals just traded one of their goalies to Buffalo. In his sixth game with his new team, Clint Malarchuk's throat was sliced by a player's skate. With a severed artery and a clipped jugular, he clutched his throat as blood gushed onto the ice. He lost almost two liters and needed 300 stitches to close the wound. Malarchuk almost died.

One week later, my dad and I set foot in our hotel's restaurant. At a table 20 feet in front of us, a man sat with a giant gauze pad wrapped around the front half of his neck.

My dad whispered in my ear. "That's Clint Malarchuk."

"Can we say hi?"

"No, I think we should leave him be."

My dad insisted we let him eat in peace. It was incredible seeing him days after the horrific injury that caused players to vomit on the ice, 11 fans in attendance to faint, and two to suffer heart attacks.

Soon after, I started wearing extra throat protection, and saw my position in a whole new way. Safety mattered for the first time. My equipment wasn't thick and didn't cover everything, so I was often getting struck with pucks where there was little or no padding to cushion the blow. It hurt, but it was no big deal unless I missed snaring a puck in my glove because the last shot left me dead-armed. A throat being sliced open is different for a kid.

Playing all this hockey made a few days of P.E. class each year especially fun—for me. From the time the teacher said we were playing hockey on our gym floor, the grumbling began. Captains were chosen before the all-important moment when they learned who picked first. It's the only sport I was consistently taken first.

Whoever selected second dropped their head and kicked the air. "Man, we're going to lose bad. I don't want to play." So did everyone else unfortunate enough to wind up on that team. P.E. class never saw such lopsided outcomes in anything we ever played except hockey.

Looking back, I may have been a bit selfish, but everyone on my team enjoyed watching me snake through a gym of "get out of his ways" with the puck/ball to score a goal, then race back to play goalie, make a save, and repeat that a dozen times. It was exhilarating for exactly half the class.

Who wants to see Connor McDavid or Wayne Gretzky against my P.E. class?

Years before all my kids joined soccer, Ethan played hockey shortly after our divorce. The Capitals goalie, Michal Neuvirth, visited the rink and tugged Ethan around the ice by his stick. After practice, we asked him to sign next to 15 other player autographs we attained on Ethan's 5-foot-long, red-white-and-blue team banner, the only wall hanging my dad didn't throw away.

Ethan skated for a season and played his last game as a goalie. This proud papa watched him pitch a shutout.

Around that time, my ex-wife phoned me in tears. "What's wrong?" I asked.

She reminisced over one of the saddest days of Colin's young life. "I was looking at Colin's face," she said, referring to the several-inch scar marring his forehead since infancy. "I'm worried people will make fun of him."

"I have an idea," I said. "Let's get him into hockey. You know hockey players have scarred faces, and many girls find that attractive."

"Okay," she said with new resolve in her voice, probably reliving some of her own crushes on pro hockey players. Good news for me—a puck ripped open my chin a few years back, and I needed six stitches to seal the wound.

But, unexplainably, my ex-wife stopped bringing Ethan to hockey the following season and Colin never signed up.

Years later, we explored soccer, which was far cheaper, didn't require as much costly travel or equipment, and seemed similar enough. We agreed to enroll the kids.

After watching them play one season, I got the coaching bug. So, I began watching pro soccer—a lot of soccer—to learn about the sport and its rules. I fell in love with Liverpool, who won championships year after year in the 1980s while I spent my youth idolizing a Capitals team that routinely blew 3-1 series leads in the playoffs unlike any team in history.

Over the summer, I grasped enough to enlist as a coach that fall. Coaching was perhaps my favorite activity with my kids. Somehow, I lucked into repeated gigs as head coach even though my assistants played soccer.

At the first practice I ever led, the team's top player said, "You're the best coach I ever had." I loved coaching.

Just like his dad, Ethan played goalie. He was fearless. I taught him to be aggressive, but he took it to another level. "I've never seen a goalie so far up the field," said an opponent when we trailed by a goal late. Of course, Ethan was just imitating his favorite goalkeeper, Germany's

Manuel Neuer of Bayern Munich. He often clattered into oncoming players to snatch the ball before they shot, thanks to a drill I devised. I either kicked the ball at him hard or gently nudged it forward. Without knowing, he had to save the shot or dart out and smother the ball. Ethan excelled at it.

I coached all three kids' teams for five seasons. We met lots of families, and they made many new friends. Ethan even played with his longtime best friend from school. They also played *Minecraft* and *Roblox* over *Skype* together with other buddies as they chatted online for hours, building worlds and destroying enemies.

Colin and Lucy were that way, too. They loved video games because it allowed them and their friends to spend plenty of time together after school. Their riotous laughter made me smile. It's these same children to whom I allegedly told creepy stuff, and lost custody of my kids as a result. That was the only reason the judge gave for forcing me from their lives.

On the witness stand in 2017, my ex-wife's lawyer asked if I believed Ethan was lying. I said, "He also said I tell his f—". About to say "friends", the lawyer interrupted, demanding a yes or no answer. Ethan's friends were my initial thought. The accusation was absurd and targeted countless others, so I assumed the judge would recognize its falsity.

"Of course he's lying, yes," I said. "What father would tell friends of his on *Skype* about something bad that supposedly happened to his little sibling ten years ago?"

The trial was on its fourth and final day. It required this extra October appearance because the three in August weren't enough. Contrary to the BIA's wishes, the judge didn't let Ethan testify in August because he hadn't yet written the essay required by the juvenile court that handled the case from him slapping me. With the open criminal case, the judge didn't want him to incriminate himself by testifying. My lawyer's idea to file charges against Ethan worked—for a time.

For months after being slapped, I considered whether to press charges against my son, and was leaning away from doing so. But at a pre-trial hearing, when the BIA said she wanted Ethan to testify, my lawyer whispered in my ear. "Now you have to press the charge." It prevented him from testifying for the three days in August, but Ethan completed the essay to close his criminal case in time for him to appear in October.

I had no clue the judge took the absurd allegation seriously until her ruling over one month later, when she uprooted Colin and Lucy from the life they were so used to, and ended any chance at reuniting with Ethan.

10

Do Not Go After the BIA

T HE KIDS WERE DOING WELL before they met their Best Interest Attorney. They spent half their time with my ex-wife where they celebrated Christian holidays, and half with me to partake in Jewish festivities. It's sad their parents were no longer together, but we had a parenting plan that worked for them. They maintained good grades in the highest-level public-school classes, and they enjoyed plenty of extracurricular activities.

When the marriage dissolved in 2009, my ex-wife took her cats and left me our beautiful tan lab-mix named Mandy. I was blessed to keep her, but I also got to keep all the kids' old, stained clothes and outdated toys. Not upset about that at all.

Mandy and I kept each other company during some forlorn years. She wandered into the room. "How are you?" my doggy friend asked through her soulful eyes.

"It's depressing not seeing my family."

"I'm depressed too," said Mandy. "My gimpy owner refuses to walk me."

After about seven more years, which included less solemn moments once custody was restored to 50/50, Mandy grew sick. My mom nurtured her final weeks in her bedroom, placing her food and water bowls by her face because she no longer walked around. Then she stopped eating.

At the vet, we agreed it was time to say goodbye. My ex-wife remained by Mandy's side when the lethal meds were administered while my dad and I waited outside in the parking lot. We couldn't bear to watch. My ex-wife might have been a good vet assistant, which she briefly went to school for, but not an undertaker. Oddly enough, a few days later at Mandy's funeral, my dad and I viewed her body to ensure it was her. My ex-wife couldn't do it. Bizarre. That day, the kids watched my ex-wife and me embrace as we mourned the loss of our beloved family member.

A week or two later, Lucy performed in a concert at school. My ex-wife and I sat side-by-side in the auditorium as Colin and Ethan climbed back and forth on our laps playing. A nearby onlooker would've had no idea their mother and father divorced. She and I were getting along great, and the kids, with fantastic grades and a multitude of friends and after-school activities, were benefiting from it.

Around that time, unbeknownst to me, my ex-wife placed a dating profile online and met somebody. The guy met the kids a few weeks later and moved in with them after six months. I didn't know he existed until after he began living there, which the BIA admitted was problematic. We finally met two months later, when he threatened me with the weed whacker in front of the kids.

On our way home after that incident, I looked at Ethan and said, "He just held a weed whacker to my face."

"I know," he said. "I saw it." Colin and Lucy didn't because their view was obstructed from the back seat by another vehicle. But Ethan witnessed everything from the front.

Later that night, I realized I should file a charge against the boyfriend. Ethan came to the police station, though they never asked him for a statement. While there, I filed a peace order and unknowingly made my earliest mistake in the case.

The police explained I could file one peace order for myself and include the names of the children in it, or file a separate one for each of us. They cost about $75 apiece. To save money, I included their names on mine, but that was a disastrous move.

At the peace order hearing days later, the court ignored the additional names. That meant I could be protected, but not the kids. Had I filed separate ones for the kids, the judge would've heard the cases on their behalf.

Ethan was in the courtroom for the hearing to testify, but the boyfriend didn't contest the peace order safeguarding me alone, negating Ethan's need to testify. So Ethan never went on record.

Further troubling matters, when the boyfriend agreed to the peace order, it meant I couldn't be near my kids when they were with him. So much for keeping them safe—it made it illegal for me to do so.

During her closing argument a year later, the BIA voiced only one issue with my ex-wife. The BIA said she shouldn't have moved the boyfriend in without telling me, and I should've been introduced before he even met the kids.

The BIA acknowledged that my ex-wife's failure to follow her rules from the beginning caused every subsequent problem that opened litigation. Had she followed the BIA's standard, that man wouldn't have threatened me in front of the kids the day we met. However, the BIA disregarded it. She was unsupportive of the victim every step of the way.

After the weed whacker incident, I told my ex-wife I didn't trust the boyfriend around the kids. For their safety, I said she was fine taking them if the boyfriend wasn't there. But she repeatedly refused.

For two-and-a-half months, my ex-wife chose to live with her boyfriend rather than her own children. Only for two weekends did she prefer her kids over her boyfriend. Across 83 days, she welcomed them for six, when she could've had half had she agreed the boyfriend would be absent.

Neither the BIA nor the judge cared she chose this guy over her kids. Why would someone find that acceptable for a mom to do? Especially one you're about to give full custody to.

When the BIA questioned me about this on the trial's last day, the judge jumped in, wanting to assert some judicial wisdom.

"Can I interject just one moment?" The judge spoke to me in an arrogant, egotistic tone, as if she was offering the world's greatest advice to the world's worst father.

"I'm saying this as a teaching moment. Your children's safety goes beyond physical safety. From the court's eyes, your children's safety is also to their emotional health, their wellbeing. And their emotional health and wellbeing comes from having a good relationship—a supported relationship—with both of their parents. Not just one of them, to the exclusion of another. Do you understand it can be detrimental to the children to have that limited a visitation with their mother for that long of a period of time? Equally damaging as anything that caused you to withhold the visitation."

"Yes, I do," I said. "And that's why I was asking my ex-wife every week to arrange to see the children."

"When you say that—well, I'll address this later."

She addressed it one month later by damaging my children's emotional health and wellbeing when she excluded me from their lives by assigning even more limited visitation for a much longer period of time.

Consider me taught.

The BIA and judge were equally okay supplanting me with the boyfriend, insisting he become the kids' new father figure the same year they met. They insisted, without speaking to Lucy or Colin, on placing the kids back in his care and sending custody his way. The judge stuck them together 99.4% of the time, while I was supervised for the remainder.

In the years since, the only quarter the kids did well in school was the quarter the boyfriend broke up with my ex-wife and moved out. He left in September 2022, months after the emergency hearing. That quarter, Colin took eight classes and earned five As and three Bs. Lucy had four As and two Bs. But Colin failed three classes the very next quarter, and Lucy failed two, as they resumed their yearslong decline.

I'm still here, but our bond has become so severed from years of a harsh reality, my impact is meaningless. The kids have no paternal role model in their lives and they're suffering.

When the BIA first joined this case, it was amidst the 83 days my ex-wife repeatedly refused to take the kids as scheduled. For obvious—and less obvious—reasons, I didn't want the boyfriend around. She hadn't seen them in nearly a month when the BIA hatched a plan. Days before officially recommending the kids move back in with the boyfriend, the BIA arranged for my ex-wife to take them to her mom's house for the weekend, without him present. The kids returned here Sunday night.

Monday morning, the BIA met Ethan at his school, where he suddenly sided with his mother, just like he did weeks later with the Philly trip. Ethan had written he saw the weed whacker threat and said it worried him, but after visiting him in school, the BIA told me that Ethan was fine with it. Imagine how that made me feel. Then, without speaking to either Colin or Lucy, she insisted all three kids immediately resume living with the guy.

When I broke the news to the kids, though Colin wasn't thrilled, Lucy's reaction worried me. She was lying on the bed when I said, "You'll be going back to your mom's house." Lucy said nothing. "And the boyfriend will be there." Upon uttering that, she convulsed for a good five seconds. Without making a sound, her empty eyes flipped into her head as her body shook. Lucy snapped out of it, but of course it concerned me since she'd never done anything like that before, nor since.

I told the BIA. Again, she blew me off.

She said the kids needed therapy to adjust to living in the midst of a hostile relationship. That was her solution. They didn't require therapy before, but let's give them an explosive environment to adapt to that necessitates therapeutic intervention. The BIA added that it would be a good idea to extend the peace order indefinitely. At that point, according to an email from my lawyer, I was still in line to keep the 50/50 custody I had.

Other lawyers and their assistants couldn't fathom why the BIA wouldn't demand at least a temporary restraining order against this unknown man who appeared off the internet. My lawyer told me to comply if I wanted to maintain my relationship with my kids since I could not confront or persuade the BIA because she was deeply rooted in the court. Along with her long-running friendships with the chief judge and others, she served her yearlong term as President of the Bar Association in Frederick County throughout my case.

She accused Ethan of not expressing his true beliefs when they benefited me. But she trusted his words when they favored the other side. Thanks to Ethan's in-school statement, the kids, including my panicked daughter, went back to my ex-wife and her boyfriend. Another wedge drove between me and Ethan, and the BIA exploited it.

He criminalized me over the Philly trip and sided with this new guy who wanted me gone, perhaps even dead, disregarding his own father. In the weeks that followed, I distanced myself from Ethan because his presence became painful. No longer would I take a bullet for the kid, and that's a disheartening feeling.

Thanks to my love of geography that began in preschool with my wooden United States puzzle and was soon amplified by hockey travel, I was teaching myself to build a geography Apple app. It's not nearly as straightforward as website design. The day that broke our bond, I was fiddling with my app next to Colin as he played on the computer beside me. Ethan entered and innocently conversed with Colin about a video game they were playing.

By then, I was so detached from the kid, I couldn't believe he didn't recognize that I didn't want him around. As I struggled to concentrate on my app with him standing two feet away, for no apparent reason, I shouted at him. "Ethan, get out of here!" Shocked, he left the room. Colin looked at me, startled, but continued playing alongside me. I never yelled at those kids, so it must've been difficult.

Ethan remained quiet the rest of the weekend. When he returned to his mom, he never came back.

That year, God placed Hanukkah on December 24th. Ethan's last day here was the 22nd. I needed to break the news to my lawyer that my Hanukkah present was losing Ethan, but earlier in the day, I received an email from her reiterating what she'd been telling me for weeks:

"I do not agree with you going after the BIA. It will not give you any positive result. The BIA has some concerns with what she considers your controlling nature regarding the children. I understand your concerns regarding the boyfriend and the BIA views you asking Ethan questions in front of her as controlling and not necessarily what Ethan really feels or thinks. Right now, we are in a position to maintain the custody you have. The BIA wants all the children to be in therapy as soon as possible. You need to work with your ex on that immediately. Do not go after the BIA."

I was paying my attorney to be the BIA's relay person rather than my advocate. For two months, she barely helped me. So, if I told her Ethan was no longer coming, she wouldn't care.

The night I lost him, I fought back tears as I wrote her a scathing letter quoting several policies from the *Maryland Attorneys' Rules of Professional Conduct* that the BIA was breaking. Because my lawyer was guilty of them too, it was a veiled threat to force her hand. My lawyer responded the next day by sending the BIA the first useful letter she ever sent on my behalf. Only then could I share Ethan wouldn't be spending Hanukkah with me.

I got her on my side, though it didn't last long, so I fired her a few months before August's trial.

Ethan and I reunited for that one therapy session located a few minutes from the offices of both my lawyer and my ex-wife's lawyer. Despite its success, the BIA insisted it was too far from our homes. In the added time apart, Ethan became more alienated than ever and eagerly lied to the court as retribution for his juvenile assault charge.

After the ruling, to cope with losing their father, all three kids began therapy in town at the Jesus place. Turns out that's a good thing.

Therapy was organized without having me involved and I had never met the therapist. Unknown to anybody, The Post was a year into examining the case. Neither the therapist, BIA, my ex-wife, nor my kids had an inkling.

The therapist contacted me. We agreed to meet in person—one time only because I limited my communication due to The Post's involvement. After suffering multiple arrests for saying too much early on, I was afraid to repeat that blunder.

The meeting lasted an hour. I produced audio clips and emails, including two expressing Colin's refusals to go to my ex-wife.

"Are you aware that Colin was refusing to go?" I asked.

"No. I had no idea."

"Back-to-back weeks, he insisted on staying at my house. The only reason he returned to his mom was because of my dad. He was running late for work when the kids needed to go back to their mom. Again, Colin was running, hiding, crying and screaming not to go back, but my dad whisked him away and said, 'Come on, Colin. I don't have time for this.' He carried Colin to his car in tears and brought him to his mom."

"Wow," she said, clearly concerned.

"I had told my dad we wouldn't physically force him to go, but would try everything else. We tried talking to him. We stepped away and had Lucy try talking to him. But nothing helped. Late for work, he forgot."

"I didn't know any of this."

"Lucy has complained of breathing troubles since she returned to her mom," I said. "She missed school several times thinking she had asthma, but the doctor diagnosed it as stress. The kids' lawyer never cared."

"That's awful."

"There's more. Aside from what I'm about to show you, I can't say much more than that because there's a powerful investigation ongoing."

I shared three witness letters, ten emails, and played audio of the judge's rulings that stated the reason for my custody loss and supervision. The therapist examined everything, then expressed her belief in me.

"Do you want to repair your relationship with Ethan?" she asked.

"Of course I do." I thought we'd reunite in the coming weeks or months.

When the meeting ended, we shook hands, and she said perhaps the most uplifting words I've ever heard. "I admire your courage and valor fighting the court. I had a divorce too, and the court system sucks."

11

Murphy Bit Him

M Y EX-WIFE AND I MARRIED under bright autumn skies on a stone balcony tucked into the large forested hills Maryland calls mountains. It was a year, a month, and a week after 9/11. The Circuit Court clerk who signed our wedding certificate also signed our divorce papers. She remains the clerk over two decades later, having known the BIA and judge all that time.

The Justice of the Peace who married us foreshadowed the end of our marriage. "Brian, if you take her to be your wife, say, 'I will.'" Our vows were affirmed with the words "I will." Because wills go into effect upon death, our marriage was destined to end.

Halfway through the humble reception inside the wood and stone cabin, our hired musician asked, "What's your wedding song?"

"Uhh…" My ex-wife and I both looked at each other. "Crap!" she said. "I forgot about that."

The musician asked, "How about Louis Armstrong's 'What a Wonderful World'?"

We said, "Okay," and danced.

As I was hearing how wonderful our world is, she leaned into my ear and whispered. "I hate this song."

"Really? You should've said something."

"I didn't want to."

That's the day I learned I'd be the one caring about her problems.

Before we met, I was assistant manager at a pizza delivery store. We delivered to the University of Maryland, so we stayed open two hours later than our county's other stores. On Sunday nights, all stores in our county had to bring weekly paperwork to the main office in Virginia. Because the others closed first, they brought theirs to me and I carried them down.

That's how I met her brother and struck up a friendship. I knew he had a sister, but we only spoke briefly. A few years after we became friends, I quit working and returned to school while they moved in together with her one-year-old son from a short-lived marriage.

On September 7, 2001, I moved in with them. It's easy to remember that date, because four days later, her brother stormed into my room, screaming.

"Dude! Wake up! Wake up!"

"Shut up. I'm trying to sleep."

"Wake up! Planes are flying into buildings! They hit the World Trade Center and maybe the Empire State Building."

"Seriously, leave me alone. I'm sleeping."

"Planes are crashing into buildings! You need to get up!"

I thought he was pranking me on one of my first mornings there, but he wasn't.

My college shut down. In school full-time aspiring to become a homicide detective, I had nowhere else to be for the next few weeks, so I glued myself to the one TV station his ancient rooftop antenna picked up.

The most scarring moments were witnessing those who chose to jump to their deaths rather than being consumed by flames and the buildings tumbling into enormous clouds of twisted debris. Save for one aunt and cousin, my entire extended family lived in New York. The World Trade Center towers were the first buildings visible when nearing the Verrazzano-Narrows Bridge whenever we drove up to visit. I couldn't believe they were gone, along with the thousands of poor souls we lost that day.

The following week, I rode the Metro train to see, firsthand, the devastation at the Pentagon.

One of the most surreal moments of my pre-Washington Post life was opening night of the Capitals' hockey season less than one month later. My ex-wife's brother and I bought tickets behind the nose bleeds, in the last row that counts towards attendance. With an eagle-eye view, we joined an entire arena immersed in a chilling rendition of *The Star-Spangled Banner* so loud we couldn't hear the on-ice singer through the speaker system.

The Caps won the game 6-1, and we celebrated wandering around the city. We hung out with a plastic-bucket street drummer for an hour and gave him the rest of our money. Because of that, we missed the buses, the Metro shut down, and we lacked cash for a cab. It left us walking home 25 miles from the arena in short sleeves on a chilly October night. That's the kind of dumb stuff we did.

My ex-wife loved animals, and cats in particular. One day at her brother's, she said, "Brian, there are kittens under the trailer."

"I wanna see."

"Look, there's two of them."

Good future husband I was, I said, "I'll get them out." I called them several times but remembered cats never liked me, as they ducked further under.

I stepped back, and she said, "Come here, guys." They were out in two seconds.

Our cat count reached four, but the sister kitten never tamed, so she ended up at the pound. Her two pre-existing cats avoided people, but not this long-haired, orange critter that we rescued. He was my dog before we got one. Our cat, who acted like a dog, was named Bear, and he lived with my kids for almost 20 years.

My daughter's Facebook page features a precious photo of him sleeping on her bed, months before his 2022 passing. He meant so much to Lucy that she blamed her poor grades on his death to a magistrate that summer. But her grades sucked when he was still alive. It was my disappearance, not the cat's, that caused the sudden, lasting downturn.

But before she was born, Bear joined our ever-growing family in 2002 and we moved from her brother's to a townhouse in Frederick with my three-year-old ex-stepson, a few months after Ethan was born.

My ex-wife and kids love cats, but my mom is terrified of them. There could be a cat on the sidewalk in front of her, and two rival gangs across a busy highway. She'd cross six lanes of high-speed traffic and risk her chances with a dozen hoodlums who've just drawn their weapons to avoid the cat. "And the funny thing is," she said, "I've never been hurt by a cat. But dogs have bitten me, and I love them."

Every time she visited, she forewarned us. "Make sure you put the cats away." When she knocked on our door, she asked, "Are the cats away? Be sure they're not out."

One time I lied. She took off running outside and refused to come back for 20 minutes.

Meantime, my ex-stepson struggled to say what all kids love most. He had a firm command of vocabulary and pronounced everything well, except candy. He called it teena.

My ex-wife and I tried to teach him to pronounce it.

"Say can."

"Can."

"Say dy."

"Dy."

"Good. Now say caaandy."

"Teeeena."

I took my ex-stepson to one baseball game. I'd been to dozens and never caught a ball, but he brought me luck, at least during batting practice. Standing behind the center-field wall at Oriole Park at Camden Yards in Baltimore, a batted ball skipped off the outfield grass, right into my hands. A few hours later, as the Orioles struggled to score, seats began clearing out by their dugout. With our baseball in hand, we snagged a seat nearby.

After the deflating seven-run loss, every Orioles player made a bee-line for the clubhouse, except for one. At the far end of the dugout, out-fielder Larry Bigbie signed autographs for a few fans. He turned for the clubhouse, but before he disappeared, I yelled. "Hey, Larry! It's his first ballgame." He smiled, strode over, and signed the ball. For years, my ex-stepson raved about his Larry Bigbie baseball. "Larry Bigbie's my favorite player."

My ex-stepson, whose due date was the same as my nephew's but chose to be two weeks younger, picked his room because he loved the angled floor in his closet above the stairs.

About a year after moving to Frederick, my ex-wife walked in the room and said, "You need to buy a pregnancy test."

"Uhh...why?"

"Because I didn't have my dealie this month."

But this was God's test. My ex-stepson was four and Ethan just turned one, so I wasn't eager for another kid. God knew.

Weeks later, I stepped through the front door. My ex-wife looked like she witnessed a tragedy. "I think I lost the baby," she said. "We should go to the hospital."

Then it dawned on me that I really wanted that baby. God knew.

During the week I took off work to mourn with her, we rented *Miracle*, the film about the U.S. hockey team's improbable win over the Soviet Union in 1980. One miracle led to another, and we conceived another baby within two months.

Though the unfulfilled pregnancy was upsetting, I thank God, because I wouldn't have been blessed with Lucy the following year.

As Lucy began speaking, hearing her and Ethan call me "daddy" made my ex-stepson, with his non-matching blond hair and tan skin, feel left out. He sat on our living room couch when my ex-wife raised the subject.

"He says he wants to call you 'daddy'. Is that okay?"

"He can call me whatever he wants," I said, "as long as it's not derogatory." From that humorous moment on, I was "daddy" until the breakup, when "Brian" gradually returned.

Because my ex-stepson, Ethan, Lucy, three cats and a ferret weren't enough for our compact three-bedroom townhouse, we found a free doggy on Craigslist. We met Mandy's owner at a local park, fell in instant love, and brought home our 4-year-old super sweet lab mix to discover she had a special surprise in her. She was filled with puppies!

As the day drew near to deliver, we placed a plastic kiddie pool in the dining room that acted as our computer and game room. Lucy had a few days' reprieve of Mandy's tail whacking her face as she learned to walk, and our new dog gave birth to five adorable lab pups inside the pool.

Three were black, one was tan like Mandy, and the other was bleached blonde. We named them after *The Simpsons* characters and sold most through an ad in The Washington Post, but I wanted to keep the biggest boy, a black lab named Homer. My ex-wife hated that moniker, so she renamed him Murphy. But I was more subtle about the switch, preferring to call my new doggy friend Homerphy for a while.

Murphy grew bigger than his mom, and our 1264 square-foot townhouse had more than enough pets. My ex-wife thought maybe it was excessive and suggested finding Murphy a home, but I reminded her of the night he might have saved her life.

She and the kids were home while I was working. The main door was open to allow fresh air through the screened, front glass door, which permitted a clear view of my ex-wife's back as she washed dishes. The kids were playing upstairs when an unknown man entered through the unlocked door and approached her, concealing a hand behind his back.

Murphy darted into him, so he fled.

God only knows what may have happened if Murphy wasn't there. Family safety, along with my unconditional love for our four-footed friend, was a major reason we kept him.

During our marriage, in 2008, Murphy turned two and my ex-stepson and Ethan's first day of school arrived. My ex-wife was stocking shelves at a large-chain retail store for a sweet just-above-minimum wage while I was hammering out the details on Social Security Disability forms post-vasectomy. So, I was charged with getting the kids ready.

As the kids made one last backpack check by our front door, we heard a loud growl, mixed with angry dog sound.

The next second of silence was pierced by hysterical wailing. Baby Colin was screaming beside the bowl, with blood leaking on the floor from a gaping wound that stretched from his hairline to the bridge of his nose, barely missing his right eye. Murphy had bitten him.

My phone died as I dialed 911, so the kids and I jumped in the van and rushed him to the hospital. My ex-stepson played a hero, putting pressure on a towel on the way to stop the bleeding.

Once he was stable in the ER, I phoned my ex-wife in tears. "Colin's eye is okay."

"What?"

"Colin's eye is okay. Murphy bit him badly and we're at the hospital. But his eye is okay." I was worried about his eyesight and kept reassuring myself that he'd be fine.

While waiting for his surgery to finish, I took Murphy to the pound. "You're in God's hands now," I said as I wished him a fast farewell. To this day, I can see his sorrowful eyes wondering where I was going.

I've always blamed myself for the incident and felt responsible every time I saw the 20+ stitches and eventual scar. Because of that, I gave Colin extra attention, but the kids never noticed. They always wanted to play, and I often obliged. But not always. When Colin wanted me, I never said no. That's the least I could've done for him.

At school, playgrounds, and parks, kids frequently asked him, "What happened to your face?" It was painful hearing him explain again and again that a dog bit him.

Partly thanks to Murphy, but also his endearing personality, Colin and I were inseparable until the court separated us. When I told him and Lucy they were leaving, he took it the hardest. The poor kid had no clue why he lost his dad and best buddy at only ten years old.

Upon losing custody, however, I was getting fast revenge. Or so I thought. Because The Post took immediate and aggressive action, I assumed things would make rapid progress. But I learned the hard way, it doesn't work like that.

For five years, I never mentioned the allegation or The Post's involvement to the kids during our supervised visits. Despite the chaos after exposing the investigation to police, they remained unaware. I missed several visits while locked up in mental health wards and jails, and they made the one-hour round-trip trek for me to not show up. That must have been heartbreaking for them.

After the divorce, I dated nobody. I loved those kids, and they were by far my best friends. I've seen how stepparents change the dynamics of a parent-child relationship, and I never wanted to risk that. It's the first time I truly wasn't there for them.

I can't imagine how agonizing it was for them to lose living with dad abruptly, then within two months have dad disappear behind bars for half a year so bizarre, you'll want to keep reading.

Technically, I was behind glass, and it was freaking hard. I got a little too close to the glass door one day while performing air elbow attacks in a show of force and Chapter 20 to the guards. My elbow struck the door, and it swelled and hurt for over a year. But aside from laughing Cheeto dust from their mouths while I went hungry, the guards didn't mess with me.

My disappearances into jails must have anguished the kids, though, to this day, we've never discussed them. The way my ex-wife has spoken about me, I can't fathom what they've heard. Locked up with The Post clearly involved, I never knew how long I'd be incarcerated, so I didn't call the Mental Health Association to let them know. I figured my kids would soon reap the benefits of The Post's interest as much as me.

After seeing each other every week since this awful supervised arrangement began, I missed a visit while stuck in the Allentown hospital. The next week, I got locked up for 11 days because I had too much fun in a dumpster. As a result, I failed to visit them a few times in a row. They drove an hour, and I was nowhere to be found. I'd always been a rock in their lives, so those mysterious absences must have crushed them. Why doesn't daddy want to see us?

After three weeks of mishaps, we resumed our weekly visits. I brought in our Xbox to play a co-op game we used to love at home, only to discover the system was broken and most of our hour was wasted trying to fix it. But the day a staff member noticed a hot-air balloon outside the hallway window was a treat. We gazed at its brilliant colors drifting over the city, a vision of the outside life we were forbidden from enjoying together.

Three visits took place before they were ditched again for months, as the crime spree I was deceived into reached its climax. It's one of the more heart-wrenching aspects of this entire ordeal.

During those three weeks of visits, other arrests occurred. But they only jailed me briefly, so I missed no visits. The last arrest, however, led to over six months of imprisonment, so from the kids' perspective, I inexplicably disappeared from their lives.

I don't know how many times they made that hourlong drive for me never to arrive. Now I feel horrible about it, but at the time, I was lost in a wave of weird and I thought only of us imminently reuniting outside that mental health facility.

From March to October 2018, the kids never saw me while I served time for honesty to police. I know others can claim that unfortunate distinction, too. I was released from jail the day the Capitals' season opened, months after they won their first Stanley Cup in franchise history.

Finally a free man, I convinced my dad to get tickets to witness the Stanley Cup banner raised to the rafters that night. For once, it paid to get the cheap seats because we had the best view of the banner all game. Not a bad get-out-of-jail present, but I probably had a better one 15 years earlier.

That celebratory evening, our longtime captain, Alex Ovechkin, skated the Cup onto the ice, something I thought I may never witness. Sadly, his dad recently passed away, but he loved Lucy. We watched the team practice when she was one, and the elder Ovechkin made her giggle quite a while, leaving me with a wonderful, lasting memory.

Freedom was amazing after six-and-a-half months of unwarranted lockup. Fresh varieties of food tasted fantastic, but everything burned the skin on my mouth's roof because it had been so long since I downed a hot meal.

Meantime, a tough task lie ahead to mend my splintered relationship with my kids as we resumed visitation.

Every time we saw each other, I held onto a giant secret, so it felt like I was stringing them along. I pretended to be a normal dad, in the back of my mind thinking some great reunion party would soon unfold. However, they entered under the giant "Mental Health" sign to see a dad recently released from jails. And that reunion never transpired.

As months became years, nothing changed other than the kids growing taller.

I didn't know what I was supposed to do. While imprisoned, I learned to be calm and patient upon my release—but that was it. No timeline was specified. Was I missing some trigger? How long does it take to investigate decades of illegal court antics and vet hundreds of witnesses?

The kids and I were stuck in a supervised setting that was so *anti-reestablishmentarianism* toward a normal parent-child relationship, we needed help. That's why I returned to synagogue. Surely, if a secret needed unlocking, God has the answer.

Much of my life, I've said, "God doesn't give us more than we can handle." Before I became a firm believer, I believed that.

While in constant pain from the vasectomy, that credo got me through. Not yet 30, I got dinged up by a doctor and saw all my life's hard work and future goals drift out of reach. But my kids kept me moving. I was single and officially damaged goods—in more ways than one—but I never felt purposeless. Those kids needed me.

I never imagined I could love three little people so much. But their ongoing absence these past many years highlights endless wasted opportunities.

Rather than stay home, each lost in our own universe, we should've ventured out and enjoyed life as a family. We could've traveled to more museums, parks, nature centers, concerts, and sporting events. We should've hiked nearby mountain trails; spent some days at the state park's lakeside beach, playground and campground; visited countless D.C. sites; gone ice skating again; eaten more family dinners like Taco Night; watched another episode of *We Bare Bears;* or played just one more game together.

Perhaps most importantly, I should've properly shown them the ways of their Jewish faith. One of our most important prayers instructs us to impress our Jewish values upon our children. But they don't know that prayer, and we missed holidays. I can't say that we celebrated Passover more than one or two years, if ever. Passover, which recalls our exodus from slavery in Egypt via the marvel of Moses splitting the sea, is the most family-centered day in all human history. It's something we retell with our children year after year, and I have no recollection of sharing it with my kids.

Vivid 35-year-old memories exist from my childhood of preparing for the big day. The whole family stayed home and adorned the table with wine, unleavened matzah bread, and a Seder plate loaded with bitter horseradish, parsley, salt water, and other evocative symbols of our lives in slavery. Every spring, we gathered round to read the Passover story—highlighted by the adorable tradition of the youngest kid asking Four Questions wondering why tonight is different from all other nights—reminding ourselves of being freed by God's mighty hand. I kick myself for not having a memory of Passover with my kids.

And don't get me started on Sukkot. I don't think they've ever seen a sukkah, the temporary outdoor hut built and colorfully festooned each year to recall our desert wandering and trust in God for protection. My best memories of Hebrew school involved heading outdoors each October to decorate and dwell in the sukkah. But my kids never experienced that.

I've built a sukkah in my yard for the past three years. Of course, the kids haven't seen it. I suppose I'm attempting to atone. Even though Ethan and Lucy have reached adulthood, and Colin's almost there, it's never too late to show you're sorry. God lets us repent because God wants us to change. That's why I'm liberal.

Missing the final years of their youth and frittering away much of the rest devastates me. However, I remind myself to view my mistakes, not as missed opportunities, but as lessons learned for next time. No moment should ever be squandered.

A psalm by King Solomon teaches this. "Children are a heritage from the Lord, offspring a reward."

Why waste something so precious?

12

THE NEWS MADE ME FAMOUS

I MISSED FAR TOO MANY birthdays and holidays after the court dismantled my relationship with the children. Jail housed me for some while Covid interrupted others. Our supervised visits rarely coincided with these special occasions, so the only way I could show them I cared was to surprise them at school.

I brought gift bags filled with presents, a few of which were memorialized in a keepsake photo or two, knowing I'd never see them again. A few times, I filled enormous gift bags with eight days of Hanukkah presents.

Once I brought so many Hanukkah goodies, including electric menorahs for them to light, Colin struggled to carry his Star of David themed bag back to class. After that, I figured gift cards would suffice, but it's a terrible feeling giving just a gift card to your own young kid. It's even worse when you don't know what store to get it from.

One Hanukkah during Covid, I gifted a $350 drone to Colin and Lucy. Buried at the bottom of Colin's gift bag, I requested he share it with his sister. For the next several months, I imagined all their excitement flying high above town, snagging cool video. Then I finally saw Colin again. "How do you like your drone?" I asked.

"We couldn't get it to work. We tried a bunch of things, but never got it flying properly."

By then, it was too late to return or replace it, so my thoughtful present was nothing but frustration for them, and a fair amount of money wasted.

Then I brought our new German Shepherd puppy to visit them at school. They pet her for a minute, then returned to class. Very anticlimactic. But, infrequent as it was, the school let me see the kids whenever I went.

That all changed when Lucy became a senior in 2022. The school suddenly refused to call her to the office, touting a no-contact order listed in their system. I could see Colin, but not Lucy. The school reached out for my ex-wife's permission, but she ignored them, so I missed seeing her for Hanukkah that year.

Colin had his presents for a couple of weeks, but I was struggling to get Lucy hers. Following winter break, I surprised Lucy by her bus stop on her way to her mom's house. The bus stop plan worked, but it was very uncomfortable—not like two-minute surprise visits at school were much better. Because her mom waited for her a block away, and I didn't know if she'd show up, I made it quick.

Hanukkah should be days and nights of family opening gifts, cooking, playing games together, and reveling in the glow of the menorah lights. Instead, I surprised her and said, "It's okay, Lucy, I'm not staying long. I just want you to have your Hanukkah presents."

Then came Lucy's 18th birthday four months later. God gifted her an April birthday, providing her with the most beautiful of all birthstones, a diamond. I got the ugliest. However you say peridot, August means you're gifted a puke-green gem.

For her welcome to adulthood present, I loaded her bank account and planned to sign it over.

I attempted to meet her at school, hoping whatever prior restriction that prevented me from seeing her disappeared. But they turned me away again.

The next day, I tried her bus stop only to discover she no longer rode the bus when my ex-wife drove past with Lucy in the passenger seat.

For the next few days, I surveilled the school parking lot, hoping to catch her leaving the building. But the one time I saw her, she was already opening the door to her mom's van, so I gave up.

The following week, my lawyer met me to discuss the case, and she asked that I obtain the kids' official records from school. When I arrived at the front office that continually refused to bring Lucy forward, they called a student escort to walk me to the records office at the far end of the building. I realized I was going inside, so as I awaited the escort, I ran to my car and grabbed Lucy's birthday card and bank account info.

Earlier that week, I read about alienated parents like me who were vilified and ostracized by their community. Because allegations were often embarrassing, everyone from school officials and teachers to sports coaches, families and religious communities looked down on these wrongly maligned parents. That's one thing that never happened to me.

The student led me to the records room. The records person invited me to wait for everything to print out, and we chatted amiably for the next 20 minutes. As the last pages printed, I asked if she could call Lucy so I could give her the birthday card and gift. She did without hesitation.

Lucy opened the door.

"Happy birthday, Lucy!"

"Thanks dad."

"I got you a special gift for your 18th birthday," I said. "I've had a savings account for you for many years. The bank said that we'd have to meet there in person to sign the account over to you. My phone number is on the receipt, so you can call or text me when you want to meet. The bank is two minutes from your mom's house."

"Thanks dad."

"I love you Lucy. Happy birthday." As I turned to leave, the records person yanked Lucy's arm and dragged her into an adjacent room. I caught half a sentence as the escort guided me outside. "Lucy, I am so sorry—"

Confused by that interaction, I glanced at the pile of records as I strolled the hallways. The top page said Lucy was forbidden to have contact with me. The records person must have seen that during the minute I was talking to Lucy, so she must have thought I was some creep trying to lure my daughter with a large sum of money.

I appeared even worse to Lucy and never heard from her.

Although I didn't have to deal with daddy issues like Lucy, high school wasn't great for me either. My highlight was working at a real estate agency, where I entered pro athletes' names in the system and later drove past their houses. The Washington Wizards' (née Bullets) 7'7" Gheorge Muresan's jeep was fitted with an extended headrest and one of the all-time Capitals greats, Calle Johansson, was out front of his surprisingly modest townhouse gabbing with a neighbor.

It sure beat another high school memory of the only NFL football game I ever went to with my dad. On the third day of Hanukkah in 1993, the Washington Commanders (née Redskins) were hosting the New York Jets (née Almost an Actual Football Team). I brought another Hanukkah present to the game, a small $100 computerized baseball stat machine. I wanted that thing for months, so I tucked my new little gadget into my coat pocket.

As my dad and I were battered by cold December gales while seated in the upper deck, I watched Washington lose by just about the most boring score possible. It was the league's only 3-0 game over a 25-year stretch. The only thrilling moments were observing punters boot-ing balls high into the wind, the same freezing wind that broke my new baseball toy.

I graduated from Bowie High School a few years later, in 1996, after attending from sophomore through senior years. I had a bunch of Bowie elementary school pals dating to 6th grade, but we lost touch when I transferred half an hour away to an Annapolis private school from 7th to 9th grade, and never reestablished those friendships when I returned to Bowie.

Key School in Annapolis admitted me because of my brain, not my grades. They assumed I wasn't challenged enough in public school, so the School of Hard Reading thought I'd excel if they pounded me with strenuous work. But I never enjoyed reading books, so formidable translations of *Beowulf* and *The Odyssey* were reasons to play ball by myself rather than read my homework.

My biggest achievement was a blank-map quiz. On an empty map of the African continent, we labeled every country. The kid that always finished first and best was my only classmate with a perfect score besides me, but I finished two minutes faster.

In the same class weeks later, I thought I aced another test. Imagine my disappointment when I got 6% on the 90-question exam. That kid got his A.

After struggling for a few years, I returned to public school, where my old pals ignored me. I preferred instead to hang out with hockey buddies and private school friends from Annapolis.

How bad was Bowie High? The senior class president ran his campaign on, "Every bathroom will have toilet paper." He should've added, "and a door on the stall." A necessary bathroom break became a perfect excuse to walk the mile home while my parents were gone working. I think I missed over 40 days my senior year, especially afternoon classes.

Departing the school became harder when they decided to chain shut every exit except two. It's a good thing school shooters and fires weren't a big deal in the '90s. Well, fires were, but that didn't stop them. Getting outside was a matter of waiting out the police officer stationed by one of the two accessible exits.

Without my mom influencing my Bowie High teachers, I wouldn't have graduated. I wanted to work and earn money instead of attending school, so I barely reached graduation day, then almost got kicked out before it began.

Our school held its annual ceremony at the since-demolished Capital Centre, the same arena where the Capitals played, and where I won my shootout trophies.

One of my friends from outside school knew somebody who made his own barrels of wine. As a connoisseur of anything alcoholic, I had two unlabeled bottles of red wine in my car. I downed one in the parking lot outside the arena before getting in line as a more talkative version of myself.

While waiting in the tunnel under the seating bowl with fellow graduates, a staff member who once argued with my mom stepped past. Five seconds later, I yelled his name and screamed an obscenity. I don't know how he zeroed in on me so fast, but he spun around and steamed over. Red-faced, he speared his finger toward my nose and threatened to kick me out of graduation if I said another word. So, I kept quiet until I reached the next line.

During the ceremony, they dished out diplomas alphabetically. As they neared Kotler, I vacated my seat for a line long enough to allow several pranks to spiral through my mind. It was difficult driving sober to the arena because my new shoes were too big, but that thought evaded me when I stood beside the arena stage and drunkenly said to the guy behind me, "Watch this."

I planned to trip on the stairs. I didn't plan for the white-haired woman doling out diplomas to catch me. At a party later that night, a girl who never spoke to me said, "Hey, you're the guy that tripped!"

A year later, the Capitals opened a new arena, where I was interviewed on TV's morning news.

After suffering one playoff disappointment after another, year after year, the Capitals made it to the Stanley Cup Finals for the first time. Radio messages said Finals tickets were going on sale early in the morning. So, after closing the pizza shop, I drove downtown to stand second in line at 2 AM. With $500 to spend and my dad's birthday around the corner, I prepared to gift him the two best seats I could afford.

"Why did you come down here?" asked a news reporter on camera.

"I've been a fan my whole life, and I wouldn't ever miss this."

By about 8 AM, the box office doors opened.

"We're selling individual tickets to the playoff series only if you buy a season ticket plan for next year," the sales agent said. I didn't have money for that, but I had a few more words for the reporter after leaving the arena.

"They never advertised that you needed to buy season tickets to get seats for one Finals game. I've been standing in line since 2 AM for nothing."

I was so peeved by the incident, when the Caps were swept in four straight games, I thought they deserved it.

I made up those wasted hours standing in line the following year. For my 21st birthday, to keep me sober, my dad took me on a trip to Cleveland and Detroit.

While we were in Cleveland at the Rock & Roll Hall of Fame, we saw a lengthy line that encircled the adjacent stadium. The Cleveland Browns were unveiling their new football stadium to the public. Unwilling to wait for hours in line, my dad wanted to leave. But I said, "No, follow me." So he did.

The half-mile line was three people wide until it fanned out near the entrance, where the biggest Browns fans waited all day. Since my dad is an unassuming guy, I figured we could meld in front of two old ladies.

A couple minutes after the gates opened, we entered with the die-hard fans that waited for hours instead of being stuck wrapped around the stadium with the sucky fans and out-of-towners like us. The old ladies, dressed in brown-and-orange team hats, jerseys, and necklaces, proved as die hard as they come. Upon reaching the section that houses the team's rowdiest supporters known for peppering opposing players with batteries, eggs and Milk-Bones, the old ladies shouted with glee.

"Can you believe it!? We're in the Dawg Pound!"

"This is the Dawg Pound! I can't believe it!"

The next day, at a Detroit Tigers game in the last year of Tiger Stadium, I officially turned 21. "Dad, I'm going to the bathroom." I came back with 32 ounces of beer breath. "Sorry dad, the line was long."

In my post-Post jail stay, I was prohibited from joining lines. I can't imagine why. But as part of their make-me-appear-mentally-ill scheme, I was transferred to the state hospital, who permitted it for the two months I spent there while The Post continued their investigation unfettered. Other than one almost-fight, those lines proved uneventful.

Locked away in that state hospital for my 40th birthday, I got a cupcake and a card from the Christian clergy. Great as it was showing off my cupcake to the sad-sack losers that didn't have one, it didn't top the prize for sinking all the billiard balls in the rec room.

The recreation woman dangled an entire bag of Chips Ahoy minis as a reward for completing her challenge. She placed ten balls in specific spots on the table, and our task was to drain every ball without missing one. Despite my limited skills, I won and was high on cookies the rest of the day.

It was an even greater moment than my other you-don't-have-to-be-in-good-shape-to-be-good sporting achievement of bowling a turkey and finally breaking 120 to every pro bowler's pump-up song, "Hit Me Baby One More Time" by Britney Spears.

I mentioned my jail time was bizarre, which really is an understatement. They labeled me a troublemaker since my first hours in the facility, and sequestered me in solitary for the first few months. Interactions with "normal" inmates were limited to occasional chatting through the air vent to the guy above me.

The first day in my cell, he blasted a tune down the vent that I'd listened to on *YouTube Music* the previous few weeks of freedom. As Camila Cabello's Cuban Capital blared down the vent, he asked, "Do you like this song?"

"Yeah, I love it."

"Me too. I have a radio up here, so I'll play music for you down the vent."

That night, he called through the air vent. "Brian!"

"Hey, what's up?"

"Get ready for dinner. We're having KFC."

"That sounds great."

"Yeah, we're having chicken nuggets."

I jumped back in bed, excited that my unique status came with more perks. Within seconds, the hatch in my cell door jolted open. I caught a big whiff of the Colonel's secret recipe and hurried to the door for chow. The guard held a tray containing the most disgusting, limp, undercooked hot dogs. The spicy KFC aroma was gone, instantly replaced by the stomach-churning stench of low-grade cow and pig hooves. I was stunned.

How on earth was I smelling things? My universe was contrived.

Weeks passed without music—not loud like this day or soft. Then overnight while the cell block slept, as I voiced dismay about being imprisoned, a few loud notes and two words from a different song on my

YouTube playlist pressed through that air vent. "I'm bulletproof." Then silence. And never any more music.

Years later, the same afternoon I wrote this portion of the book, an ad on a religious radio station grabbed my attention while driving through the center of Hagerstown. "We hacked into your account and stole your *YouTube Music* playlist." Why would a religious station advertise computer crime and theft?

In jail, a few days after my arrival, the cell block was filled with typical commotion. The cacophony of 30 or 40 bored souls banging, talking, shouting, laughing, and flushing toilets was a daily constant. A half-dozen guards chatting and going about their routines added to the unrelenting noise.

As I laid on my thin mattress being poked in the head by a medieval pillow, I channeled my high school and pre-marriage days beating on my drum kit, about which my mom said, "I hate those things!"

I began tapping a beat with my fingers on the metal bed frame, listening to each piece of steel produce different pitches. Within seconds, the entire cell block fell silent.

Recently, I took a trip out west where I visited seven national parks in as many days. The deathly silence atop Golden Canyon that epitomizes Death Valley took me aback. The cell block loomed that quiet as I banged out tunes for the next 20 minutes, without hearing a single other sound.

Gradually the noise resumed, but these impossible daily experiences instilled the understanding that I was someone special. The next day, eager for some peace and quiet, I repeated the process. To my chagrin, my metal music only shut them up for a minute and never silenced them again.

One of my least fond activities was having to eat so much pepper. Not green peppers, red peppers, or black pepper. Jail doesn't have that stuff. Theirs comes in spray form.

They first doused me a couple hours after arriving for asking where food was, then found more reasons every so often to light me up again. Thanks to that, I remained in solitary confinement the first few months in jail. The benefit of pepper spray was the shower soon afterwards. Because I often went days without one, I was happy to get washed.

After getting streamed then cleaned one day, I arrived in a new solitary cell across the block for an unforgettable incident. One of the friendly guards banged on my glass door and said, "The news made you famous. Say it."

"The news made me famous?"

"Louder."

"The news made me famous."

"Louder."

"The news made me famous!"

"Louder!"

I screamed as loud as I could. "THE NEWS MADE ME FAMOUS!!!!"

"LOUDER!!!"

I howled the line with everything my lungs could muster several more times when my upstairs air vent buddy from the old cell approached the glass door, smiled, and winked at me.

Unlike jail, the state hospital allowed me into the general population. Whereas jail offered two brief 2 AM opportunities outside my cell for rec in a fenced cage reminiscent of a dog kennel, at the hospital we listened to whatever radio station we wanted while playing basketball in the gym midday. Almost every day that summer, we enjoyed fresh air outdoors in a walled-in grass field large enough to play kickball, volleyball, and football. It was a welcome respite from the dim, dingy 1960s sanitarium vibe inside.

Like us inmates, the hospital staff had their quirks, too. Cletus was hillbilly stern, so the day he caught me jumping up and down, scratching my head, making monkey noises in full conversation with another inmate, I thought I might lose some privileges. Unlike most other infractions, he laughed it off.

Cletus was a good guy from whom to hear the Capitals won the Cup, though he won't unseat professional announcers with his lackluster call outside my bedroom to a fellow guard down the hall. Fifteen minutes after being forced to bed a few minutes before the final horn, Cletus' unmistakable voice uttered the words I waited four decades for. "Yeah, Washington won." It was the closest thing to being there.

Though being around people was sometimes enjoyable, the isolation jail offered had its advantages. Instead of sharing one or two dayrooms with over 20 men from sunrise to bedtime, I had my own mostly peaceful cell to myself.

Jail also featured the most intense events. The most intimidating, disturbing, and terrifying of which landed me in the state hospital for months. It began when a guard said, "We're sorry we have to do this, Mr. Kotler," and ended with a round of applause.

13

FAIL THE KIDS, PASS ON BILLS

T HE LENGTHS I WENT THROUGH for my kids are extreme. Because I was fighting people with significant legal power, The Post's smokescreen needed to be drastic. For that same reason, I knew going into my trial there was a chance I could wrongly lose custody. Plus, that's how my life works. So, I planned to take a trip if the unthinkable occurred.

Following the court ruling, I was so angry that my life's first pounding migraine took hold. My time with my kids was done.

No more trips to Hersheypark. No more stops on the way to Hersheypark.

Colin, Lucy, and I found Autobahn Indoor Speedway for some high speed go-karting. Racing adults, I got the fastest lap. Racing kids, Lucy took a good thump into the barrier while Colin was first learning the difference between an accelerator and brake.

After the court's decision, all I could do was peer at the Autobahn cards in my wallet and think, "These will never be recharged."

To escape, I bought a plane ticket to Colorado two days after I lost custody, with a return flight eight days later.

I left for Colorado with an angry migraine but returned home more hopeful and optimistic than I'd ever been. I had no hunch I was about to gather witnesses and approach the news within three weeks.

The majesty of the mountains and legalized marijuana migraine relief were just what Dr. Kotler ordered. I always wanted to call myself that!

Then again, maybe not. Though some doctors show compassion, like our longtime family doc, they can be condescending. I delivered pizza to the guy that insisted his name was Dr. So-and-so. At his townhouse door, I pushed the doorbell and waited. There was no answer, so I pressed again. After standing outside for a minute, I knocked on the door. Before long, it opened.

"Why did you bang on the door?" he said. "You shouldn't do that. There's a doorbell right there." He pointed to the button deliberately. "You're supposed to push it."

"I did."

"No, you didn't."

"Yes, I did. I pushed it twice."

"If you did that, don't you think I would've heard it?"

"Well, I did."

"Watch," he said, like he was teaching a toddler how to ring a doorbell. He pushed the button. "Hmm. I guess it's broken."

Out in Colorado after losing the kids, things got off to as bad a start as that pizza delivery. After dozing off at a hostel thanks to the sweet smell of weed, I awoke to the suffocating stench of human stink glands that enveloped me and my luggage, worse than the *Seinfeld* smelly car and *Friends'* smelly cat combined.

As I cruised the mountains in my rental, reeling from the reek, an Imagine Dragons song instilled some much-needed mojo regarding the court and my kids.

"Break me down and build me up, whatever it takes.

'Cause I love how it feels when I break the chains

Yeah, take me to the top. I'm ready for whatever it takes."

Well, it took wasting three days to rid the odor by washing everything I owned, returning my luggage to Walmart, trading in a brand-new Jeep Cherokee for a broken-down old minivan before receiving a complaint-driven upgrade, and switching from the hostel to a run-down Denver motel before landing a rustic ski lodge in the mountains.

Colorado will be remembered as the trip of highs and lows. It was the most beautiful, worst smelling place I'd ever been. Filled with the sweetest people, it was a needed respite from the evil I encountered back home.

All the ups and downs I experienced felt like a premonition that instilled a recurring thought. "The worst moment of my life happened back home. Am I about to have my best?" It gave me hope.

Back in Hagerstown, after my nephew's monumental gesture got my wheels turning, that worst to best feeling was coming true.

The kids had no clue The Post was present at visitation. My ex-wife didn't either. I concealed those families' letters from them and the BIA, imagining they would spark a surprise revelation that never materialized.

My interaction with the newspaper smoothed after my prolonged jail stint. In jail, informants' directives coupled with too many unsettling experiences taught me patience and to stop bickering with my parents. I eased the arguing and focused on everything helpful they've done for me my whole life. God commands us to honor our parents. I owe that advice to a mostly peaceful life since.

By April 2019, six months after jail released me and nearly a year-and-a-half after I lost custody, there was a child support hearing.

After far too long not visiting the kids, our one-hour weekly visits at the mental health facility had resumed under a new supervisor. But thanks to the craziness of jail and mental hospitals, the only custody improvement being offered was an increase in supervised visitation from one hour to two. That day, I figured The Post would swoop in like Superman and save us. But they never sent Clark Kent.

Ahead of the April 2019 hearing, I prepared a statement to the court. I could hint at an investigation without revealing The Post's involvement. In the ominous brick courtyard out front of the courthouse, I confirmed via email with The Post to proceed with the statement.

I stepped inside, thinking my life might change the moment I walk back out. "Maybe this time, reporters will finally be waiting for me outside the courthouse."

The courthouse was strangely empty. Our case seemed to be the only one docketed in the entire three-story building. The halls were quiet, and the benches sat barren. Years later, when the case reopened with a new lawyer in 2022, the emergency hearing was held in a similarly desolate building. My 2022 lawyer said, "This is weird. I've never seen the courthouse so empty." I thought, "It was exactly like this the last time I was here."

At the April 2019 child support hearing, I provided a useless piece of evidence that served to freak out the BIA, but was otherwise insignificant. Without the financial wherewithal to bring witnesses into court, thanks to hearsay, I couldn't submit the families' letters. So, I only produced the following email that I sent to Colin's school days before shipping everything to The Post.

"I'm sure most, if not all of you are aware of the sudden, severe custody change regarding me and Colin. I am not allowed to be unsupervised based on allegations that I am inappropriately telling my child and 'friends they're talking to and people they're Skyping with' about something bad happening to my child.

"The accusation is that I do it 'all the time'. If true, the allegations are awful and I deserve the custody arrangement I got. Also, if true, the 'friends they're talking to and people they're Skyping with' part alleges I am targeting the children at the school. So I reached out to the families whose children would have been my alleged primary targets.

"Overnight, my 50/50 time with my kids became one hour a week supervised in an institution—based solely on allegations that I am targeting my child and these two families.

"I will be separately forwarding their emails to all of you. Please have them for your record."

Inside the courtroom, our case was called by the same judge who ruled our trial. After the judge read that letter, lawyers informed her of our successful supervised visits. Upbeat, she said, "Good, so there's progress."

The judge wouldn't read the families' actual letters because they're hearsay, one of our more ridiculous laws. (You can't say what they said. But you can say what they did. Well, they did say something. But you can't say that.)

Since she read the email that I sent to the school, she was aware others vouched for me, but she was in no mind about modifying custody. Knowing I had an unlimited supply of witnesses and The Post in my back pocket, I addressed the court as the BIA's face withered 20 years in seven minutes.

"Good morning. I'd like to refresh the court's memory back to day four of the trial. On October 10, 2017, at 11:16 AM and 15 seconds, judge, you began stating, quote: 'Ethan expressed concern of dad frequently reporting that his child has been abused. He reports that this is brought up all the time, that he tells this to everyone, including that child, the other children, people he's Skyping with, friends he's talking to. This is a frequent topic of conversation to, and in front of, the children.'

"So, according to Ethan's claims, I've been targeting every child my kids have been in contact with—close friends of theirs, classmates on their school trips I've chaperoned, every teammate of theirs on the ten soccer teams that I've coached.

"But it seemed that everything that Ethan testified was believed. And judge, the BIA's custody suggestion was based on what Ethan told the court, and you followed it to the letter. You based your entire ruling only on what Ethan said, even after he admitted to you that he was upset that he got in trouble during that altercation, and I didn't.

"Judge, I specifically recall you said you were great at recognizing when a kid is lying for one of their parents. There was written evidence on record that Ethan was a proven liar. He wrote two statements that he witnessed the weed whacker threat, then spent a year saying it never happened. Either Ethan lied to help me early on, or he helped his mother by lying for her later. Either way, he has proven willing to lie for a parent, and you should have known his word could not have been trusted. I feel that too much weight was given to Ethan's testimony while my evidence was overlooked.

"During trial, I had no way of knowing Ethan would make such an outlandish claim that I was targeting the entire communities of Hagerstown, Williamsport, and Boonsboro. Had I known in advance, I could have paraded a hundred witnesses in on my behalf for the trial. I didn't have the chance then, but I can bring forth a number of witnesses, including families from every soccer team that I coached, and all my kids' friends and classmates. They can all testify about Ethan's falsifying facts on a number of issues.

"Additionally, I testified at length regarding the BIA's bias towards me, though the court did not attribute much weight to that, unfortunately. The BIA even opened her close saying my ex-wife should have had me meet the boyfriend both before he moved in and before he even met the kids.

"On October 10, 2017, day four of trial, at 6:47 PM and 25 seconds, the BIA began stating, quote: 'In an ideal world, if I had anything to do with it, every parent—before someone moved into their house—they would tell the other parent before they ever told the children. I try to tell clients, before you're even going to introduce them to the children, introduce them to the other parent. I'm not making an excuse for [mom], but I suspect that her position was, I know it happened last time this happened, and I don't want it to happen again or at least I want to avoid it for a while from happening again. So, it's very unfortunate that dad didn't know that [the boyfriend] was moving in.'

"The BIA admitted on record that my ex-wife caused every problem with her new boyfriend by failing to meet both her standards of introducing him to me. My question is this: Why, BIA, did you recommend so strongly against my ex-wife's original behavior of keeping her boyfriend secret from me? I know in this case, it created serious mistrust and communication problems. Yet, in spite of acknowledging my ex-wife caused every single subsequent problem, the BIA awarded my ex-wife with custody for creating such an inappropriately hostile relationship. Why did you reward the problem causer and punish the one who was victimized by someone failing to follow your own rules?

"And judge, do you recall when [the BIA] wanted to put my oldest son, Ethan, in criminal jeopardy by forcing him to testify in this case while he had an open criminal case? The BIA didn't care about my son's best interest on that day, and she never has. The President of the Bar Association forced my 14-year-old son to commit perjury against his own father.

"And I'd just like to point out the reason for my sudden legal and mental health issues that popped up. There was about to be a massive leak in the investigation that was prompted by the email that was sent to the school, and it was made to look like I was a criminal nutcase in case that leak got out. So, I sucked it up and did it because this was too much injustice and too psychologically traumatic for my children to continue to allow the court to prey on other families the way it has destroyed mine.

"Judge, at the end of your ruling, you said you want my child to know for certain whether or not abuse occurred. The only way my child's going to know is from their mom, brother, and the court when it's publicly proven I never said a word.

"My child didn't learn this awful thing happened from me; they'll learn it from the court and BIA. Unfortunately, because I believe this is about to be such a big story, they'll have no choice but to hear what the heck really did happen. It's all on public record. And now all three of my children have suffered and are the biggest victims of all."

Then the judge spoke.

"Thank you, Mr. Kotler. I will tell you I'm very disappointed because I had hoped we have had some improvement in your ability to look into your own behavior, and to examine how that behavior impacted the outcome of that trial. It's clear to me that we once again are back right where we were before, and I think that is really very sad."

Was she even listening?

I asked the judge if she believed people were vouching for me, but all she said was, "You're done talking," three times and "YOU'RE DONE TALKING!!!" once.

She added that I wasn't telling Ethan's *Skype* friends, I was telling mine. For the record, I didn't use *Skype*, and at the time, I had no friends. My parents and kids were my best and only friends. I did everything with them.

Days before the hearing, my ex-wife asked permission to get the kids their passports so her deceitful mom could take them abroad. I said I'd discuss it at the hearing. They asked again before entering the courtroom, and I told them to wait.

After tearing into the judge and BIA inside, we proceeded to the waiting area, lined with sets of seats along walls made of the same sinister red bricks that wrap the exterior. The BIA, my ex-wife, her mom, and her lawyer huddled—a typical sight. Then my ex-wife's lawyer approached me, close enough to smell his breakfast, and asked again. "Will you sign the passport form?"

"No."

"May I ask why not?" He used the same condescending, snarky tone he displayed throughout the trial.

"Because I don't trust her mom with the kids." My Leo personality shined as I roared back at the question, pointing toward my devious ex-mother-in-law. It's all those frustrating years Leos can't celebrate our summer birthdays in school. "I'm not letting her mom take them out of the country. When you asked her how I was abusive during the trial, her response couldn't possibly have happened."

Whenever we exchanged the kids, the pickup parent drove to the public gas station nearest the other's house to start their kid time. Our custody agreement ordered this arrangement. According to my ex-mother-in-law's testimony, I cursed out my ex-wife as she picked up the kids near her house, not mine. Supposedly, the kids witnessed it as they began their week together. The scenario was impossible, and I was never abusive toward her daughter in front of the kids. Not there. Not anywhere.

With The Washington Post involved, I refused the passport because I feared she could remove the kids from the country, and I'd have trouble retrieving them. When I finished speaking, the BIA turned to my ex-wife's lawyer, half in rage, half in tears. "See, I told you he wouldn't do it."

I fired back. "I have a hundred witnesses to support me. I lost the kids over a lie, and you know it."

Bordering on frantic, she screamed in the middle of the three-story courthouse, whose polygonal glass railings allow each floor to see and hear the next. "Get away from me!"

She tore past and ascended the poorly lit, open stairwell, pausing to hear my final words. "You know I did nothing wrong." In a blink, she was gone from sight for the next three years.

After this confrontation and my statement to the court, I had no shot getting the kids back the conventional way without outside intervention. When would The Post intercede? Maybe they were waiting outside.

I left the eerily quiet courthouse to find nobody. No camera flashes or crush of reporters. The only other poor soul was another God-fearing person lamenting over getting shafted by the court.

Six more months passed, and the investigation was still a well-guarded secret. The kids continued to fail school and I let the BIA, my ex-wife, and her lawyer, hear about it. Nothing helpful was ever done. All the BIA did was charge me money to read the emails about their poor grades and pass them on to my ex-wife's attorney. Below is one complete email from May 2020 that she billed $70 for:

> "The children are having extreme difficulty with my ex-wife and her boyfriend as their at-home teachers under the Covid-19 distance learning that is required. I have attached their grades.
>
> "Ethan is currently failing 5 of his 6 classes for the 4th Grading Period (including a 19% in English, a 43% in Math, and three classes with 50% grades that state 'Base grade; actual achievement less than indicated.') All five of these teachers comment that he either 'needs to exert more effort' or has 'failure to exert any effort' while also stating that he is missing multiple assignments. For the 3rd Grading Period, Ethan failed two of his three Honors classes with a 45% and 46% in History and English, respectively, while also receiving the same comments. He also had a D in his Math class.
>
> "Lucy's 4th Grading Period is even worse, with her best grade being in English where she has a 50%, but the comment states this is the 'Base grade; actual achievement less than indicated.' In her other four Honors classes, she has a 0% in Biology, 33% in U.S. Studies, 36% in French, and 45% in Math. Every teacher says she 'needs to exert more effort' except for her Guitar class, where she has 'failure to exert any effort' in achiev-

ing her failing 50% grade. They also routinely state that 'several assignments are missing or incomplete.'

"Colin may be the worst of the bunch: He has a 0% in Band, a 16% in Arts, a 17% in Magnet Science, a 25% in Merit ELA, a 59% in Magnet Math, and is barely passing Merit Social Studies with a 64%.

"You have destroyed these children's education, and their mother and the man you want to be their father clearly are not equipped to help them through these difficult times. My children will, at best, no longer be able to stay in their magnet and honors programs, and at worst, have to repeat their grades—all thanks to you looking out for their 'best interest'. It is not in their 'best interest' to be failing out of 6th, 9th, and 11th grades because they are stuck with incapable parental figures.

"Again, their grades are attached so you can see for yourself the dramatic harm you have caused to the future of these three children."

She billed me 0.2 hours to read that and examine the grades. It takes me three minutes.

I responded to her bill:

"You are disgusting to charge me $70 for reading a 3-minute email that was sent only due to how awful all three of my children are doing at school, while you're making it impossible for me to help them. Why am I being billed for something that is COMPLETELY YOUR FAULT? If these children were with me, they'd be doing fine like they were, and I wouldn't have had to send you that email.

"If you're going to bill for reading emails, you may as well send me another one for a couple hundred dollars for reading the attached email that I originally sent in mid-December 2017 to the families who are helping me. It explains everything you have done to destroy my family. I can't wait to see how much this one will cost."

Attached was the five-page story I sent to The Post. That was her first opportunity to read it, though she was unsuspecting that I emailed it to the media two-and-a-half years earlier. She never billed me for reading it, but she also did nothing to help the kids.

Those 83 days post-weed whacker threat when my ex-wife chose her new boyfriend over her kids should've raised eyebrows. But as with suffering school grades, the BIA prioritized my ex-wife's lawyer's interests over the children. He got his reward for giving the BIA this lucrative job.

But before she insisted they go back to the boyfriend, the extra time with my kids felt like make-up time.

When my ex-wife and I first separated in 2009, I lost my spouse, two jobs, school, newspaper work, my website, and my health in a matter of months. I was editor of an interfaith congregation's newsletter and the school paper, and those were gone too. But losing my kids hurt more than all the others combined. I was empty inside without them.

My ex-wife said we were splitting up and asked me to leave the house. Thus, I had to abandon the kids and found life impossible to enjoy without them. For that initial week, I ate nothing. The moment they arrived, a full meal went down. The appetite flourished all week, but when the kids disappeared, hunger vanished too.

A couple of months passed before I could stomach the idea of a meal without them. After all, the kids and I hung out every other week, so life wasn't that bad. Then I lost that.

14

QUICK AND SIMPLE

FIVE-YEAR-OLD LUCY SAID to my dad, "Mommy won't let daddy drive." I didn't hear Lucy's comment, but my dad was steamed about it for years—not at Lucy, but at her mother.

It didn't matter that I owned a clean driving record and every pain-management stipulated drug test confirmed proper usage of my pain medications. My ex-wife insisted I was misusing them and wasn't safe to be around the kids alone. Of course, she had no problem with me driving the kids to and from school, or leaving me alone with them while she worked or hung out with friends toward the end of our marriage. But once she left me, I was no longer competent and was suddenly restricted from driving.

One evening, my dad drove me and the kids to the grocery store in the blue Dodge Grand Caravan that I eventually plowed into water for The Post's amusement. I bought it months earlier, a few years used in great condition. While on the dark four-lane road, I noticed a deer in the distance standing across our travel lanes. "Dad, there's a deer in the road. Stop the van."

"Huh?"

"There's a deer. Stop driving."

Though he slowed a few miles per hour, my dad never saw the deer that he killed several seconds later. The crinkled front driver-side fender remained unfixed to the day the minivan met its watery demise. There was no reason those kids weren't safe with me behind the wheel, but they thought less of their dad because the court favored my ex-wife's nonsense.

Two years before the accident, doctors prescribed powerful opioids to relieve unrelenting vasectomy pain. Pain management doctors force patients to submit to drug tests regularly and randomly, but a year of clean test results didn't prove to be enough. My ex-wife accused me of abusing them, so my custody was reduced from 50/50 to a supervised Wednesday dinner in a church each week. Soon after, my parents were allowed to oversee us, and two weekends a month at home in Frederick were tacked on.

It was a massive strain on my dad. To provide us Wednesday dinners, he drove 90 minutes to get the kids from my ex-wife, 30 minutes to bring them to me, 30 minutes back to my ex-wife and another 90 to get home. Four hours of driving let me see my kids for three, and D.C. traffic often made it worse. That drive awaited him every other weekend, too.

In a lawyer's office recently, he cried recounting games of spaceship on those drives. Grandpa was the ship's pilot, Lucy was supply officer, Ethan was his navigator/gunner, and Colin was the cute kid who played mascot.

"Enemy at three o'clock!" Pilot grandpa warned of approaching aliens as he spun the radio dials to control their spaceship. "Man your battle stations."

"Got him in my sights!" Ethan pretend-blasted an outer-space intruder as mascot Colin giggled humor into the affair.

"Phew!" shouted Lucy. "That was a close one. Is anyone hungry after that? I've got peanut butter cracker sandwiches, boxes of raisins, and one fruit roll-up."

The weekends he spent away from my mom took a serious toll on the whole family. With her health in decline, she often stayed home alone in Bowie while my dad spent weekends with us an hour away.

After one such weekend, he returned home to find my mom ill with pneumonia and she was hospitalized for the next few days. Afterwards, our weekends included her in my childhood Bowie home. I loved seeing the kids have free rein where I did decades earlier, but it was two extra hours of driving for my dad. When I mention my parents being there for us, this is what I mean.

The court order stated that, to end supervision and reinstate driving privileges, I needed to complete regular and random drug testing. No time frame was specified. The wording said to use a place "such as [one in particular]". Because it named that specific company as an example, the restrictions dragged on for two-and-a-half years.

The named place did not make random phone calls, so I could only go of my own accord to get their drug tests. All tests came back as they should, but my ex-wife and her original attorney (not the guy that asked for the BIA) refused to accept them because they weren't random.

I tried other drug testing facilities since the order clarified that I wasn't restricted to the one named. The test results were compliant, but were refused because I chose when to go. I wasn't randomly called. The lawyer insisted on one specific place that didn't make random calls, and the court agreed.

Meanwhile, I chalked up additional random and regular tests with pain management, but they were never good enough.

Two years passed. I hired a new attorney who met with the master (a subordinate appointed by a judge) and the opposing attorney in the master's chamber. My ex-wife's attorney confessed to knowing the place they insisted upon did not perform random drug testing. So, I lost two-and-a-half years unsupervised parenting of my kids because of BS.

The kicker is my ex-wife was ordered to undergo drug testing once every three months for the duration of my supervision. That should have spelled ten drug tests across that 30-month period. Twenty-four months in, she took none. She finally relented by taking one after two years of complaints, but the court was fine trusting her with primary physical custody the entire time. My plethora of out-of-pocket drug tests only cost me more money and aggravation. She had the kids. Not me.

The initial BIA on the case for those first years completed her degree in Women's Studies and was CEO of a shelter run by women for victims of domestic violence, so I understood why she always sided with my ex-wife.

Eventually she was replaced, and my new lawyer worked an agreement using a different testing center that randomly called me. Within three months, I was completely cleared. Supervision ended and I could drive the kids, but I was still stuck with the all-too-common 14% of custody time because my ex-wife claimed I was incapable of getting them to school.

Because I missed raising the kids, I asked my ex-wife to meet me at a local restaurant where I floated the ridiculous notion of getting back together. But, thankfully, she had none of it. She did, however, concede to allowing the kids to sleep over Sunday nights instead of returning them. That meant she trusted me to bring them to school on Monday mornings.

I met with my lawyer a short time later. As she drafted a motion for a separate issue, I mentioned the incident, prompting the coolest thing I ever saw a lawyer do. She stopped writing and tore the motion in half. "I wish you told me sooner," she said. "You just got your kids back."

She was right, but so much irreplaceable childhood vanished.

Substantial dollars went to those various drug testing facilities, but it paled compared to the cost of pain management's tests. I discovered that the hard way when I arrived at a routine appointment, like I'd been doing every two to four weeks for a year.

"We can't see you anymore," the woman at the front desk said. The office manager emerged. "You owe us $2,500 because you no longer have insurance." I learned my ex-wife had removed me from the family health plan without my knowledge. Those drug tests cost a fortune at over $400 apiece, but were worthless for getting custody.

When things seemed perfect pre-divorce, my ex-stepson, who was three years older than Ethan, lived 90% of his life with us. With four impeccable children to care for, my ex-wife and I returned to school seeking to start new careers. Student loans let us learn more while working less. The plan was to earn four-year degrees by the time the kids reached school age. With our youngest four years away, the timing fit.

She wanted another kid, but we were living paycheck to paycheck, in need of sporadic help from our parents. I was 29 years old, and she was 27. Our savings was empty, so it made sense to stop making family and start making a living.

Because a vasectomy is much safer than the female equivalent, I preferred not to subject my ex-wife to it. I didn't want to hear the post-procedure nagging. Though that's a joke, the awful reality was neither did she.

Step one was a group information session at the medical center, where we gathered in a conference room around three long tables connected like a U. Half of the 30 chairs were filled. Some patients, like me, sat by themselves while others brought their partner.

The doctor gave a presentation discussing how vasectomies are simple procedures, but not foolproof guarantees against pregnancy. After explaining the straightforward post-op care, the doctor asked if we had questions. I never ask questions; this time I did. "Can we be asleep during the procedure because I'm squeamish?"

Responding to the entire room, he said, "No, it's quick and simple. You'll be fine."

Nervously awake the night before the vasectomy, I researched what to expect. Some suggested asking for Valium upon arrival to calm the nerves. Many were asleep for their procedures.

My appointment was 8:30 in the morning on June 30, 2008. As requested, I arrived half an hour earlier, only to find the office door locked. Fifteen minutes passed before the nurse, clad in blue scrubs, heard my knocking. There were no other patients inside where she asked me to wait.

Five minutes elapsed before the nurse acknowledged me again, at which time I inquired about the medicine with ten minutes to spare before my scheduled appointment.

"I read online to ask for Valium to soothe my nerves."

"The doctor isn't here yet," she said. "I can't make that call." Minutes before my procedure, she phoned the doctor who was still on his way in.

The nurse brought me to the operating room and requested I strip from the waist down. Lying under a paper sheet on the operating table, I gazed around. A computer, clipboard, and orange pill bottle rested on the counter to my left. High on the wall was a clock, on whose hands I fixed my attention. Inches from my feet, a large silver tray held a dozen glistening surgical tools. Not an ideal prop for surgery-phobic people. I refused to look at it.

At 8:40, the doctor entered.

"I'm told that you're asking for Valium," he said as he sat to my right, on a round stool that barely squeezed between the operating table and stale white wall.

"Yes, because I'm extremely nervous."

"I wish you said something beforehand."

"I asked to be asleep for the procedure, but you said, 'No.'

"Usually it's not a big deal," he said. "But you're my first appointment of the day and I was planning to start right away. It'll take too long for the medicine to take effect."

"But I can't do it like this," I said, shuddering at the thought of knives and needles neutering me.

"Give me a minute." He stood, stepped out the door, and slammed it behind him. In the hallway, he yelled at the nurses. "Why the hell did they schedule him for 8:30?!? I've told them not to schedule anyone before nine!"

That should've been my cue to throw my pants on and run, but I was naïve. The doctor returned and plopped on the stool, falling forward in dismay with his face tucked in his hands. Out came his laundry list of grievances.

"If I give you Valium, by the time it takes effect, I'll be late for every appointment the rest of today. Plus, I'll have to call the hospital and tell them my surgeries will be late. But you're a patient too."

"When can I make another appointment?"

"The next isn't until July 31st."

I didn't want to wait. I couldn't afford another month of healthcare, and knowing my luck, we'd get pregnant again in my sleep.

The doctor departed, and as 9:00 rolled past, I heard other patient's voices. Fifteen minutes later, the nurse walked in. "The doctor is deciding what to do," she said, ducking out the doorway. Sometime after, she reappeared, and marched straight to the orange pill bottle that I stared at for an hour. She pulled out a Valium and had me wait in the lobby until it took effect.

Long after my scheduled appointment, my dad, who accompanied me, was surprised to see me again without the procedure having been done. After 30 minutes, the meds kicked in and I went into operating.

That metal tray of torture tools became a manageable sight. As I waited alone for the doctor to begin, I tried determining what they used each device for. That cuts me open. No, that cuts me open. Wait, does that cut me open?

Over two hours after I arrived, the nurse and doctor entered. "Ok, you're going to feel a painful pinch," the doc said. God made sure of it. The nurse held my hand as the doctor pierced me. "Ouch!" the nurse yelled. "You hurt my hand." She angrily fled the room and ditched me to be alone with the doctor and that metal tray. Those tools didn't seem so interesting anymore.

As the doctor worked on the left side, I felt soreness from the injection, but that was it. Minutes later, I yelled. "Oww! What was that?"

"I'm doing the other side now," he said. Without warning, he pierced me with an ineffective injection. The first injection numbed properly, but this one didn't.

As he yanked and maneuvered my innards, he said, "Stop moving!"

"I'm trying not to." I began to hum loudly, attempting to occupy my mind.

"Try not to move."

"I'm trying, but it hurts." Unlike the left side, I felt every tug, slice, and needle poke. He couldn't have finished fast enough.

Years later, my dad recalled the nurse speaking to him during the procedure. "The nurse said, 'He's having a bit of a rough go in there, but he'll be out soon.'"

I staggered out, picked up my pain medicine at the pharmacy, and headed home to recuperate. After days of the "gentle narcotic" not helping, I hobbled into urgent care. The large national HMO that performed the procedure supplied doctors with many specialties on one campus, including urgent care. They prescribed a less-gentle narcotic. With a hefty supply, I assumed I was done with doctors, but it was only the beginning.

A week after the vasectomy, I returned for my follow-up appointment with a different doctor in the same office. Despite having been to urgent care, the pain remained more severe than expected. I shared my experience and the doctor's denial of my request to be knocked out for surgery. That surprised this new doctor. "Why would he tell you that? That's the only way I do my procedures."

A few weeks of prolonged pain passed. They referred me to pain management, who prescribed additional pills. Because of my high tolerance for drugs, they escalated the dosing quickly. Afraid what tripling my opioid dosage in two months meant for me long term, I asked for an alternative. The pain specialist prescribed a stronger narcotic, however insurance didn't cover its $1,000 price tag each month—but it helped.

I scheduled an array of appointments with handfuls of doctors from varying specialties and medical providers, but they had no answers. Nerve blocks temporarily made things worse. An at-home TENS unit pointlessly shot electrical pulses through electrodes, in fruitless efforts to dull the flashing pain in my thigh. Plus, there was no solution to lessen the discomfort radiating into my abdomen.

Imagine needing to use the bathroom. It's on your mind until you do. That's chronic pain, but you never get relief.

Sleeping was difficult. A side-sleeper my whole life, it became too painful, so I had to adjust to sleeping on my back.

Ice and meds were my saving grace. Most of each day, I reclined with an ice pack tucked between my thigh and the incision. The ice even helped me fall asleep at night. In other words, the doctor roasted my chestnuts, and I was Jack Frost nipping at my nose.

Every four hours, like clockwork, I downed my pain pills. How else could I keep up with little ones aged eight, five, three, and nine months?

I met countless doctors outside the insurance company. Visit after visit, there was no fix. Doctors said, "There's nothing I can do," or "You'll have it the rest of your life."

Struggling for hope, I sought the best. So, I booked an appointment with the country's top-rated urology department's head urologist. He referred me to a quack of a surgeon. The guy waddled into the room and said he'd perform an out-of-pocket procedure costing tens of thousands. He guaranteed new numbness in unaffected areas, with no promise of improvement in pain.

I searched the internet for other examples of my injury, but found nothing. Nobody's post-vasectomy pain symptoms matched mine, and I'd been to pain management for quite a while without a specific diagnosis.

Long after the vasectomy, my pain doctor handed me a form for a handicap parking placard. As I limped into Motor Vehicle Administration, I read the form and there it was for the first time. My diagnosis was ilioinguinal neuralgia—nerve damage to the ilioinguinal nerve.

I hit *Google* the moment I arrived home. That was it. The doctor nicked my ilioinguinal nerve during the vasectomy, through an incision a quarter-inch higher than on the other side, where the ilioinguinal nerve begins. Pain ran from the incision up into the abdomen, then down my inner thigh, tracing the ilioinguinal nerve precisely. It's the first time my symptoms matched.

I researched, wondering how often a vasectomy causes ilioinguinal neuralgia. Relatively commonplace after hernia surgery, it's exceedingly rare from a vasectomy. Shortly after my ex-wife left me, I discovered exactly one other man who endured my ordeal over a decade earlier. So, I spoke to his lawyer from neighboring Philadelphia, Pennsylvania. He said he remembered well the largest payout of his career.

"The defense appealed the $930,000 verdict," he said. "But on appeal the award was upped to $22 million. The judge didn't think the defense could pay $22 million, so the final settlement was $4.3 million."

"That's what the guy got?"

"Yes."

"Is he feeling any better nowadays?"

"No. He's about the same."

"How about his family? Is he still married?" I asked from my parents' house, the childhood Bowie home I frequented much more often after my marriage disintegrated.

"They had troubles early on before the case, but now they're doing just fine."

"Can you take a case in Maryland?"

"Unfortunately not. I'm licensed in Pennsylvania, New Jersey, and Washington D.C."

"My surgery was performed five miles from D.C. in Maryland. Can you recommend an attorney?"

"Not down that way, sorry."

Despite that, I was enthusiastic. My injury had a name, and a huge settlement acted as precedent to entice an attorney. The lawyer referred me to his nearby doctor, who performed a lengthy, videotaped procedure that was entered as evidence to win the settlement. I met with him and shared my story.

"This is déjà vu," the doctor said.

"What do you mean?"

"It's exactly the same thing the other guy had."

"So you can perform the same procedure on me?"

"No."

"What? Why not?"

"That was almost 15 years ago. I can't do a seven-hour procedure anymore."

"Do you know anyone who can?"

"No."

"Does the procedure have a name?"

"There's no name for it. It was just exploratory surgery with the intent of fixing it. On the videotape, we saw what the doctor did, and proved the damage was from his procedure. They tried to argue it was from mine, but there was no way. So we won the case."

Already more than a year in, I'd need luck finding a doctor to perform an unnamed procedure before the statute of limitations expired.

I phoned a major law firm that routinely advertises on our local TV stations, and the head lawyer answered. Seconds into describing my situation, he interrupted. "Unless you're paralyzed or lost a limb, we're not interested."

Another lawyer never let me consult with his doctor before he rejected my case. Because I contacted another attorney while waiting weeks for this guy, that one also refused. Apparently, only one lawyer may be sought at a time.

Amid this, I struggled to see my kids, so I focused my attention on them rather than on money. Before I knew it, the statute of limitations passed. I had no diagnosis for the first third, and no results at the end.

15

THE PRESIDENT'S MOVIE

I VISITED FAMILIES' HOMES SELLING educational software for their kids at the time of the operation. That's how my dad raised our family, but with encyclopedias instead of computer programs.

The software was expensive, but supposedly aligned with each state's curriculum, significantly helping children with school. Because I assumed I made a positive difference in these kids' lives, I earned the most sales of all rookie salespeople in the company. For my reward, I won a suite at a famed beachfront hotel in south Florida.

The problem was, I also won the software. Hard to install and even harder to use, it didn't match what my kids learned in school. They found it boring and cumbersome, and so did I. Though I continued on sales calls, I stopped making sales. By the date of the Florida trip, others said I'd quit the moment I hopped aboard the homebound plane. They were right. By the time wheels touched earth, I was done.

Before my vasectomy and brief stint in educational sales, I worked a few years as a courier, probably the most likable job I ever had. Familiar with the courier company for years, both my dad and another family member worked there, dating back to my high school days. Almost a decade later, I joined my dad delivering for them. As an independent contractor, I set my schedule and earned enough to care for my family.

Delivering packages around the D.C. area and the Mid-Atlantic afforded me tons of freedom. Because I love to travel, visiting new cities and towns was right up my alley. Longer drives of a few hundred miles offered plenty of sightseeing and food-tasting opportunities. Since I may have been their quickest driver, I received profitable runs and could choose my work. They appreciated me like family.

When I was still a teenager in the mid-'90s, I met the company on a fishing trip. I never fished before, but was excited about the prospect of an underage beer on a chartered boat.

The Chesapeake Bay is known for three culinary specialties: blue crabs, oysters, and striped bass (aka rockfish). Fifteen of us set sail in search of the biggest bass, with everyone tossing $20 into a sweepstake given to catcher of the largest fish. I never got a beer, but I got the big bass. Though I won $300, I was stuck mourning the massive fish that clogged our freezer for months, never to be eaten. What a memorable introduction to the company that helped me raise my family a decade later.

When I delivered to ABC News in Washington, the security guy sent me upstairs. Outside the elevator and around the corner, I figured employees seated at computers would sign for the package. As soon as I passed through the doorway, they were terrified when I asked for a signature. They waved me out as they pointed right. I glanced over to see a teleprompter, lights, cameras, and possibly George Stephanopoulos' back. I was the only background prop standing and looking in the cameras on live TV. They never let me back upstairs.

There were plenty of interesting shipments, like frequent private movie screenings and deliveries to secure government facilities. A few stars from the *Cops* parody, *Reno 911!*, debuted their movie in downtown D.C. The actors who played Lieutenant Dangle and Deputies Junior and Williams surprised the theater audience. Upstairs, in the private film booth, they signed a movie poster to my ex-wife and me, which she stole when we divorced.

Perhaps that was retribution for another delivery, when movie reels had to reach Camp David during George W. Bush's reign. The delivery took me through my hometown, so I called my very pregnant spouse and asked her to gather the kids for the scenic drive.

We arrived at Camp David to find a 12-foot board filled with dozens of DO NOT ENTER signs in various colors, fonts, sizes, and verbiage.

"We shouldn't go there," said my ex-wife.

"But I've got a movie to deliver, and the President needs it now!"

Two small words were obscured by a hundred agreeing with my ex-wife: DELIVERIES ONLY. "Oh good. That's me." On ahead we went. We rounded a few bends through the lush mountain forest before reaching some orange cones that prompted police and military to swoop in. They radioed me to exit my vehicle.

"Why did you think it was a good idea to proceed to the entrance?" a cop asked.

"There was a 'deliveries only' sign."

"Didn't you see the 'do not enter' signs?"

"Yes. I also saw a 'deliveries only' sign."

Then I explained the countless shipments to government agencies, my familiarity with showing ID, having my car searched and answering questions—a process that lasted a few minutes, at most. But this one tortured my eight-month pregnant ex-wife for hours.

The cops requested she exit the van and wait on the opposite side, leaving the kids in their car seats. They confiscated our cellphones and flipped through every photo. For nearly two hours, the police kept me and my ex-wife apart so we couldn't communicate or see one another.

It was fascinating getting paid to chill on the ground surrounded by natural mountain beauty and Camp David's buildings that the public never sees. The kids were fine entertaining themselves, shaded by mature oak trees showing their first hint of fall colors. After two hours, a pair of military guys signed for the 60-pound box of movie reels. We piled in the van and drove off.

I looked at my ex-wife. "That was so cool!"

She glared back. "I could kill you." That was unexpected. "They made me sit on the ground for two hours, not caring how pregnant I am. It was so uncomfortable." She should be proud. It strengthened our baby.

I felt bad, so I made it up to her by taking her on vacation to Pittsburgh during another delivery, my last for the company.

A month before our surprisingly enjoyable Steel City weekend, I arrived at work like any other day. Job security seemed high because I was an extremely reliable worker for a company we knew for years, so when I entered the friendly office and they greeted me differently, I was stunned.

"The company was sold and they're shutting down our office."

There was no inkling our workplace would close, leaving me 30 days before I was jobless without severance pay. Little did I know, this marked the beginning of the end of my marriage.

Many colleagues transferred to another company on the wrong side of town, so my dad and I followed suit. D.C. became difficult to drive into and the airport was even further. The extra driving was met with less work and much less money. The hour's drive from my Frederick home to the office, plus the gas used between deliveries, often cost more than my day's earnings. Eventually, I was forced to leave my adopted family for a courier on the right side of town, two blocks from our old address. They paid more per job than the original courier; so much that it was unaffordable to customers.

I regularly arrived at the new company's office after morning rush hour to deliver one or two local jobs all day, paying $20 or $30 apiece. Long-distance profitable runs were scarce. Unlike the other couriers, this one paid $35 extra for late-night work after 11 PM. So, I almost always hung out as late as 2 or 3 AM, hoping one job would arise, so my day's pay was reasonable. Often it never did. But one very late night, God blessed me with an article in *The Washington Times* while I killed boredom.

The article informed of internet bloggers writing about the Washington Capitals and being accepted into the press box as legitimate journalists.

A short time earlier, my mom spoke about my dad helping her find a career path. She sought a more meaningful and higher paying job than her secretary position when my dad asked her a brilliant question. "If you could do something for free, what would it be? That's your calling."

My mom returned to teaching. With a Latin degree from Queens College in New York and teaching experience decades earlier, she found work in middle and high school foreign language departments. She even returned to school for her master's degree at Bowie State, Maryland's oldest historically black university, once named Maryland Teachers College. Poor health, sadly, forced an early retirement.

I gave the idea some thought after having just discovered a talent for writing in an unusual way.

Months earlier, while struggling to eke out a living after the office closure, I stumbled on an ad that said a pizza delivery chain was hiring managers. Since I had plenty of experience, I walked in and applied. They hired me as an assistant. Without feedback for two weeks, I was prepared to return to the courier since I applied to be a manager, not an assistant. I asked the supervisor, who had barely said a word to me since my arrival, what his plan was. "I've heard nothing about getting promoted to manager."

"You're doing great," he said. "I'm about to fire somebody and put you in charge."

Surprised by his response, the highest volume store, which delivered to my townhouse, became mine. I couldn't have hoped for a finer position. Sure, I had to gain favor with the dismissed manager's sister, mother and fiancé who still worked there, but after a week of glares and behind-my-back whispering, we became friends.

The incompetent supervisor who priced cars online when he visited was another story. After a month of disagreements, I quit. Outraged that I withdrew from a potentially ideal job, I penned a three-page letter to the owner. That was a first. I stopped by the store and showed a copy to the new friends I left behind.

"I can't believe you picked up on all that in a month," said one.

"This is really well written," said another.

Writing had been my biggest deterrent to enjoying school. I could skip reading assignments when multiple-choice exams were offered, because I'd at least earn around 25%. Though I often found myself asking, "Why did I get a 15 when I should've gotten 25? Oh. I guess C wasn't the most popular choice."

I always appreciated sitting next to the kids who cheat. "Yeah, you can copy off me."

But essays on exams were the worst. Having to guess people's names and describing random events out of thin air is harder than it sounds.

With newfound confidence in my writing ability, I figured I'd combine my passion for hockey and seek work as a hockey reporter. Upon reading that newspaper article while awaiting a delivery to cover gas expenses and provide a little to take home, starting my own blogging website sounded like the perfect method to fast-track myself into a dream job.

The next day, I checked out a book from the library on creating websites. Within a month or two, I launched it, days before the Capitals fired their head coach with the worst record in all of hockey. I didn't care. The team was terrible, but this was the job of a lifetime. A bright future was on the horizon, but I invested tons of time and was spending money on the site, not making any.

Within a month, the 2007 Hanukkah and Christmas season arrived. But I didn't have cash for presents like years past. So, my ex-wife floated the idea of teaching the kids the true meaning of the holidays since we couldn't afford to provide the typical American version of buying out the kids for another year. I thought it sounded like a great idea, so I agreed.

Holidays were simple to this point. When we got engaged, we discussed religion.

"I'm not converting."

"I'm not converting either."

"Let's celebrate all the holidays."

"Okay."

That was the extent of our conversation. It was so straightforward, it worked.

I was so excited to celebrate our first Christmas, I bought my own ornament and strung Christmas lights out front in Hanukkah colors. And we began our tradition of leaving the 7-foot tree up way too long. Being festive during the Christmas season was new to me and I went all out. The glowing lights and overabundance of green-and-red decorations dwarfed the small menorah and blue-and-white bears holding a candy dish under a music box dreidel.

All was well, at least for the first five years.

As 2007 rolled into 2008, my ex-wife joined her mother's new church with the kids, who previously attended preschools at different local churches and came back better. So I thought nothing of it. But this place was different. Within a week or two, the whole family shifted mindsets and turned against me.

The spouse switched every preset radio station in the car. Gone were all the pop songs of the past in favor of Christian talk and music. My ex-stepson glowed over reading Bible verses to me from his New Testament, complete with case and Jesus-fish zipper. Five-year-old Ethan forced three-year-old Lucy to affirm her love for Jesus before unbuckling her car seat.

"Lucy, do you love Jesus?" Ethan asked. She said nothing. "Lucy, say you love Jesus."

"Please unbuckle me."

"Say you love Jesus."

"Please get me out."

"Not until you say you love Jesus. I'm not unbuckling you until you say you love Jesus."

I watched her say it, and he unbuckled her.

The kids used to playfully "Attack daddy!" as they jumped me from every direction. But during family breakfast before school, one of them thought it more appropriate to shout, "Attack the Jew!"

Arguably worse, my spouse began calling me a "bad Jew" and threatened divorce for the first time. One Sunday I was working while my ex-wife took the kids to church, then to a family gathering. When we reconvened at home that evening, she said, "I should just listen to everyone and leave you already."

One of my favorites was the day she said, "If I knew you wouldn't convert, I never would've married you." So much for the effective conversation that lasted five years.

"Baptist churches are fine," my ex-wife said, defending the church that lured her to swiftly spurn her Jewish husband. "It's Southern Baptist churches you need to worry about."

I read aloud the first sentence on their website. "We are a Southern Baptist church."

"That's not true," she said.

"Why do they call themselves that if it isn't true?" I learned there's little reasoning to be had with those who are convinced they're right, like my parents all these years later.

I did everything in my power to save the marriage.

An interfaith congregation welcomed us. I liked the rabbi, but I really liked the Southern Baptist-raised pastor who stoked an atmosphere dedicated to learning and celebrating our religious traditions.

Their approach to youth was far different from the church, whose website said, "We love the unquestioning faith of children." In stark contrast, the interfaith website said, "We encourage children to ask questions."

I insisted my ex-wife stop attending the evangelical church, but she complained the interfaith wasn't spiritual enough. I admit, it differed from a synagogue experience, but they were friendly and inviting to our family, and would have taught us about the holidays as my ex-wife intended. When she said she wanted the kids to learn the true meaning of the holidays, I assumed she meant both Christmas and Hanukkah. Southern Baptists didn't know much about the Festival of Lights.

My ex-wife ceased taking all three of our kids to that church. But because my ex-stepson, who lived with us most of his life and called me "daddy," wasn't technically my kid, my ex-mother-in-law continued taking him. She used to send cards thanking me for treating him the same as my own kids. Not anymore.

"He's not your child," she said. "You can't stop me." Through the end of the school year, she brought him, until summer vacation was enough to break the twice-a-week cycle. After months of arguing around the time of my vasectomy, she truly hated me. Eleven months later, as the vasectomy pain debilitated me, my ex-wife separated.

My inability to continue work and school was the opportunity my ex-mother-in-law needed to coax my ex-wife to leave me. We learned disability took time to receive—too much for them.

Had she stayed, we'd have been better off. The money spent for two residences, plus the additional financial compensation disability would've given her, were a lot of money lost. Most depressing of all, hundreds of thousands went to lawyers instead of our own kids.

I never understood how my ex-wife could leave me, knowing she'd be giving up tons of time with the kids. But a decade passed when I recognized I made that decision too. Had I converted to Christianity, we could've worked things out, and I'd have seen my kids every day. Without realizing, I never second-guessed choosing Judaism over an intact family. I didn't know why, but I knew I'd always be Jewish.

Without God, who freed us from Egypt, I wouldn't have children for whom I care so deeply or any other joys of life, so I made the right choice.

16

My Favorite Number

GROWING UP, I HAD MORE than a few favorite players on the Washington Capitals. One of our leading scorers, a Swede named Bengt Gustafsson, topped the list. He played on the Caps for a decade from the time I was a year old, and I loved his number 16. And since I had nothing against neutral Sweden, I figured I could like the guy.

My Bowie Bruins won the opportunity to scrimmage against the Caps at the Capital Centre after one of their practices in 1989, his last year in the league. We won 2-1, but Scott Stevens knows his goal was hogwash. Sure, he's a Hall of Famer known for captaining his team to Stanley Cups and smashing people into another realm of consciousness, but he also knows that was a wuss shot. I saw the puck the whole way, but my skate caught in a rut, preventing the save.

I suppose they could've scored another, but they didn't. Bengt Gustafsson, of all people, grabbed the puck and flew full speed up the ice, as my team froze in awe. He wound up for a slap shot, hockey's hardest shot. Because I wore thin pads that didn't cover me completely, shots from kids my age hurt, so I wasn't going to test his. As I ditched my goaltending duty, leaving him an empty net, he succumbed to laughter and never fired the puck.

Upon later discovering that I was born at 16:16 on August 16th, I had abounding reason to love the number. I guess Bengt and I were written in the Book of Life all along.

Like everything else in life, though, the number 16 isn't perfect. My longest stay in post-Post jail began on the 16th of March 2018, about four months after losing custody and one month after Dumpster Night, thanks to the number 16.

But two weeks earlier, as the last night of February ticked into March, I found myself in my shortest stint behind bars.

Knowing I was being followed, I routinely hit the nearby Appalachian Trail, visible atop the flat green mountain ridge seven miles east of town from my children's bedroom windows. The cold late-winter weather couldn't chill my enthusiasm for experiencing the outlandish wonders The Post prepared.

One sunny day on the trail, my jacket overheated me, so I slung it over my shoulder. After ten minutes of hiking, I noticed it disappeared. As I backtracked to search, a couple approached.

"I was wearing a brown, wool-lined jacket. Have you seen it?"

"Yeah. It was hanging on a tree a little ways back," they said, motioning toward my starting point.

 How is it hanging on a tree? It was draped over my shoulder as I traversed the wide, rocky trail. I retraced my steps but found nothing. Later, while I was in jail, one of the head guards donned my jacket over his uniform. How does he have my coat? I bought it in Colorado.

On the last night of February, I roamed the trail well after dark under a full moon. Logs and branches laid across the path diverted me off-trail down the mountainside. With every moonlit plant visible and leafless, it was easy walking amongst the trees.

Bam! Something snagged my foot and flung me forward, smacking my stupidly hard head against a fallen log.

As I wandered further down the mountainside, a distant bright light flashed on. Moments later, the light disappeared, but I proceeded that direction as I ventured further from the trail. Every so often, the light flashed on and off, hundreds of feet ahead of me, progressing at my pace.

Wham! I was jolted again. A second pitfall stole my shoe and sent me flying. I knew I wasn't alone in these woods.

With my footwear gone and my foot hurting, the icy temperature made water puddles soothing to step in. Eventually, the steady porch light of a mansion greeted me at civilization's edge. I rested on a patio chair behind the house, thinking my life might change inside.

The unlocked sliding glass door glided open, so I welcomed myself inside to warm up. I figured someone from The Post would provide a compassionate reception, but instead of hearing, "Thank you, sir," like at the hospital, a couple said, "Sit down. We're calling the police."

The cops arrived and kindly placed me in their heated squad car. "You should knock next time before you enter," said one of the officers.

"Why?"

"Because that's the lowest possible crime you could commit."

"Oh, okay."

The cop smiled and carted me to the Frederick jail that was a five-minute walk from the townhome I once shared with my ex-wife and kids. The burglary was a weak misdemeanor. Imagine if I knocked first.

After receiving a foot X-ray in jail, which was too conveniently located between the reception desk and my cell ten feet away to make sense, they prepared me for release and permitted a phone call. With my car parked 20 minutes away and the clock past midnight, I dialed my parents. Repeated attempts yielded the same recording about a Caribbean vacation. Maybe they're sending me out of the country!

Instead, they released me about 2 or 3 in the morning into sub-freezing temperatures with a dead cellphone, no wallet, and no ride.

Without a clue what to do, I trudged five minutes to my old townhome wearing my new black canvas and Velcro jail shoes, holding a clear plastic bag that contained my soaked freedom shoe. In front of my old townhome on the public sidewalk, I found a scooter. The obstacle course of an adventure that led me to the burglarized mansion and an hour in lockup had me curious for something better.

I rode the scooter to the back patio and left it. But other than the new homeowner telling me to scram, nothing interesting happened. For that, police later charged me with theft and trespassing, though I was gone before their arrival on scene.

I slept behind the kids' gymnastics center across the field until sunrise. As morning dawned, I searched the adjacent industrial street for a bathroom to warm my frozen hands and feet.

Then I continued to the UPS facility where I worked for six months, loading and supervising the loading of UPS trucks in the wee hours of the morning before delivering FedEx SameDay packages later each day as courier. Neither one knew about the other.

Outside UPS, a parked truck appeared to have been bombed. Literally bombed. Severely blackened and mangled, with its side wall, rear gate, and roof torn to shreds, a potent bomb must've destroyed it. The truck carcass, with a mostly intact front end, melded with the absurdity of the evening perfectly.

Stuck wandering in Frederick that March morning, I stopped at McDonald's for breakfast and balloons, then headed back toward my old townhouse community. A Thomas' English Muffin factory was across the street. So, I went. At the front entrance, I buzzed the intercom and asked for that singer the cops told me about, then waited outside bouncing a basketball while standing on four-foot boulders.

Two cops rolled up. "You're looking for a singer?" one asked.

"Yeah, a cop told me about her a few days ago."

"I'm not sure you'll find her here. Put the basketball back and I'll drive you to your car." We discussed former co-workers of mine on the way.

The evening's burglary, theft, and trespassing charges were eventually dismissed because no witnesses appeared in court. But in a matter of hours, I was charged with three crimes at two separate locations.

It occurred at the midway point between my initial 11-day jail stay for risking catastrophe in a dumpster and the much longer sentence that book-ended the crime spree.

That evening at home, my dad said, "They want me to take you to the hospital." I didn't know who "they" were, but every day was a new adventure, whether it was wandering the Appalachian Trail and encountering a prefab night encampment with a talking fireplace or ending an overnight on the Chesapeake & Ohio Canal with a low-flying aircraft pass over. What did they have in store now?

I said, "Okay."

In my psych ward room the first night, a nurse, who looked like a former hockey teammate, began taking my blood pressure.

"You like exactly like my old teammate," I said.

"Wow, you're good. How do remember that?"

"And the other nurse looks like my former classmate."

"You know," he said. "We've lived your entire life."

"Huh?"

"We know everything about you," he said, grinning widely. "How's this for a fact? This is your first girlfriend's name."

Two weeks after that first burglary, they staged my second one. The afternoon of March 16th, while driving on the interstate highway that runs through Hagerstown into Pennsylvania, a local radio station went to commercial break. The night before, I was home indulging in some whimsical self-banter. "How great would it be to have a giant hot tub on our back deck? I'd dive in from my second-floor window!" As I approached the Pennsylvania state line, an ad played on the radio. "Head now to the Auto Auction right off Exit 3 in Pennsylvania to get a hot tub. They're practically giving them away."

Since I was a few miles from the exit, I headed over. On a cold, cloudy late-winter Friday, I arrived to find nobody in sight, and no hot tubs. There weren't even cars for an auto auction. But there was a small cul-de-sac with trailer homes that looked very similar to the one where I met my ex-wife and lived with her brother years earlier.

One trailer stood out from the rest. At cul-de-sac's end was a trailer whose house number was four digits long. Two digits were upside down; the other two were 16.

Two weeks earlier, when they arrested me for burglary during my late-night mountainside walk, the cop's words stuck in my mind. As the Maryland officer suggested, I knocked on the back door. It pushed wide open.

I walked in and was greeted by a framed photograph of a former employee of mine. But nobody was inside, so I waited to see if someone showed up.

As I listened to music through my cellphone, I heard chatter from walkie-talkies outside. After a few minutes, I grew interested in that noise. The moment I opened the front door, a laser dot hit my chest. "Freeze! Hands up! Get on the ground!" The place was swarming with cops ready to haul me to jail.

"But I knocked first. The police said this is a nothing crime, so aren't you going to release me?"

"What cop told you that?" his brother in blue asked.

"I don't know his name, but it was in Maryland."

"Haha! Burglary is a felony here in Pennsylvania."

"Even if I knock?"

"Yeah, knocking doesn't matter," the cop said as he reveled in my predicament. Then we played a guessing game on his computer. "No. PSP doesn't stand for PlayStation Portable," the cop said. "That's Pennsylvania State Police."

We rode to a small private building on the outskirts of town to meet a judge. I've encountered far too many judges in my lifetime, but this one stands out. Why would a judge make a special trip to meet one criminal at a crummy private office that featured a flickering ceiling light which continuously triggered a second cop's epileptic twitches and seizures?

So began my six-plus months in jail and a state hospital. The October day I was expecting to be released, the knock on the cell door arrived. Freedom, at last—but not so fast. God had one more trick up the sleeve. "You're being released to Maryland," the guard said. "So you have to wait another week."

Months after they discharged me from jail, I checked the map and learned the trailer home with the non-latching door was across the street from the granite warehouse where I spent Dumpster Night. They set me up twice, a thousand feet apart.

Upon my reintroduction to civilized society, I still observed tons of unusual stuff. I took copious photos and videos to coax my parents to understand what was going on. In jail, The Post taught me to be patient and stop fighting, but nobody said not to gather evidence.

Over the course of two weeks, I repeatedly took short five-minute strolls around the block by my home. Every time, something crazier happened than the day before.

A few days, I videotaped rows of red vehicles creeping past. The street isn't busy, so seeing three or four red vehicles in a row every day is rather unusual. Despite witnessing this, my parents still thought I was nuts and my jail stay was deserved.

I couldn't whip out my phone fast enough to catch the red car whizzing past at double the speed limit, complete with blinking turn signal, on its mission to kick dust through the red light.

The next day, I captured video of an incident I thought finally got through to my mom.

During my standard jaunt around the block, I stumbled upon some police cars and began recording. A red car sat atop a tow truck as its transgender owner screamed at the cops. "Stop calling me sir! I'm a woman!" Along the main road, mostly red cars were caught on camera driving past as I inched closer to the scene. The confrontation eased, so I turned for home, still recording. Before I could cross the street, a red car passed from each direction.

After watching the video, my lift-chairbound mom said, "I'm starting to believe you. And it's weird."

Then she tuned back to Fox News.

The next day, I chanced upon a winning scratch-off ticket lying in the street by that same intersection. I showed my parents. One day later, I found another winning lotto ticket in the exact same spot. Before I finished my loop around the block, I was approached. "Don't show it to anybody. And stop taking pictures."

Neither my mom nor my dad again believed that the news was helping.

17

PIG AND A BLANKET

PIGGY JOINED OUR FAMILY WHEN Lucy was two. She finished choosing new books with her brothers and we headed for checkout at the bookstore. A handful of stuffed pigs rested on the bottom shelf near the registers. She clutched one. He had floppy ears, fuzzy pink skin, a blue-and-white polka-dot tie, and the cutest squiggly tail. "Can I have him?"

Consumed by her glowing smile, my mom said, "Of course. Grandpa and I will get him for you."

Lucy brought Piggy everywhere. She refused to go to school without him in her backpack. Her teachers knew how valuable he was so they could keep him safe. As Lucy aged, he still went to school. Piggy followed her every time she shifted between my ex-wife's house and mine, tucking him into her bookbag on exchange day. I think she forgot him once. Piggy arrived that same night.

She took him to a Washington Nationals baseball game. The most well-loved stuffy in the stands, he watched her and Ethan run the bases with four beloved presidential mascots after the game.

Since losing the kids, I haven't seen Piggy once. After a few years, I asked about him. "Lucy, how's Piggy doing?"

Colin said, "Piggy died," and the world never heard a girl get so defensive.

"No, he didn't!"

"She lost him."

"No, I didn't!"

After learning Piggy was fine, I knew he was in excellent hands for a long time.

Colin had his own love—Bear Blanket. They met the day he was born, and a photo survives of him wrapped in Bear Blanket leaving the hospital. The fluffy blanket was filled with as many tan and brown bears as the white that separated them. Colin carried him around by day and slept with him at night. But as Colin grew bigger than Bear Blanket, he disappeared.

My ex-wife and I searched all over but couldn't find him. We asked our families, but nobody had seen him. For months, we continued asking people and kept our eyes peeled, without success. Then my ex-wife found an exact match online and purchased it.

Colin was somewhat uplifted. "But it's not Bear Blanket," he said, whimpering. A few days passed. "I want to name him, but I can't think of anything." Colin has a hundred stuffed animals, and everyone has a name. Naming them is what he does. Bear Blanket meant so much to him that he drew a blank for the first time.

"How about Bruin Blanky?" I asked. He looked at me weird as I explained. "Bruin is another name for a bear."

"I don't know."

"The hockey team I played on as a kid was called the Bruins."

His eyes brightened. "Okay, Bruin Blanky."

Bruin Blanky sufficed, but he was never Bear Blanket. Several times over the next few years, Colin began crying out of nowhere.

"What's wrong?"

"I miss Bear Blanket," he said, sniffling.

I felt so bad because I knew what it was like to miss a blanket or stuffed animal, and I can't imagine the scene if Lucy couldn't be so defensive about Piggy's good health.

Colin made do with Bruin Blanky when he received the best news. My ex-wife left it at her brother's house. Several times over the years, she asked him about it, but he said he didn't see it. When he found it, he said, "I've seen it so many times, I was wondering whose it was."

It was agonizing to pack those two blankets into Colin's backpack the last time I dropped him off for school. Of course, I made sure Lucy had Piggy, too.

Before Ethan was born, I tried getting him hooked on a blanket, but failed. I bought him a baby blue blanket with a satin edge on one side and complete satin on the other. Because I enjoyed rubbing those satin-edged blankets growing up, this looked great. My mom called the satin edge "the plastic part". Whenever the plastic part wore off, my mom bought me a replacement.

Ethan, however, preferred sucking on a pillowcase. The fabric had a dark floral design and belonged to my ex-wife's old sheet set. Ethan discovered it tasted way better than the blanket.

Over 20 years later, I still have the blue satin blanket. Colin liked it as a third little blanket to carry around, but when he left that last morning seven years ago, I hid Blue Blanket. I wanted a reminder of him, and Bear Blanket and Bruin Blanky overfilled his backpack, anyway.

Unlike the blankets of my childhood, the satin hasn't frayed. After the kids left, I only rubbed it a little, but it became a bit of a problem, so it's lived in the linen closet for the past few years.

Colin had a bedtime routine that included those three blankets and a whole lot more. "Colin, it's time to go to sleep."

"But I'm not tired."

"School starts early. Your stuffies are waiting for you."

"Not yet."

"Come lay down. Your pillow will make your head cozy. And I'll put this sheet on to keep your body heat in."

"Okay. I'll try it."

"I'll wrap Bear Blanket around you to help the sheet. Then this thick blanket will help keep the cold out. And just in case, here's another blanket to make sure any chilly breezes don't make it through. Bruin Blanky will lie above your head to keep heat from escaping through your hair. To make sure your feet stay warm, I'll wrap Blue Blanket around them. And we'll tuck your stuffies next to you." That was the hard bit, squeezing 20 feet of giant stuffies beside him.

Sure, it sounds like a sauna, but he magically wormed his way out through the night. And Colin loved it so much, he requested full explanations of each blanket's use almost every night.

Their love of stuffed animals and computers made Webkinz a natural hit in our home. Adorable plush stuffies included a code that brought them to life on the internet. After accumulating a dozen of their own, the kids insisted I get one so I could play along. It didn't stop at one.

In search of something clever to write, I sifted through the enormous pile of stuffies that represents the totality of my children's childhood here. After four Webkinz—a frog, badger, blue puppy, and tan bear—leaped to the surface, I put them down. "This is too depressing," I said.

One day, Colin, who also felt a bit down, said, "There's a girl I like but I'm not sure she likes me."

"Oh," I said. "Tell me about her."

"She likes sloths."

For the next few weeks, Colin was still fawning over his classmate whose birthday was approaching, so when I saw a stuffed sloth near a cash register, I grabbed it.

"Colin," I said. "I found this cute little sloth. Why don't you give it to her for her birthday."

"Okay."

When he jumped in the van after school, I asked, "Did she like the sloth?"

"Yeah, she liked it a lot. And now she likes me." I fared better helping Colin win over a girl in elementary school than I did for myself.

To win over my daughter after picking her up from school, I played DJ, and not the girl from *Full House*. "Dad, put on Demi Lovato." Or, "Dad, put on Katy Perry." Or, "Dad, play that song from *Frozen*."

One day I asked her, "Do you want to go to a concert?"

"Yeah."

"Who do you want to see?"

"Demi Lovato."

She appeared in Hershey that summer, so we spent the day riding rollercoasters at Hersheypark before attending the concert in the adjacent stadium that night.

Afterward, we grabbed a hotel nearby where we watched Amish horse and buggies clop their way up and down the street the following morning. "Do you want ride one?" I asked Lucy.

"Sure."

The internet led us to the most tech-savvy Amish family that offered buggy rides from their farm. After we pet their goats and sheep, they let Lucy steer their horse along country roads past their neighbors' rolling farms with her never-ending smile.

The next summer, I asked Lucy, "Do you want to go to a concert again?"

"Yeah."

"Who do you want to see?"

"Demi Lovato."

The kids had nicknames. From infancy, Colin was called Col-lieBananas, or simply Bananas. I asked him shortly before losing custody if he knew why. "Because I like bananas?"

"No. Because you were a monkey. You climbed on everything."

Lucy had some too. Thanks to the TV show that helped raise me, *Married... with Children*, I called her Pumpkin. If Al can call Kelly that, so can I. Plus, it sounded cuter when applied to my daughter. Lucy never knew her nickname's origin. She also went simply by Lulu, or less simply Lulucablulu. And I don't know those nicknames' origins either.

Ethan struggled to call her Lucy for a few years. "Hey Shloo Shloo, come here." So, to keep Ethan from feeling left out, I called her Shloo Shloo too.

Ethan's terms of endearment were a little less original. They were based on an alien and a cracker. Take a moment to guess.

This is your spoiler avoidance sentence.

Did you come up with E.T. and Wheat Thin?

Less than a month before I lost custody, Colin's 10th birthday arrived. "I want a *Minecraft* party," he said.

"Do you want to play laser tag?" I asked.

"Yeah!"

We gathered everything *Minecraft* from the party store and bought four laser tag guns that connected to cellphones. With his friends staying overnight, we wandered to our nearby school playground after sunset.

Three kids spent the next hour spraying each other with lasers while I rotated among them continually trying to reconnect the fourth. The party lasted well into the night, and by 1 AM, they had their video exposing what ten-year-olds do around 1 AM.

Hint: The football lineman won two floor mattress fights in eight seconds, and that included pausing between them to say, "Straight up laid out."

I miss everything about those kids. I miss seeing them and their friends, I miss calling them those names, I miss feeding them, I miss shopping with them, and I miss Lucy's missing socks.

She adored her sock collection. Not one of them was plain-colored. Pandas, pigs, rabbits, daisies, tulips, hearts, stripes, dogs, kittens, ladybugs, princesses, polka dots, rainbows, smiley faces, snowflakes, ice cream and cookies in every color combination filled her sock drawer. Lucy even had splashy socks with each day of the week stitched in them. And I had exactly one of each.

Every morning, I rifled through her sock drawer. "Lucy, I have 20 socks in my hands. And not one pair."

"Didn't I wear a pair yesterday?"

"They didn't match."

"Oh," she said with less interest than you could imagine. "I don't mind wearing them mismatched."

"Do you have lots of single socks at your mom's?" I was certain that was the issue.

"No."

Puzzled, I maintained her kaleidoscopic collection until it disappeared during my dad's purge.

"What would you have done if the kids came back quickly?" I asked him recently.

"I'd have bought them all new stuff."

"But you didn't have money for a lawyer. How would you have come up with thousands of dollars to replace all their furniture, toys, and clothes?"

He thought losing the kids made me nuts, but it was him throwing everything out. If only my kids were huge sports fans like him so their stuff was entirely sports-related, because that's about all he kept.

Besides the signed Capitals banner, my dad salvaged the framed Bryce Harper photo from his half-season playing minor league baseball in Hagerstown. He signed "To Lucy" when she was six years old outside the stadium where Willie Mays played his first pro game 60 years earlier. It sat beside her computer monitor atop the desk Lucy and I built, which long ago my dad tore down and trashed.

When parents have lost their kids unexpectedly, they often memorialize their room like an untouched time capsule. Everything is left exactly how their child left it. Thanks to my parents, I didn't get that chance.

Though I miss those kids immensely, I don't miss limping in pain from the vasectomy. People remembered me better, and I suddenly had more in common with elderly folks, which wasn't necessarily what a man in his thirties wants. Ethan's school principal, who materialized after my ex-wife left me and absconded with primary custody, wasn't old, but she certainly remembered me.

When my ex-wife took off, Ethan left an accelerated kindergarten class at a brand new, high-tech school in Frederick for an aging school with a noisy, open floor plan in the less educated city of Hagerstown.

I've lived in both cities for a decade, and I love them, but Frederick was half an hour closer to D.C. and had the affluence of a learned suburb. Hagerstown, on the other hand, is rural farmland on the opposite side of the mountain. Folks in Frederick have bachelor's degrees at two-and-a-half times the rate of those in Hagerstown. Education wasn't factored when my ex-wife's mom moved her and the kids out of Frederick.

Ethan was in the middle of his kindergarten year when he began complaining about his new school.

"Dad, school is boring because it's too easy."

"What do you mean?"

"We're learning how to spell words like 'and' 'the' 'an' and 'I'."

Ethan read at a second- or third-grade level.

His teacher arranged for me to view his class, and those simple spelling words filled a third of the chalkboard. During a brief meeting with his teacher afterwards, nothing was resolved. The following week, I met the principal inside the main office's conference room. After requesting the school to offer Ethan extra work on his level, she forced me to leave.

As we exited the conference room near the secretary, the principal said, "You need to go. You're endangering the children."

"What children?" I asked. "There's nobody here. The only thing in danger is my son's education."

A piece of mail arrived days later, indicating banishment from the school. After nagging the superintendent, I was welcomed for first grade's Back to School night. I arrived at the school, found a handicap spot, grabbed my cane, and wobbled my way toward the entrance.

A staff member I didn't recognize said, "Mr. Kotler! Right this way." As she held the door open, another unfamiliar woman greeted me. "Mr. Kotler, welcome. We've got a chair all set up for you." As she led me into the auditorium, a third unknown woman said, "Hi, Mr. Kotler. We have this seat picked out for you." I was in the last row.

Magnet programs in Washington County begin with second grade, so Ethan joined a science, technology, engineering, and math program at a new school the following year. Two years later, Lucy, who was more artistic than the boys, earned her way into a separate arts and academic excellence magnet school. Another three years elapsed when Colin followed in Ethan's footsteps. I was a proud father of three promising magnet-school kids working through the curriculum at an indepth, accelerated pace that's one to two years above grade level.

The court outlined our 50/50 parenting schedule. The kids spent Jewish holidays here and Christian ones with my ex-wife, so it was easy having no religious holiday disputes. We had the kids on our birthdays, alternated Thanksgivings, and she had Mother's Day while Father's Day was mine. It worked for us, and most importantly, it benefited the kids.

But in 2009, my ex-wife left me a week before Mother's Day. As empty as I felt that first Mother's Day without the kids, Father's Day has evolved into something worse.

Each of the past seven Father's Days, I've been alone, absent as a father. Visitation centers aren't open on holidays, so my kids spent the day with my ex-wife and her boyfriend, detached from the essence of the day. That's added to the distance between us, along with many missed milestones and school events.

Though I'm fortunate enough to have my dad around to share the day, when I wish him, "Happy Father's Day," he says, "Thanks." Nobody tells me "Happy Father's Day." Well, my rabbi does.

At least I can envision my last Father's Day with Colin and Lucy. My dad joined us for a day in Baltimore to see an Orioles baseball game, Babe Ruth's birthplace, and Ripley's Believe It or Not! Museum. When I see photos from that day, I'm grief stricken at how unsuspecting I was that they'd be gone in five months.

After the Babe Ruth Museum and three hours in the scorching summer sun at the ballgame, Lucy wasn't enthused about going to Ripley's. Tired, she preferred to wait in the car with her grandpa, so Colin and I entered the lobby ourselves. He looked around in amazement. "Let's get Lucy!"

His excitement was convincing, so she hopped along. We wandered the mirror maze until we nearly had it memorized and hammered it up in the funhouse mirror that made Lucy's neck as long as her legs and Colin's brain thrice its size. The world's tallest man oversaw them riding a winged wooden motorcycle. And other oddities, like an even taller Transformer and a menacingly small, tattooed freak, captivated them as they posed with a six-foot penny made of individual Lincoln one-cent pieces.

Father's Day finished at the Inner Harbor with a visit to a cartoon-like wonderland of a candy store, where Colin went all-in on lollipops and colorful flavored sugar while Lucy stockpiled her favorite Japanese and Korean sweets.

But thanks to the BIA, Ethan was nowhere in sight.

Lucy loves the Korean band BTS and owns every album, so I gifted her a BTS magazine at one of our supervised visits. She flipped to the centerfold photo of all seven guys and looked at me. "Tell me who's who. Their names are right there." She had me dead to rights. I knew little about her favorite band as she pointed to a name. "He's my favorite," she said. "Which one is he?"

I aimed my finger at the middle guy. "That one."

"Good job, dad! You're right."

"Of course I know your favorite." Feeling like a super dad, I hoped the interrogation was over, but it was just beginning. "Keep going. There's six more."

An amazing stroke of luck helped me guess the next one. And the next. Lucy couldn't believe it, and neither could I. My fourth guess was spot on too, when Colin jumped in. "That's Suga." Thanks Colin, you made this easier.

Down to the final two, I flipped a coin in my mind. It landed on heads, but I saw two guys' heads to guess, and realized the coin flip was pointless. But God was still with me when I made that 50/50 guess, and I tricked my daughter into believing I was attentive. After nailing all seven names, I studied the picture.

"Okay, so this guy has blonde hair. That one has brown."

"Dad, what are you doing?" Lucy asked.

"I'm memorizing whose hair is what color."

"They change their hair. This guy had black hair last month, and that one was blonde."

"Oh, okay," I said, as I thought, "Crap!" So, I searched for another notable feature. "Well, this one has dimples. I can remember that."

She laughed. "Five of them have dimples. You can't see the other four because they're not smiling." Can you believe they have a song called "Dimple"?

We never played the Guess BTS game again. I left on a high note—as high as a one-hour supervised visit allows.

18

LOUSY LAWYERS

J USTICE ISN'T ALWAYS A FAMILY lawyer's primary pursuit. "Unfortunately, there are cases whose outcomes are wrong and unjustified," said my current attorney. "Yours is one of them." But she can't do anything about it. Put differently, I'm not the only one exploited by the court.

Other lawyers from a big firm recently said I had poor legal representation along the way. Those high dollar attorneys, including the most expensive one I ever met, are among that impotent group.

I plowed through several attorneys in the years since I lost custody in 2017. One or two were hired with impending child support hearings docketed, while others got our money thanks to the continuing decline in my children's school grades. The latter reopened my case after years of dormancy, once my grandma's inheritance finally manifested in 2022. Thirteen years of family squabbling prevented me from using my witnesses before the two-year statute of limitations expired.

The first attorney I hired that year touted himself as a friend of the BIA, so I figured he'd use their connection to maneuver a positive outcome. After successfully securing an emergency hearing, he failed to notify me of its time change. My courtroom absence made me appear as a nuisance without a just cause to the magistrate, who said, "I think that, at some point, Mr. Kotler may be on the hook for attorney's fees for no-good-faith basis."

The court deemed my kids' grades to be so appalling, they warranted an emergency hearing. So, why would a magistrate remark, in my absence, that I filed without reason and should pay my ex-wife's legal fees along with my own?

The lawyer once said, "You're morally right." But he later recanted his friendship with the BIA, downgrading their relationship to legal acquaintances, and claimed the judge misspoke during her ruling, so it no longer favored me. After taking almost $10,000 and accomplishing nothing but turning another court official against me, he wanted off the case.

After firing this attorney, I diligently sought another. Via the most selective process I ever employed, I interviewed half a dozen lawyers before settling on one.

Along the way, I met a callous attorney with the least fuzzy personality imaginable. He said, "Your biggest mistake was sending your story to the news."

The next attorney I spoke to said, "You might have a claim for legal malpractice against the BIA. It's hard to hold BIAs accountable, but is possible thanks to a precedent setting case." The target of the precedent-setter was that unfuzzy attorney I just interviewed.

It's scary to think the court allowed that man to be the sole voice of helpless children. He worked as a BIA in a case involving a father he befriended. The father was sexually abusing his daughter, and bald Mr. Fuzzless insisted they live together. In a 2006 Maryland case, the state ruled against him, determining no malpractice immunity be afforded to court-appointed guardians, such as a BIA.

I wonder, why didn't he want the news involved?

My dad, the recipient of grandma's inheritance, funded my lawyers, so I allowed him into the consultation with the lawyer we settled on next. But his cluelessness sabotaged it. As I presented the lawyer with emails and other evidence that went to The Post, plus a pretty collage of the news agencies I contacted in June 2022, my dad interrupted.

"I'm not sure the news is doing anything."

"Dad, please stop."

"I just want to explain what I think happened." The lawyer insisted on hearing it. "I think Brian was so upset from losing the kids, he imagined the news was helping him."

The ensuing argument didn't deter the lawyer from taking the case and money, but it prevented him from taking me seriously and caring. The guy was a partner of a large firm with dozens of attorneys. Its head attorney referred us to this younger partner after indicating I had terrible representation along the way. The head, who charged over $550 an hour, also recommended we speak to one of the firm's malpractice attorneys, who was similarly disinterested. Why? "I hate family law." Thanks for the help.

Upon consulting with yet another attorney in the firm, the family lawyer I hired moved the case out of Frederick County to our hometown, in a county where neither he nor any of his partners worked, an hour from his office. For months thereafter, he said, "You should see the kids more than you do." But he did nothing to accomplish that. So, I fired him and never let my dad join another meeting with an attorney.

During the two-hour consultation with that lawyer, he noted another lawyer my dad handpicked shortly after my run-ins with the law post-Post, when I needed brief representation for a hearing. "How was she?" the lawyer asked.

"Not good."

"I'm not surprised," he said, "because she asks the most basic questions on a legal website. She doesn't seem knowledgeable."

I mentioned her refusal to learn my case. "When she asked me to explain the situation, I begged her to read the five-page story that I originally sent to The Post because it concisely described everything. She refused several times and said, 'People write differently than they speak. I want to hear from your mouth.'" The moment I began a verbal explanation, she interrupted with unrelated questions. No matter what I tried, she tergiversated. I fired her the same day. But maybe she was right after all because I've never said tergiversated aloud.

Including my current lawyer, this accounts for my last four lawyers, all hired after the 2017 custody ruling.

Now let's discuss the first four.

I have no clue how my mom found my first attorney, a pleasant woman who dedicated the bottom floor of her century-old Victorian home as her small-town law office. The office was halfway to Baltimore, half an hour east of the Frederick courthouse and an hour north of my parents' Bowie home. Her middle-of-nowhere location wasn't superseded by her reputation.

Though she meant well and offered good life advice, she's the lawyer who allowed opposing counsel to walk all over me regarding the drug tests. And if that wasn't bad enough, she insisted I chronicle everything. "I want you to keep a handwritten journal," she said. "Every day, write what you've experienced—everything involving your ex-wife and kids." It was hard enough living the lonely existence that featured only two supervised weekends per month with Colin, Lucy, and Ethan. Having to write about it afterwards was almost unbearable. The journal was never used. Instead, it served as an excruciating daily reminder that most days sucked.

She urged me to act like a rabbi toward the first BIA, who had a degree in Women's Studies and a very non-Jewish name. In my first meeting with the BIA, also a lawyer who sucked, I perceived my lawyer's advice was wrong. The BIA broached the topic of religion, citing the differences between my ex-wife's Christian faith and mine. We were both uncomfortable.

"I understand you're Jewish," she said.

"Yes." I answered proudly as I'd done my whole life, assuming we shared the same tenets of God. But within a minute, I felt I could no longer be open and honest about my Jewish background to people.

"So, you don't believe—" She caught herself mid-sentence and re-started.

"You think that—" Again she stopped.

"Do you believe—" Her tone implied that my answer would be wrong, but she stopped short of asking.

"You don't—" The BIA continued stammering, struggling to find the right words.

"So you celebrate different holidays?" That was her brilliant question she fought for a minute to fashion.

"Yes." She quickly changed the subject, but the sense was palpable that she didn't like Jews.

Thank God she disappeared from the ranks of BIAs within a couple years. But she found herself in *Baltimore Magazine* as their Top Single of 2014. The first on their list of eligible bachelors and bachelorettes, she could no longer hide her adoration for her dream date, Justin Timberlake. And her perfect fit described in three words? Sincere, intelligent, romantic. Sorry Justin, I guess she doesn't know you too well.

My second lawyer, who tore the paper and said, "You just got your kids back," won me shared custody in 2013, was last seen two years later at a family funeral, then soon after withdrew from the field of law. Like an angel, as quickly as she came, she departed. Because it took too long to pay off the bill, her old law firm refused to represent me again without an excessive double-retainer.

When I reopened the case in fall of 2016 because of the weed whacker threat, I hunted down a Top Lawyer from *Washingtonian Magazine*. The Jewish woman listed was unavailable, but her Italian partner was obtainable, so I hired her. The best advice she ever gave me was not to fight the BIA, whom she was meeting at a reception dinner the night the court appointed her. That's still not sound guidance, but it's astute compared to the several times she actively screwed me.

The lawyer told me to rent a car and secretly videotape my ex-wife's arrival home to see if the boyfriend exited her van. So, I did. My lawyer told the BIA, who disapproved of me going to such lengths to catch my ex-wife in a lie.

I asked my lawyer, "Did you tell her it was your idea?"

"No, that's attorney-client privilege." She let me take the fall.

Come winter, she threw me under the bus even harder. My ex-wife and I disputed over our winter break schedule. In my five-page story to The Post, I called this the tipping point. And upon relaying this story to my current lawyer, her jaw dropped.

As the custody agreement dictated, I'd have the kids 11 days of the 21-day period that included winter break. It's the same schedule we adhered to the previous several years without incident.

The agreement said I'd have the kids for the second half of break, including New Year's and the remainder of the "week". My ex-wife insisted on interpreting "week" as "break" because it would have given her five of my days. She'd have 15 days of the 21, meaning winter break would've done nothing but cost me substantial time with my kids.

To further solicit favor, my ex-wife claimed that my ex-stepson was in town after winter break, and wanted the kids to spend time together. She lied. He had already returned to school with his father in North Carolina.

The BIA chimed into the email chain, siding with my ex-wife. "I would like the children to spend time with their brother. I am in agreement." The BIA was happy to violate the court order, as long as it helped the other side. She never cared that I proved my ex-stepson was back in school in North Carolina, and according to my ex-wife, he returned to Maryland for good two weeks later. During the trial, my ex-wife said, "He moved back to our house after the holidays this year."

My ex-stepson was there for all the time *other than* the days for which my ex-wife convinced the BIA to approve the schedule change. The BIA believed her lie, knew she lied, and continued to back her despite it—all against the court order.

Sick of all the BIA's one-sided decisions, I replied privately to my lawyer. "The BIA is condoning the violation of the court-ordered custody agreement. She should be removed from the case, period." From her iPhone, my lawyer accidentally forwarded that email to both the BIA and my ex-wife's lawyer, a younger Mr. Fuzzless with hoop earrings.

The email was presented at the custody trial by my next lawyer as evidence of the BIA's bias against me, and the trial judge heard all about it. However, she deemed it unimportant. I hired this next lawyer three months before the hearing, after many more months of insufficient counsel by the *Washingtonian* law partner, including the following incident.

A month after the winter break episode, I was forced to threaten her with *Maryland Attorneys' Rules of Professional Conduct* to prompt a letter on my behalf. This is the same woman I had to frighten when Ethan stopped coming here a month earlier.

She finally backed me in a January 27, 2017, letter to the BIA and my ex-wife's lawyer. Like I told The Post, I went through quite an ordeal to get it. She wrote referring to my ex-wife as "mom":

> "First, I want to set forth information regarding this last winter break. Mom lied to the BIA when claiming she wanted the children from January 3rd to January 9th, which was not scheduled access time, so that the children could spend time with their half-brother. Mom's son, the children's half-brother, had already returned to school in North Carolina and was not present at mom's home during those dates.
>
> "Second, it appears that mom is in contempt of the court's Consent Order awarding the parties joint legal custody. And mom is placing the children in the middle of legal decisions and alienating them from Mr. Kotler. There needs to be a visible change, or my client will be forced to file for contempt and seek sole legal custody.

"The latest incident goes to mom's refusal to keep Mr. Kotler timely informed of doctor and dentist appointments and making shared decisions regarding dental work that is being considered for Lucy.

"In sum, two years ago, mom took Lucy to a dentist without notifying Mr. Kotler of the appointment ahead of time. The dentist recommended a palate expander and eventually braces. Since the procedure was somewhat invasive, coupled with the fact that Mr. Kotler was not present, he requested we seek a second opinion. The parties got the second opinion shortly thereafter. They were told that Lucy's teeth were fine, and the palate expander was 'highly inappropriate' for a child her age. Mr. Kotler also attended at least one subsequent appointment with the second dentist, and they reiterated that Lucy's teeth were growing in fine, and no further procedure was necessary.

"Nothing more was said until this last November when mom texted Mr. Kotler that she had taken Lucy back to the first dentist—again without informing Mr. Kotler ahead of time and without his consent. Mr. Kotler does not agree to use this dentist, nor to have such invasive procedures done on Lucy. Instead, he compromised and offered to get a third opinion. However, mom received a referral from the first dentist and went to the referred orthodontist with no notice to or consent from Mr. Kotler. Upon learning this information, Mr. Kotler researched the orthodontist and found that the orthodontist had a very low rating and many complaints against him. Mr. Kotler will not allow this orthodontist to provide any services to Lucy.

"Mr. Kotler then received a phone call from Lucy after school yesterday. Lucy was very upset and accusing him of preventing her from getting a procedure she suddenly wants to have done. Mr. Kotler tried to explain to her differences in opinion, etc., but Lucy hung up on him. Today, Mr. Kotler took Lucy to lunch to explain the situation with the procedure being suggested by the first dentist and the second opinion he received. Lucy was highly disrespectful, averted her eyes, and defended her mother, claiming her mother doesn't have time to text her father to tell him about appointments. Clearly, this is coming from mom. Clearly, she is throwing Lucy in the middle and alienating Lucy's affections for her father. This behavior needs to STOP.

"There are other examples of mom's blatant disregard of the legal custodial obligations. Those will be set forth should we need court intervention to make a change in the best interest of the children.

"Finally, please note that it is Mr. Kotler's position that mom has successfully harmed his relationship with Ethan. And she is working on Lucy now. It is also of note that when the BIA talked to Ethan on October 31st, it was directly after Ethan was in his mother's care. It's no surprise that Ethan claimed he wasn't scared by what he saw mom's boyfriend do toward his father. The State's Attorney has not been contacted to my knowledge to provide the facts of the incident as she understands them. This incident should not be shrugged off and further inquiry is not only necessary, but was promised.

"I hope moving forward mom can modify her behavior and follow the Consent Order. I am advising my client to call the dentist that mom may have chosen, and deny his consent. No medical procedure may be done on the children without Mr. Kotler's consent. Mom is to give Mr. Kotler advanced notice of any appointments involving the children. I hope that these issues may be resolved short of court."

This is how parental alienation works. Alienation isn't overly overt, but it's insidious and fostered as a routine. It's emotional abuse—the leading cause of depression among children—and disastrously, many health professionals deny its existence.

After being chided by Lucy, she agreed to the third opinion, who confirmed the palette expander was a go, and as of seven years ago, fortunately all was well. I've been kept in the dark far worse, however, since the 2017 custody ruling that still left me with the glimmer of responsibility called joint legal custody. As the judge told my ex-wife, "I want you to consult with him. I want him to have a feel for what's going on and to have a say in what happens. But in the end, you have the tie-breaking authority."

For years, I've heard nothing. Because the BIA doesn't care, she's emboldening my ex-wife's persistent alienation.

This late-January letter was the final catalyst that prompted the BIA to speak to the State's Attorney who dismissed the weed whacker case because she wanted to let the family lawyers investigate. Up to this point, the extent of the BIA's investigation was asserting the State's Attorney dismissed it, so she didn't have to examine things. But back in October 2016, when I questioned the BIA if she spoke to the State's Attorney, she said, "I will. The reason it was dismissed matters."

"Is the State's Attorney's opinion important?" I asked.

"Of course it is. If she told me something bad about the boyfriend, it could affect my decision."

But they didn't talk prior to October 31st, when the BIA threatened me with an emergency hearing and loss of time with my kids if I did not immediately allow the boyfriend around them after not seeing them for 11 weeks.

The BIA's October 31st email said she "met with both parties and the minor child, Ethan." (Notice that she didn't meet with Lucy or Colin.) "I find this of the utmost urgency," she wrote. "It is my position that the children return to the regular access schedule immediately. My recommendation for access may be more liberal to mom if we go to hearing so she can have makeup time."

I agreed, and Lucy suffered her panic attack moments later. And by spring, Colin was refusing to go.

Then, in December 2016, I asked the BIA if she contacted the State's Attorney. So did my lawyer. "Not yet," she said. "But I will." The BIA's billing shows her first communication with the State's Attorney in early February, days after receiving the January 27th letter.

The State's Attorney would've said she never investigated, as she testified at my hearing. Early on, the BIA assumed she did and dropped the charges because it was found not to have occurred. But obviously that's not what happened, and she'd have known that if they spoke.

In March mediation, I grilled the BIA. "You didn't speak to the State's Attorney until three months after you put the kids back with the boyfriend. No matter what she told you, you wouldn't reverse your decision because you'd be admitting you endangered the kids for three months. And you'd never do that."

The mediator separated us and sent the BIA into my ex-wife's room for the remainder of mediation.

To worsen matters, the State's Attorney shielded the BIA by perjuring herself during my custody hearing. She said she and the BIA spoke in October, contrary to emails and the BIA's billing statement. Because the BIA demanded the kids go back on October 31st, October is the only month that would have covered the BIA's behind.

This letter was the high-water mark of my attorney's help, and I went through hell to get it. By May, nothing continued to go my way, no contempt was filed, and communication was horrible, so I fired her.

Her successor, who represented me during the custody hearing, fought for me, but could've been more articulate and pressing. Though unsuccessful, at least I had an advocate who seemed like a decent guy that represented me during trial.

The lawyers who win and flourish are often ruthlessly disinterested about the families they represent in our so-called justice system. Destroying the relationship between child and parent are simple byproducts of their day's pay. And if visible damage is done, they minimize, deflect, or deny it, at a rate of hundreds of dollars per hour.

19

ALIENATION NATION

PARENTAL ALIENATION IS A CONTROVERSIAL topic. For every psychologist who insists it is a major problem affecting families, there's several who assert that it's a phony attempt for abusive parents to gain access to their children and hurt their former spouses. Although I recognize the validity of the latter argument, they trumpet alienation is 100% false. It's not.

I searched for help this past year, but the herculean task of finding an in-state psychologist knowledgeable about parental alienation proved impossible, so I turned to one who opposed the concept. She was surprised I reached out to her, but she offered me the name of a woman who supposedly fell on my side of the issue. After a brief phone conversation with the referral, I wrote her a letter. Days later, she called me.

"There are red flags with you," she said.

"With me? What do you mean?"

"Because you're concerned about your child having refused to go back to his mom, it doesn't sound true." Then her humility kicked in. "I'm nationally renowned and I know what I'm talking about."

After a 15-minute heated discussion, she said, "I don't think I'm the right fit for you."

"I knew that 15 minutes ago." Without another word, she hung up on me, dashing any hope of help. These are the professionals entrusted to care for children who are too young to speak for themselves.

Alienation is misunderstood because it's immensely counterintuitive. Alienated kids are devoted to their abusive parent and firmly reject a loving one. It doesn't make sense, but I've experienced exactly that.

One-quarter of divorced parents are thought to engage in these tactics, and it's proven to be a low-risk, high-reward ploy. Dishonest accusations, therefore, run rampant. And children are left with the impression of having a superior alienating parent with primary custody and an inferior alienated one they rarely see. Even if exposed to be lying, the alienating parent seldom faces punishment.

Their deceit often goes unnoticed, providing the alienator with the majority of time with the kids and child support money to match. Meanwhile, therapists, like the one who red-flagged me, make false assumptions based on faulty intuition.

Those who study parental alienation recognize that it is so deeply illogical that professionals who aren't specialists make long strings of major mistakes that prove devastating. Even experienced psychologists lack a true understanding of its manifestations.

One issue they face is how parents present themselves. The alienating parent comes across as subdued, level-headed, and credible; whereas the other is often frustrated, agitated, and angry from losing the once healthy relationship with their children over lies.

Parental alienation is recognized as psychological child abuse. Psychological abuse, as opposed to physical or sexual abuse, is the most prolific contributor to teen depression. It's a substantial problem facing America. An astronomical 57% percent of teen girls deal with depression and an alarming 30% struggle with suicidal thoughts. With 22 million parents experiencing alienation, and even more children affected, this is a major cause.

My kids were taught to keep secrets from an early age because "daddy would get mad." My shared custody agreement ordered that we could call the kids every evening they weren't with us. It said, "The calls are to be private and are not to be placed on speakerphone." That's written because it always happened. When my ex-wife called the kids, I handed them the phone and left the room because I had little interest in what they discussed. My ex-wife, however, lorded over the conversations.

Lucy was four years old when I called one evening.

"Hi, Lucy!"

"Hi, daddy!"

"How was your day?"

"Good."

"Did you do anything fun?"

"We went to the park with—" Sounds of commotion cut her sentence short and in the background, someone said, "Shhh."

Lucy resumed. "Today I played—" More sounds of disturbance resonated on the phone, followed by Lucy crying, with the phone far from her mouth. "I'm just trying to tell daddy a story." The call ended abruptly. I phoned back several times that evening during the allotted hours and it always reached voicemail.

The eavesdropping didn't end with the court order. Is it surprising the kids kept my ex-wife's newest boyfriend such a well-guarded secret?

Before my ex-wife's news of the live-in boyfriend, I heard his name once without understanding what their relationship was. And I said nothing.

The kids loved playing on moonbounces. Every month, we'd visit an enormous playland at the mall filled with moonbounces of every type. A few different moonbounces ran a hundred feet, each with their own colorful configuration of hidden sections, ladders, slides, and obstacles. Others, like the pirate ship, were shorter but featured the tallest slides, while still more acted as ball pits. From the time the kids removed their shoes, they were in an uproar.

One day, we grabbed a snack and gathered around the table.

"Do you remember the joke about the naked homeless guy?" Lucy asked her brothers. "Who told us that?"

Ethan responded with the boyfriend's name before I knew a boyfriend existed. I sat silent; daddy didn't get mad. The joke sounded inappropriate to tell young kids, but I assumed it might've been one of my ex-wife's brother's stupid friends like me. It wasn't. It was this guy a month after they met.

A concern that the red-flagging psychologist blew off occurred my first day seeing the kids after several months in jail and the state hospital. I've seen Colin cry three times since I lost custody: the night I broke the news they were done living here, the next morning saying goodbye at school, and at that post-jail supervised visit.

After not seeing him for seven months, he shocked me as he entered the room. His once neatly cropped hair fell straight and long, past his shoulders. Halfway through the visit, Colin's face puckered. "Daddy, kids at school make fun of my hair. They say I look like a girl." I felt helpless as he stared at me for an answer.

Why did his hair grow so long if he hated it? He never mentioned wanting long hair before. The self-proclaimed, nationally-renowned psychologist insisted it was meaningless, and I was wrong to use my fatherly instinct.

There are reunification programs intended to reunite alienated children with their badmouthed parent. Typically designed as a four-day program with added travel expenses and follow-up treatment, they are accessible only to affluent victims. They cost anywhere from $25,000-100,000+ leaving people like me and my kids in the lurch.

Unfortunately, they're sometimes accessed by wealthy abusers of children who were not actually alienated. Because of these instances, many deem the whole concept of reunification as corrupt and demand an end to them, denouncing parental alienation as a bogus theory.

However, children might wrongfully report a quality father as abusive because of alienation. Ethan did.

Other children can easily become sufferers of Stockholm syndrome—which describes victims who empathize with their abusers—especially when their abuser is a loving parent. After all, how bad is mom if she only "tells the awful truth" about dad? She doesn't physically or sexually abuse the child, so, outwardly, there's nothing wrong with her from the child's perspective.

Children can falsify their own experiences in their minds, believing something terrible was done to them, even if it never happened. Human minds can be manipulated, and children are particularly susceptible. Studies have revealed that false memories may be accepted as truth if the person receives new or suggestive ideas and misinformation, such as what occurs from parental alienation.

The problem is, kids are poisonously learning they're half bad. "If mom or dad is so awful, something's wrong with me, too."

Those negative thoughts snowball into the steady decline toward those miserable fatherless statistics where kids are several times more likely to be on the bottom rung of society. With 22 million American parents reporting alienation from at least one of their children, a vast portion of our future generation is vulnerable.

Because alienation is often based on falsehoods, why aren't lie detector tests admissible in court or widely used? It's the best tool God's given us. They're between 88% and 98% effective, which is far better than the human intuition we rely on now. One might further surmise that test accuracy would improve by leaps and bounds in the coming years if it became a staple of our justice system.

For the amount paid to one lawyer for one hour of work, a polygraph test can be taken. How many hours are spent by therapists, custody evaluators, BIAs, and parents' lawyers trying to decipher the truth? Polygraphs could reduce costs and aggravation for parents, who would be less likely to lie if they knew a lie detector was awaiting them. Unknowing children would be the biggest beneficiaries and that's most important.

Sure, lie detectors can be beaten, and that stinks, but their accuracy could be a tremendous relief to courts, parents, and children alike. And it would be a wonderful deterrent to corruption.

In theory, because polygraphs are 90% accurate, courts shouldn't rule against "truthful" parents over 10% of the time, meaning goodbye to siding with attorneys that helped finance the judge and court-appointed professionals. That 10% number can be referenced to analyze the performance of judges, BIAs, and psychologists to siphon those guilty of repeated backroom dealings out of our family courts.

If a judge rules against lie detector tests 25% of the time, why? They shouldn't. With that amount of clear and objective scrutiny, corruption could be killed.

Thankfully for me, my son's allegation can be refuted by hundreds of people, which should one day establish the truth. But often that's not the case. With no method to prove their innocence, what do parents do when they're alleged to target only their own children who may have already unfairly turned against them?

Not all my experiences with mind manipulators have been bad. I had an amazing therapist after the weed whacker threat. Every week, we discussed my worries regarding the kids, my ex-wife, and the boyfriend who threatened to disfigure my face. She used EMDR light therapy to chill me out, something I'd recommend for anyone going through PTSD.

Then, after I lost custody and contacted The Post, we met again. "I was skeptical when you first started coming here," she said. "But you really are a victim. You've been through a lot, and you've been mistreated by a lot of people."

Soon after, as insane scenarios cropped up again and again, I conveyed my certainty that The Post was helping and something positive should emerge.

"You seem very sure about this," she said.

"I am."

The next few weeks became our last. As the extraordinary encounters heated, it was harder to keep them secret.

"This is my last session," I said. "Thank you for your help. I think they'll take over from here."

"You know, Brian. I'm impressed with how you're handling everything," she said. "You're a badass."

"No, I'm not."

"Yes, you are. I'm telling you that you're a badass, and I mean that in a kind way. From things you did as a kid to things you're doing now, you're a badass."

What kind of badass is terrified of getting on a motorcycle?

20

PROVING MY STUPID

I GREW UP THE YOUNGEST in a household of four. My dad queues corny jokes before stepping in line at the supermarket to see if the cashier is one of the few who gets it. With his sales presentation background, he has no problem explaining the same repetitive punchline to people over and over.

"Did you hear the story about how hot it is today? The news showed a dog chasing a cat, and they were both walking. Do you get it? It's so hot, the dog and the cat were walking. Am I embarrassing you, Brian?"

On Sundays, he bought a half-bushel of steamed crabs that we devoured during football games. Once when my cousin and I were kids and she was visiting, my dad bought live crabs. They made for great crab races on the back patio. We discovered sprinkling water on them quickened them up, though they still never reached the finish line.

My dad sold encyclopedias and phonics programs in some rough neighborhoods. One day, he received a phone call. "We're notifying you that this ends the Drug Enforcement Agency's six-month wiretap."

Then there's my mom, who called the DEA back. "We got a phone call saying we've been wiretapped. Are we in trouble?"

"Ma'am, if you were in trouble, you wouldn't be calling us back." It's a good thing I wasn't yet a teenager when our lines were tapped.

My panicky mom screams at the sight and sound of tossed balls and dropped feathers, but sits through TV gunshots and crash scenes like they're calming lullabies. Her favorites are westerns, which she'll watch all day. But she's still ignorant about guns, horses, drinking, and fighting. Then again, I've watched hundreds of hours of *Dancing with the Stars*, which hasn't helped me tango like an Argentine.

She once exhibited an unusual style of parenting. "Brian," she said. "If you don't eat that banana, I'm shampooing it into your head!"

"I hate bananas!" I yelled back. "I'm not eating it!"

We both kept our word.

I don't know who looked stupider that day. Me covered in mushed banana? Or my mom as she spent the next hour cleaning it from my hair?

My mom once handled honeybees well. A stray ball landed under our pear tree amidst its discarded fruits when I was in kindergarten. The moment I retrieved it, a swarm of bees that were enjoying their delicious rotting pears became angry. Though smoke would've worked better, my mom opted to use ice to remove the coat of a hundred bees I was wearing. Without a single sting to either of us, she tossed my sweater aside, and the bees relented.

Whenever my parents didn't want me to understand what they said, they spelled. After I learned to spell, they spoke French. After I began taking French, I pretended to understand so they'd stop.

Finally, there's my older sister, who reminds everyone she's a law-yer by constantly threatening them with litigation. Watch what this book does. I can hear her now: "I'm going to sue you for saying I threaten people with litigation."

I was born at Holy Cross Hospital in Silver Spring, Maryland on August 16, 1978. The hospital, which overlooks the Capital Beltway just north of D.C., is Maryland's top baby factory.

On my first birthday, my parents bought my childhood home in Bowie, Maryland, the last of four Levittown planned communities in the country. Four different types of mostly identical homes were built between D.C. and Annapolis in the early '60s. The Washington Post described my house as "roomy, basically simple, well-planned, sturdy, and in the Levitt tradition of maximum living space per dollar—minus extras or frills."

Bowie was so middle-class, the 1965 West German film, *Suburbia, U.S.A.*, dubbed Bowie "middle-middle-class America".

My Papa Sol, a house painter, couldn't identify what material the walls were made from, but tennis balls bounced well off them. After countless days of diving catches with my baseball glove that won me hundreds of Gold Glove Awards, dozens of MVPs, and I don't know how many Game 7s, I'm the right one to attest.

We lived on the first main street in the city, with its center double-yellow line and repeated postings of its 25-mph speed limit. The constant traffic that rolled past our driveway made it a boon for new ball acquisition. My mom said, "If you lose one in the street, don't chase after it. I'll buy you new ones." Since I liked throwing balls off the backyard roof too, her offer enticed plenty to be tossed completely over. "Sorry, mom. I threw it over by accident."

Beasley, who became our dog when he was four and I was 15, was a liver-and-white English Springer Spaniel that weighed as much as a German Shepherd. He didn't get my mom's memo.

As a car barreled down the road at a speed less than I was accustomed to driving, his ball took an unfortunate bounce. Beasley froze as the car screeched its brakes. Thank God it stopped five feet before hitting him.

He grew up in D.C. running for miles alongside a bicycle through Rock Creek Park. The exercise enlarged his heart and made him extraordinarily strong. Couple that with his fondness for stealing hats off people's heads and his complete disregard for men in uniform, and you've got yourself a true Beasley story.

A cop led Beasley back to his first owner's home, still in a blocks-long tug-of-war over his police hat.

"Is this your dog?" the cop asked.

"Yes."

"He won't give me back my hat."

My friends visited wearing baseball hats, and left complaining that my Springer Spaniel sprung, snatched their hats, and chewed them to shreds. I grumbled too. "I told you not to wear hats. My dog loves them."

Ducks were his other obsession. Do you want to get him riled up? Just say, "Beasley, ducks!" He launched himself into the Chesapeake Bay off a two-story yacht when ducks floated past. Lucky for the ducks, several moments passed before he resurfaced.

Beasley joined our family with four tricks up his sleeve: sit, speak, shake, and lay down. How his first owner taught him to speak, I have no clue. But he did. I added "roll over" to his repertoire by rolling him over when he laid down. That wasn't too hard.

We had our own trick. When we wanted him inside, we grabbed a slice of American cheese. "Cheese, Beasley! Cheese!" He came flying. Want him to perform his tricks? Same thing. Show him cheese and say his tricks one-by-one. After a month, he memorized his trick order, so when he saw cheese, he'd roll through all five feats in about a second, before we even asked for the first.

As a little kid, long before Beasley, I pressured my parents for a dog. After years of complaining, my mom finally caved. "I'll get you goldfish." Within a year or two, Abbott and Costello grew too big for their fishbowl, so they earned their own ten-gallon tank and some new tropical friends.

They lived atop my waist-high Pine Factory bookshelf by the windows that matched the bed I passed on to my daughter. All eight pieces of my coordinated childhood furniture were pine, which I stained dark brown. Below the fish tank was my trophy shelf. They became stained the furniture's color when my root beer spilled, but I cleaned them years later.

All my sports statistics rested on the bottom shelf—my *Baseball Weeklies, Baseball Encyclopedia,* and *NHL Official Guide and Record Books*. I spent more time wrapped in the statistics of baseball than watching or playing it. Because I enjoyed math much more than reading, baseball stats were childhood Zen.

I knew too much from every era. My dad once asked, "What famous baseball statistic is 511?"

Without hesitation, I said, "Mel Ott's career home run total." Rather than the much more obvious all-time wins record held by Cy Young, the man whose name is affixed to baseball's most illustrious pitching award and a record that will probably never be touched, I opted for the obscure 14th place guy on the home run list from the 1930s whose name few ever heard of. He's since fallen to 25th place while Cy Young's record appears more unapproachable than ever.

Among the pages of my handwritten, stat-filled notebooks were repeated autographs of my name. What began as simple, cursive "Brian Kotler", slowly evolved into, "I can see the B." In my early teenage years, I thought I'd be famous one day and would be signing oodles of autographs, so I practiced scribbling my name as quickly as possible. It turned out, instead of signing oodles of autographs, I can barely afford Oodles of Noodles.

Roofball didn't become known until decades later on *YouTube*, but even then, the Roofball Federation of America's World Championships entailed grown men throwing footballs off the roof of their parents' house.

Long before everyone became transfixed with computers and cellphones, I devised my own fun and consumed excess energy. But despite constantly throwing balls off the wall and knowing that Three Finger Brown's 1.04 ERA in 1906 is the best in a season ever—and he actually had three fingers—I never played much organized baseball. I wish I did.

I graced the Bowie Boys & Girls Club diamond by the city's long-forgotten horse racetrack one year. The baseball trophies were cooler than the ones my hockey team presented. I earned one for being an All-Star shortstop, though the actual All-Star Game was canceled that season. The smallest was my favorite, which was awarded for being the league's defensive player of the year. And you thought I wasted time throwing balls to myself.

Perhaps I quit after one season because my pitching career was derailed by stupidity. I struck out the first three batters I faced, all kids I knew. The next game, a couple of hitters reached base, so the coach paid me a mound visit where he forced me to change my four-seam fastball to a two-seamer and I couldn't pitch again. Every time I'd revert my grip to what I was more comfortable throwing, he'd yell. "Switch it back!"

Despite not offering All-Star Games or league-wide awards, my Bowie Bruins hockey team was more prestigious. Unlike the Boys & Girls Club, our names were sewn into our jerseys, which mimicked the NHL's Boston Bruins' black-gold-and-white with the same spoked-B logo. Plus, we traveled out-of-town for games and tournaments.

But rather than achieve league-wide recognition, they offered only team-wide trophies. My least favorite hockey award was labeled "Most Shutouts on Team". I was the only goalie, and shutouts are goalie-only stats. I had one that year.

After moving out, my parents disposed of my broken backyard basketball hoop in favor of an award-winning yard. But maybe if my friends listened, my rim wouldn't have been so ramshackle.

With the hoop lowered to a height shorter than most basketball players, they slam dunked the ball.

"Uh, guys, I'm not sure you should be dunking that hard. The hoop says it's not intended for dunks."

They grabbed the ball and jammed again. "Well, if they can do it, so can I."

Thanks to that extra practice, I almost played a full season of organized basketball, but I broke my ankle chasing a loose ball during recess days before tryouts. By the time it healed, the season was underway, and I was coming off the bench, missing shots on a full-sized hoop for the crummy, middle-school JV team at my Annapolis private school for the academically gifted. That's academically gifted, not athletically gifted. Too bad the rims weren't tilted to one side the way mine was.

I received a scholarship despite my below average grades in elementary school. The thinking was that hours of homework a day would motivate me. But they couldn't have been more wrong.

The most I put my head to good use in three years at the school was the day some kid got mad in music class and smashed his plastic recorder on my skull, then had the nerve to blame me. "Brian broke my recorder!"

Though my lackluster musicality earned me solid, just-above-failing grades, my even worse singing ability saved me from much deserved punishment in English class. While discussing the 1931 novel *The Good Earth* by Pearl S. Buck, a "riveting" tale of Wang Lung's rise from impoverished peasant to prosperous landowner, the teacher asked the class a question.

"Who helped Wang Lung?"

"His wife," someone said.

"What was his wife's name?" asked the teacher.

I shouted. "Sarah!" The teacher glared at me, so I guessed again. "Theresa?"

"Brian, her name is O-Lan. Don't shout in the middle of class again."

So, I belted out the famed 1960 Brenda Lee hit song. "I'm sorry. So sorry. That I was such a fool!" The teacher laughed and left me be the rest of the semester.

The school featured enjoyable multi-day trips, like canoeing 17 miles around Wye Island in the Bay among rays and ospreys. The island state park was known for its 500-year-old white oak tree, once the largest in the country. Sadly, it since met its end during a nasty thunderstorm, though a cloned sapling grows today inside the remains of its 31-foot circumference.

A year later, we trekked to the southern tip of Maryland where the Bay meets the Potomac River and the beach sand is more of a mud that should never again be used as shampoo.

Another excursion saw us hike and camp in Shenandoah National Park, where a giant downed tree acted as a bridge across a deep ravine leading to a stream. We waded through the crystal clear, ankle-deep mountainside water. Midway across, my Ensolite pad, used for insulating the sleeping bag from the cold autumn ground, broke off my backpack. It began floating its way downstream, so I raced after it. But two steps through the sparkling water was an unseen drop-off. I fell into the frigid, waist-deep water. My sleeping bag and half my clothes were soaked, and I never recovered that useless pad.

Later that chilly fall evening, we huddled together under a huge tarp in our sleeping bags for a brisk night's sleep. The girl I liked stayed warm in the guy's sleep sack next to me while I grimaced my way through the frosty night curled in the last third of mine that remained somewhat dry, alone.

A hockey friend, who later attended an Ivy League college like his parents, encouraged me to enroll at the Annapolis private school. Though I discovered I was no future Ivy Leaguer, I made some of my best friends there, which included innumerable late-night memory fragments.

Before my kids taught me maturity and responsibility, my whole life sounded like an Olivia Rodrigo song. "It's a bad idea right? Whatever. It's fine."

Having never tried alcohol, my best friend prepared the cocktail, another supplied his dad's docked sailboat, and I was the entertainment. My friend placed the half-filled gallon milk jug on the galley table beside a deck of cards and revealed what was in the neon-green alcohol concoction. "This morning, I opened the liquor cabinet, found ten types of liquor, and poured some of each into the jug. Then I added a can of Bud Light." Ask God how it turned neon green, not me.

After two hands of cards, our drinking game quickly devolved into three teenage boys staking their claim to their own sides of the boat, offering that downed alcohol and our recent meals to Chesapeake Bay crabs and fish. A while later, when we could finally speak again, we uttered a shared thought. "Why the heck do people drink?"

About that time, I began smoking cigarettes with my best friend of the two, opting for Camel because we thought their cartoon mascot, Joe Camel, was cool. But we liked Marlboro better, so we switched. When they killed off Joe Camel a year later, we said, "Good riddance. Nobody's going to trick us to smoke."

After learning we were supposed to inhale, cigarettes made us so lightheaded, we wondered how it was legal for people to drive and smoke. Once tolerance built up, the haziness subsided and the addiction kicked in, so we began rollin' down the street smokin' and sippin' like Snoop Dogg, wishing one day we'd be a Shiznit, too.

But the first time we smoked pot, like cigarettes and Bill Clinton, I didn't inhale, so nothing happened. A year later, with my longtime best friend from hockey who was born the same day as Shakira, that all changed.

The HFStival was an annual rock festival held at RFK Stadium in D.C. A group of a dozen of us bought tickets and made ourselves home in the middle of the field.

Then news came back: they were selling everyone and anyone alcohol—no picture ID necessary. Though I was 17, I've always looked years younger, which is great now that I'm 46. But not back then. Despite my appearance as a recent middle-school graduate, my friends insisted I could buy my own. I came back with two giant beers. Never again did I successfully purchase alcohol underage.

After polishing off those beers, our hometown guy, Dave Grohl, closed the show, and I closed my lips on a cannabis joint for the first time. Half the thing found its way into my lungs, and the Foo Fighters became the Blue Fighters. Ocean and sky merged inside RFK that day, and I was sold that pot and concerts were good.

Hard liquor and concerts, not so good. Bush was my favorite '90s rock band, so my hockey friend and I grabbed tickets to their concert with his brother. My friend drove while I pounded ten shots of Bacardi 151 on the hourlong drive. He parked his truck outside the arena; I stepped out and parked my face on the asphalt. As I staggered my way into the arena, I repeated my sentiment. "I was fine until I got out."

Crammed into the arena floor crowd, seventy feet from the stage, the opening band, No Doubt, was a few songs in. I tapped my friend on the shoulder and shouted through the noise. "I'm going to puke!"

"What?"

"I'm going to puke!!!"

"I can't hear you!"

I motioned my hand like a fountain, arcing from my mouth toward the floor. He looked at me funny. Then all went dark as I lost rum from my tum onto the arena floor.

That crammed throng of bodies fanned out in a circle 15 feet wide, glaring at me alone in the center, disgusted. My friend and his brother were among them.

At some point, they escorted me to seats on the side, where we watched the rest of the show far from some nasty guy's repulsive upchuck. Can you believe somebody was that gross?

Of all my friends, he was around the longest. Twenty years ago, I moved an hour northwest of Bowie, and he moved his family an hour east. We haven't seen each other in decades, but I remember the start of our friendship like it was yesterday.

I was seven years old, and he was eight. The new hockey season began, and our first practice reached its anti-climactic end. As always, when a new season starts, new kids join the team. One of them approached me as I was leaving the rink. "Do you want to come to my house?"

Under helmets and facemasks, faces aren't recognizable, so I didn't even know he was a teammate. To this day, I've never been approached to begin a friendship so randomly and unexpectedly. I visited that weekend, and we remained friends for 15 years.

One night during our high school years, we ventured down a rural road along the Patuxent River with a sack full of Roman candle fireworks. Parked in an empty field, he lit his candle and watched colored balls of fire blast dozens of feet high. I lit mine simultaneously, and nothing happened.

So, I peered down the barrel to determine what was wrong. Five seconds later, I realized how stupid it was for a non-pyrotechnic specialist to stare into an ignited firework, so I tilted it away. Within one second, it functioned correctly, and I was spared a trip to the trauma center thanks to my quick thinking.

During senior week in Ocean City, my friend oversaw a pull-up competition between me and another guy. After I won easily, the guy said, "Of course you won. Look how little weight you have to lift."

I pulled up my sleeve and showed my arm. "Look what I have to do it with."

"Good point," he said as he trudged away, having been beaten by Olive Oyl, not Popeye.

I recently stumbled upon an old high school project completed around graduation. Its Table of Contents lists everything from my personal resume, religion, humor, mementoes, my favorites, my family, and my friends—which indicates he's my best. There's also a page titled "25 Things I Want to do in My Lifetime." I lived out the dream that's listed first, "Drive a racecar."

I sped down a residential street in D.C. behind the wheel of my 1994 Dodge Shadow, with less than 100 horsepower, at 70 miles per hour. A parked cop saw me blow by. He hit his lights, so I turned down some side streets in an unfamiliar neighborhood. After speeding through stop signs and making several turns to lose the fuzz, I found myself driving sanely, back on the main road. Of course, every turn was a right-hander, so I basically did a circle, and passed that same cop from moments earlier. This time, he got me.

"Why are you in such a rush, Mario Andretti?" the cop asked. Like Andretti, I fulfilled my dream.

Though that cop offered unexpected restraint as I imitated one of the greatest race car drivers ever, another was having none of my friend impersonating the police. We drove down country roads with a bright spotlight mounted on the roof of his pickup. A black-and-white pulled him over. "Who do you think you are pretending to be a cop?" the officer said. "Take the light down."

He introduced me to his friend who was a car mechanic. After becoming close ourselves, my new friend said, "Your dad came into the dealership, had some work done, and left a review. My boss used it for training." My new friend learned to repair cars from my dad, who doesn't know the first thing about car repair.

Late in our relationship, my old hockey friend said, "You're the smartest person I've ever met." Considering he attended a prestigious athletic high school, and arguably a more illustrious community college, that's saying something.

He was wrong. To get financial aid for my community college, I took an IQ test. I scored 134. One point higher would've placed me in the top percentile. But I got that. It sucks knowing I can walk into a room of 100 people and there's always someone smarter than me.

Getting into college wasn't straightforward. The night before taking the SAT exam, I got drunk. While reeling from a massive hangover the next morning, I slogged into the classroom.

The math test was first. I shook off the "I don't want to be heres" and scored 660.

Then came verbal. My least-favorite-subject-because-of-all-the-reading headache meshed with the hangover one.

Meanwhile, the restless girl beside me sat with her legs crossed, foot dangling in the corner of my eyes. It's hard to describe how fast her foot was shaking, but think of the fat guy getting blasted in the gut with a cannonball. Imagine his stomach fat jiggling for 90 minutes straight—it wasn't nearly that funny.

After trudging out with a degrading score in the 300s, my mom insisted I study and retake the SAT sober. My respectable 530 proves I didn't read or write a thing throughout middle and high school, and I'm probably not all that smart.

21

TOO MANY PEOPLE LIE

SOON AFTER TAKING MY SAT, I hopped a plane to Spain. A year earlier, as my Spanish grade teetered between a D and a C, my teacher said, "Ask your parents if you can invite a Spanish student to stay for a month. If you can, I'll bump your letter grade two notches."

Because my parents were always impressed by As and Bs on my report card, they said yes. An amazing summer that was highlighted by an Ace of Base- and Spice Girls-filled bus trip to New York's Statue of Liberty was appreciated by him returning the following summer and bringing me back to Spain for 16 days.

My mom wanted a special gift. "Since I know you're old enough to buy your own alcohol there, you will. So, bring me back a bottle of Tia Maria. It's a coffee liqueur." Though I've never seen my mom drink, I went to Spain to bring home the taste of Jamaica made in Italy that she could've bought down the street.

Good son that I am, I scoured the twisting maze of medieval cobblestone streets in Palma, the large Spanish city on the Mediterranean island of Mallorca, for a more unique surprise. The sheer, earth-toned handmade scarf that I discovered became her favorite accessory to wear while teaching.

The trip enhanced my love for travel, and I aspired for a job that let me go further than six miles beyond the pizza delivery shop. Since travel agents received all kinds of vacation perks, my mom helped me find a business school with a business & travel diploma.

There, on the second and third floors of the glass-encased office building, I took school seriously for the first time and made Dean's List with perfect attendance.

But halfway to graduation, the internet exploded in popularity. No one needed costly travel agents anymore because people could book their own trips for little or no charge.

So, that plan was out the window. But the school offered one major benefit: Those of us in the business & travel program received a class trip. My class of a dozen mostly girls chose to go to Jamaica. Disillusioned by the uselessness of my career path, I chose to stop attending.

Months later, after missing out on that trip, I returned to finish the diploma. I joined the next class who selected a Caribbean cruise. A week before the date we were scheduled to leave, I learned I'd be left off the plane and ship because my tuition's trip money was already allocated for Jamaica. As their plane flew away, I played an Oasis song over and over in angst. "As the day was dawning, my plane flew away...So, don't go away."

I graduated, but my grandma was annoyed that she came down from New York for a ceremony I refused to attend. Two failed interviews for flight attendant later, I was out of the travel business for good.

One redeeming feature of the school was typing class. Beforehand, I hunted and pecked my way to 30-40 words-per-minute. By the end, I became certified with the third fastest typing speed in class at 65 words-per-minute with three errors over a 5-minute span. Being able to type almost as quickly as I thought drastically improved my writing.

Out of school, and having missed out on two trips, I packed my bags for Europe. More specifically, Amsterdam. The lure of legal weed on a continent I treasured ignited my one-way ticket purchase. Without an itinerary or planned date of return, I set out on the cobbled canal-lined streets the morning the plane touched down. I took the long route to stock up on marijuana. Who knew they liked putting red lights and pretty women in windows? Since the best weed wasn't found there, I continued on.

The one must-see in town was Anne Frank's House. A few days into my trip, I roamed the attic from which she penned her diary, which infused a lump in my throat that dampened the entire day. What those poor people endured is impossible to comprehend.

After sleeping off the horrors of the Holocaust, I reestablished my will to wander aimlessly through the city. As day became night, I stopped at a local coffee shop and ordered a hashish space cake. After downing the dry, hard-to-eat brain food with a cup of hot chocolate, I moseyed about town awaiting its effects as night became late night.

While after-hours stragglers strolled up and down the busy street one block over, only me and a pair of guys drifted on mine. They rushed over brandishing a knife. "Empty your pockets," they said, as they reached in and grabbed about $10 and a bit of hashish. "Give us your backpack!"

Do you know that ridiculous belly band we're supposed to wear abroad under our clothes to safeguard ourselves from pickpockets? I hated wearing that thing, but it still contained my valuables inside my backpack. My passport, traveler's checks, and hundreds of dollars in cash stood to be stolen if I handed it over. "No, you're not getting my backpack."

With fight-or-flight mode in full effect, I prepared to do both.

"Hey! What's going on?" A guy yelled down the street, spooking the muggers. They fled.

I spent the next few hours floating in the Amsterdam air like a Dutch tulip as cops sped me around town while that space cake was hitting hard. "Is that them?" they asked.

"No," I said, as the cops' blond hair melded over top of the dark hair we were looking for.

After the incident somewhat soured me on Amsterdam, I figured I'd do a bit more traveling. So, I booked a train to Paris.

I needed a drink, so I stopped in a small Parisian convenience store. "Un soda, por favor," I said. The guy glared at me. "Soda?" I asked. "Uno por favor." I'm terrible with languages, and that's made worse by me having studied several of them because I combine two or more languages into a single sentence. At the time, I'd taken at least two years of French, Spanish, Latin, and Hebrew. I've since added German, only complicating matters further.

Thoroughly angered, the convenience store clerk asked, "Do you speak English?"

"Yes."

"Tell me what you want in English."

While heading up the street with my drink, I couldn't understand why the guy was so mad at me. All I said in English was "soda". Everything else was Spanish. Oh, I was talking terrible Spanish in France. That's why he was mad.

I grabbed a map to walk several miles across Paris to the Eiffel Tower. As darkness fell, rain did too. The front of my pants were soaked as I struggled to pull out my map. It disintegrated. But I saw the tower's tip minutes earlier, so I was sure it was close by.

After locating and losing the Eiffel Tower a half-dozen times, I made it, drenched but relieved to leave the rainstorm and replace my map. The lights sparkled outside the elevator to the top, where I waved to Washington, D.C. and gave the finger to two people in Amsterdam.

The next day, inside The Louvre, I saw a lot of foreign tourists who saw the Mona Lisa up close, walked the Champs-Élysées and Seine River, and boarded a train to London.

At the London train station, a customs officer asked, "Where are you coming from?"

"Paris."

"Is that it?"

"Yes."

"Let me see your train ticket."

As I rifled through my over-packed bags, I plucked the first ticket I saw. "Here you go."

"It says Amsterdam. Come with me."

Uh oh, I think there's weed in my bag. In fact, after smoking up the last few days in Paris, I'm certain there is.

Behind the curtain, he snagged the bag of weed. "Am I trouble?" I asked.

"Not if this is all you've got." Thank God for that, because that was all I got. But the Lord shook me down twice on my trip, once using thieves and once with street muggers.

Hampered by a sore shoulder from lugging a giant duffle bag around Europe for a week, I circled the train station looking for a hotel, bummed that he got what I got. So, I hopped the train to Heathrow Airport and flew back home.

Crime documentaries prompted me to return to school once I was resettled in America, hoping to become a homicide investigator. The idea of unearthing murderers outweighed my many years glued to The Weather Channel aspiring to be a meteorologist.

Though with violent crime holding steady and climate change on the verge of becoming a runaway train, it may have been a more lucrative career choice tracking monster storms than monsters. We need to be way more careful, because God will let us destroy our planet.

Because of my miserable high school grades, except one quarter of Spanish, I opted for a two-year associate degree from community college and maintained a 3.5 GPA. I intended to transfer to the University of Maryland to complete a bachelor's in criminal justice. But the plan was derailed the final semester.

To become a detective, not only is a bachelor's degree in criminal justice needed, one almost always must begin as a police officer. They insist on clean criminal records. I had one strike against me and couldn't afford another, but God said I needed another to remain happy-go-lucky. Search for the bad in people, you see bad. Focus on the good, you see good.

Possessing marijuana back in the day got people arrested, and months after reaching adulthood, that happened.

Then one night a year later, after delivering pizza in Annapolis, I asked a co-worker to buy me a six-pack of beer. My car was unusually immaculate, with nothing inside but the six-pack on the rear seat and almost two ounces of weed in a radar detector box underneath mine—a felony amount.

I rounded the historic waterfront past shops, bars and restaurants tucked into early 18th century brick buildings painted red, white, gray, or blue. Then I reached a stop sign. Marking the end of the hundred-yard road, the sign stood before a wide, red-brick crosswalk designed for massive weekend foot traffic. But this late evening, few people used it.

Impossible to see traffic from the recessed stop sign, I crept into the crosswalk for a clear view. Several seconds of passing cars held me there as I enjoyed the warm sea breeze with my window down.

Then a voice interrupted.

"I'm pulling you over for stopping in the crosswalk," said a uniformed cop as he stepped into the brown horizontal-ladder of stones that formed its lines amongst the red bricks. "Park there."

In the center of downtown Annapolis, the gray-haired, overweight officer read my underage birth date and asked, "Why do you have beer?"

He forced me from the car, still wearing my pizza uniform. "Spill out the beer."

"Where?" I asked, as people passed from every direction.

"On the ground."

As I poured the cold, golden beverage that I'd been looking forward to all day onto the red-brick street, a guy strolling past shouted. "Hey, you got any pizza with that beer?"

After removing my pizza shirt, I continued unloading my night's fun as I pointed out everyone who ran the stop sign I stopped at.

"Look! He didn't stop. Why aren't you pulling him over?" The next car blew through the sign. "What's wrong with you? You're letting them go too?"

"Stop talking."

With six beer bottles emptied, we returned to the car, where I offered three more words to him.

"Is that it?"

"Not yet," he said, grabbing his flashlight. In the waning years of his career—and based on his health, his life—the officer steadied himself for the difficult transition to his knees so he could search under my seat. "What's that box under there?"

"It's the box from my radar detector," I said, thinking that moment would send me to prison.

Rather than taxing himself by reaching under to retrieve it, he wheezed himself upright and asked, "Is there anything in it?"

"My radar detector. I don't like using it."

"Okay, well, you don't seem nervous. I'll let you go."

It's hard to seem nervous when you're pissed.

He kept his word, so that's not what cost me a career as a detective.

This did.

Sometime later, instead of delivering, I worked as assistant manager at that same pizza store. I was about 20.

Annoyed at a recent break-up with one of our drivers, the owner of the hair & tan next door became incensed with another driver because she didn't like where he parked. She screamed and spat on the kid, then kicked him for good measure.

A third driver and I watched everything in the tiny parking lot out front of our store. After the minute-long incident, I told my abused driver we should call the police, but he was easygoing and didn't want to fuss, so we didn't.

Soon after, we learned the owner pressed charges against both of us. The owner, who likes to file frivolous claims and has an extensive court record dozens of cases long, as both a plaintiff and mostly a defendant, accused my driver of assault and me of indecent exposure.

With separate court dates, the driver's was first. I testified on his behalf and the court found him not guilty. The third driver was witness for my hearing and I, too, was ruled not guilty.

Jump to age 23. Months before we married, my ex-wife was home pregnant with Ethan. On a toasty summer day, my car windows were wide open as I pulled into the grocery store parking lot, blocks from our home. Two women strolled up and one approached my passenger-side window. "Do you need something?" she asked.

"You can keep walking."

Her friend said, "We should call the police on this guy." Spooked, I never went into the store and just drove home.

Back home with my expectant ex-wife, a knock at the door disturbed our merrymaking. She answered, and seconds later said, "Brian, the police want to talk to you."

"Your car matches a report from the shopping center," the cop said. "You're under arrest."

"For what?"

"You know what you did. You've done it before."

"Done what?"

"You know."

In the back of the squad car, I didn't know why I was under arrest and headed to the police station. Sometime after arriving, I learned I was accused of indecent exposure again. For hours, I denied and denied any wrongdoing, but the detective pressured me with the same repetitive questions. Countless times, I said, "I'm telling you what happened."

Eventually, he asked, "Is that your story?"

"Yes, that's my story." The moment that left my mouth, he dipped. In my head, it always sounded like I lied—like I was making up a story.

After my interrogation, police escorted me to Seven Locks, the same county jail boxer Mike Tyson was recently released from. At least that seemed kind of cool.

Fifteen years before, my dad bumped into him on the streets of D.C. and got his autograph on yellow, lined legal paper. "To Brian, Mike Tyson". In disbelief, I compared it to his signature in the instruction manual for my Nintendo video game, *Mike Tyson's Punchout*, and sure enough, it matched.

After showing it off at school, someone stole it—much like many of my Nintendo games.

Before games could be rented at video stores, they could be rented from me. I shared my extensive library with classmates, who paid a few dollars to borrow the game for a week. Unfortunately, it was difficult retrieving my games from some. Years later, I learned rental stores gathered credit cards on file to secure rentals. If I'd only known that when I was seven.

At Seven Locks, a county jail named for the nearby Chesapeake & Ohio Canal, I met the commissioner through her security window, expecting to be released.

"You were found guilty of indecent exposure a few years ago," she said. "So, I can't release you. You'll go out and do it again."

"No, I wasn't. I was found not guilty."

She pointed to her computer screen. "The system says you were guilty."

Then it clicked. That's why the police said I knew what I did because I'd done it before. A clerical error from years earlier ensnared me a second time for the same thing I still didn't do.

I used my phone call to request a family member head to the courthouse the next day to fix their mistake, and I was released. But a few months later, I sat in tears in the courtroom as my crappy lawyer advised me to plead guilty. "You have a baby on the way," he said. "If you plead guilty, you'll get a slap on the wrist. If you don't, it would make things a lot worse."

The detective was present, but the second woman listed as witness was not. Still, I listened to my lawyer and wept my way through a guilty plea.

What was that slap on the wrist? I mixed kitty litter into disposed paint cans and trimmed the lawn around Seven Locks to wistful waves through narrow windows from inmates that contested their charge rather than plead guilty.

That was enough to cut my dream short of helping victims and their families mete out justice for one of humanity's most heinous crimes. I dropped out of school and focused on work, seeking promotion from driver to general manager of a pizza delivery place.

Miscommunication led to me violating probation months down the road, so they arrested me again. Hours later, they released me, and I arrived late for work. After not eating all day, I got high on my own supply shoveling pizza into my mouth, when the owner made an infrequent surprise visit. I feared reprimand for eating in plain view of the customers. It's a no-no.

"Congratulations!" he said. "I'm promoting you to your own store." This post-jail event may have topped the Stanley Cup banner.

———

I excelled in the job, winning manager of the month and earning promotion to a higher volume store within a few months. Then I learned of a couple missing money deposits affiliated with the first store. Having occurred the evening of my shift, of course, I was the prime suspect.

The franchise owner took stealing seriously. He once arrived with police at a store during the busiest hour of the week to arrest a manager for pocketing a few hundred dollars. I insisted on my innocence, but thousands of dollars were missing, and I was held accountable. My supervisor said, "The only reason you still have a job is because of how well you're doing."

To account for the missing money, the owner was illegally withholding my paychecks until he recouped all the money. A few times, strangers helped at the gas station to fuel my car for the 30-minute commute to work while my weekly salary dropped to zero dollars.

A month or two later, moments before a managers meeting at the headquarters, which was a pizza store-sized office next to a pizza store, the owner called me into his personal office.

"Good news," he said. "The bank found the money. It was an inside job. The teller stole the deposits, and you're cleared."

Though I recovered the withheld pay, that wasn't the end of money issues.

Every month, besides our salary, we received a bonus check as a percentage of the store's profit. Without ever revealing a profit-loss statement, each month the owner volunteered a few hundred dollars "because he's a nice guy" since my low-volume store supposedly lost money. Other managers heard that too. At the higher volume store, he still signed over a few hundred dollars, this time for a different reason. "Because that's what it earned."

Later, in a one-on-one meeting with the owner, he inadvertently showed me a profit-loss statement that indicated I should've been paid several times what I was, but I foolishly passed it back. When I asked to see it again, he refused.

So, I wrote to Maryland's Department of Labor, Licensing and Regulation, who discovered the owner stole about $1,800 from me in one month alone. We reached a settlement so, combined with the escrow dispersed from a short-lived job installing entertainment systems in people's homes, I could get my own. I'd have been better off getting a lawyer.

After life in pizza failed to succeed, I became a courier. Then I moved into educational sales as I began attending another community college to become a hockey journalist. Hockey, writing, and traveling—truly a dream scenario.

Unfortunately, many of my criminal justice credits didn't transfer to a general studies or communications degree. I was two months away from my associate degree in criminal justice when I dropped out, but because of the new school and career choice, I needed another year.

Among my classes was journalism. Our professor was in charge of the school paper, so we discussed me writing for it. A semester later, I became editor but was reeling from the vasectomy pain. Imagine a flaming lighter held to skin that's supposed to experience pleasure, not pain. That was life—all day, every day. A nightly realization manifested: the constant buzz of pain never left my brain feeling rested.

The busiest I'd ever been in my life, I helped my ex-wife with her schoolwork and was proficient in mine while writing and editing the school paper. I worked nights in sales 45 minutes from my house, and arrived home late to watch the Capitals game and write a story for my website. Empty hours were filled by designing and maintaining the site every day. To reach as many eyes as possible, I also volunteered to edit the interfaith congregation's newsletter.

Doped up on pain pills, I interviewed the college's head basketball coach to prepare for a season-opening article in the school paper. During the interview, the long-serving coach asked, "Do you want me to call the sports editor of the city paper? I know him well." Thanks to him, my first paid gig soon followed.

High on morphine and Percocet, I watched the women's basketball team nearly win, limped to my office across campus, and wrote my only published article. The pain was worsening, my website was slipping away, my grades were tumbling, and a night's sales calls often ended in a visit to urgent care.

For posterity, I kept the oversized paycheck featuring a prominent watermark of the news building. It rested on display about three years until I became desperate for the two-digit sum on that check.

I began hobbling with a cane, but stopped to avoid elbow problems. The last walking stick propped a broken window for years inside the door of the van I flooded. Along with the van, it met its doom at the junkyard.

I couldn't sit long enough to type on a computer and the weight of the laptop was overbearing.

Ice all day and ice all night. One lousy ice pack could be microwaved and used as heat. Falling asleep with it was awful because I'd wake up to its warmth. When it already feels like fire down there, that's the last thing it needs.

Loads of doctor's appointments those first few years in search of a cure offered no relief.

After months, not years, my ex-wife took off, making a tough situation worse. The one constant I always had was my parents. They helped pay for doctor visits, prescriptions, and lawyers. When I fell short of paying bills, they swooped in with money. I don't know where I'd be today without them.

Those were such lean years. When the kids weren't with me, I didn't laugh. I was so miserable that the few times I did, I stopped laughing and wondered what was so funny.

22

HEALING THE PROSECUTOR

WHEN PEOPLE BECOME DISABLED, MONEY is sluggish reaching them. Bills roll in as work hours disintegrate and medical expenses skyrocket.

People don't choose their health, but the system punishes them for it. Maryland offers temporary cash assistance while waiting for Social Security to award disability, but it isn't much. They paid under $200 a month, barely enough for car insurance, let alone rent, food, and utilities.

Almost two years elapsed before I received regular Social Security payments. Disability awarded a lump sum to cover that period, but because of increased medical expenses, plus late fees and interest owed to creditors, none of it was mine. For a parent of three, monthly disability payments have been below the poverty line, so relief was never in sight.

As I've discovered, disability payouts don't trend with inflation or minimum wage increases. Much of my compensated employment was at a pay rate one-third of Maryland's current minimum wage. As the minimum climbed almost 300% and inflation increased 45% in the years since, my disability checks rose less than 40%.

Disability barely keeps us afloat, so when prices increase faster than income, we're in extra trouble. If not for outside aid, disabled folks face a lifetime of struggle. My parents proved my source of salvation, shielding me from severe debt.

Their ongoing help eases the post-Post horror I endured from their ignorance. It's a massive minimization to say I'm livid how things turned out after involving The Post, but if I don't discuss it, they find it easy to disregard. I just have to eat crow in some sort of passive acknowledgment that they've been right, and I've been wrong, year after year, to establish peace in our home.

Seven years on, they've settled on a hypothesis: I overcame a bout of post-traumatic insanity in the months following the loss of my kids. As my mom recently reiterated, they believe I screwed up and they were never wrong. They've never apologized nor admitted any fault.

In a recent conversation with my dad, who is familiar with a bit of this book, I said, "I'm not trying to paint you in a poor light, but I've got a story to tell."

"You're saying I'm unknowing," he said, as if he accepted the book's agenda.

"Right."

Seconds later, he rose from his desk, sauntered into the living room, and tuned to Fox News. Guess he wanted to firmly establish his will to be unknowing.

Unfortunately, that blindness to reality has screwed me and my kids for years. If it weren't for Fox News' continuous barrage against The Washington Post and other mainstream media outlets, my parents would've realized they should've spent the money on a family lawyer to help us seven years ago with newfound witnesses. Instead, because they insist The Post is corrupt, dishonest fake news, the funds went to a criminal lawyer, fines, and bail for my cover-up crime spree.

My parents' indoctrination made a mess of my life and my kids' lives. Only God can save us now.

Fox News has my mom as good as Kreskin.

For 20 minutes, the Amazing Kreskin had my mom do subservience tricks on stage before sending her off into the dinner theater audience.

"Maxine," said Kreskin. "I want you to shake her hand. You won't be able to let go until I say to."

Kreskin rambled on about something else as my mom kept telling the woman, "I'm so sorry. I can't let go."

My parents have been convinced by talking points. They don't consider their own experience. "The wealthy should be taxed less," my dad said. "We need the trickle-down effect."

"Dad," I said, "Did you sell educational stuff to people who made more money or less than you?"

"Less."

"I noticed that among my pizza customers too," I said. "People with less money tend to spend more locally. Meanwhile, the owner who was supposed to provide the trickle-down effect, stole thousands from me."

"That's true."

"Didn't you also have a boss lie and steal money?" I asked.

"Well, he promised a bonus if I hit a sales target," my dad said. "When I reached it, he offered more if I hit an even higher figure. He repeated that until the target was impossible so he didn't have to pay me anything."

Trickle-down economics is the misguided hope that tax cuts on the wealthiest few will see money pass through countless middlemen and see its way into the hands of those most in need.

Having lived paycheck-to-paycheck with four young children at home, I know when I received a tax credit, I had more to spend. My dollars were taken by cashiers making minimum wage, counted by managers who earned more than that, and deposited into the bank accounts of those affluent CEOs who were the lone beneficiaries of trickle-down tax cuts. When poor folks like me have money, everyone bene-fits. Not just the top one percent.

My brainwashed parents have lived in a daze through a fascinating world since 2017. A few weeks after sending my story to The Post, my favorite visitation observer at Frederick's Mental Health Association introduced a woman to me before my kids arrived. In what has become the most difficult situation to portray accurately in this entire book, they both walked into the room.

"Brian," my favorite observer said uncomfortably, in a half-whisper and frightened expression that said she guarded some secret and hoped she was getting this right. "I want you to meet this woman."

Shoulder-length, straight, sandy brown hair framed the excessively rosy complexion of her intense blushing. With the giddiest smile I'd ever seen, she extended her hand.

"It's nice to meet you," I said as our hands met. She squeaked al-most inaudibly as we shook. Her hand would've hit the floor if I let go. After a few moments of happy awkwardness, I did. Startled, her hand sprung to life without a single word.

The observer warily looked at me, then at her. "Okay," she said. "Let's go." They left the room. Never before, or again, was I introduced to someone formally at the Mental Health Association. Every other time new faces observed a visit, they entered like it was nothing—without any introductions.

Five minutes later, they returned to monitor my visit with Colin and Lucy. Huddled together, whispering, the woman never lifted her gaze from the clipboard.

When I told my dad, he dropped everything and yelled. "She's from The Post!" That's the first time he seemed on board.

"She never looked at us," I said.

"Oh yeah, she's from the news. It makes no sense for a trainee not to watch."

"I think you're right, dad. I didn't even consider that."

"Wow," he said, ruffling his once black, now gray hair. "This is so surreal."

"That's the same word I've continually used to describe everything—surreal."

Ecstatic that my dad finally appeared to have his revelation, I assumed our arguing ran its course. But the very next day, it ramped to new heights and never ceased until my return from jail many months later.

In need of money, I asked my dad for $50. Without hesitation, he wrote me a check, which I promptly misplaced. So, I asked for a replacement. "We need to talk," he said.

I met him at a gas station while he was running errands with my mom. It wasn't long after she said, "I'm starting to believe you. And it's weird." But after flipping her TV back to Fox News, she quickly reverted to skepticism and complained about me losing the modest check they supposedly couldn't afford. My dad suddenly shared her opinion and, from then on, refused to consider The Post was assisting.

"Dad, yesterday you yelled. 'She's from The Post!' Why don't you believe it now?"

"I said, 'Maybe she's from The Post.'" He was accustomed to downplaying or reworking event after event.

"No, you didn't. You shouted it, and nobody shouts, 'Maybe she's from The Post!' Why are you lying?"

He responded with his reflexive head shake of dissent, insisting he was right, and I was the problem.

That $50 was insignificant compared to the $20,000 they shelled out in the coming months on legal representation, bail, and fines that resulted from my criminal charges. Had they acknowledged The Post was investigating, they could've backed me with lawyers and witnesses to achieve a swift resolution of restoring my custody. Instead, because they assumed The Post was fake news and would never do such a thing, my mom melted down whenever I asked for financial help. "Where am I getting the money?!?"

"From the Washington Post investigation," I said, remarking that a lawsuit might arise. She rolled her eyes.

I parodied these frequent occasions when joking with my air vent buddy above my cell. "Where am I getting the money?!?" It turns out they had the money all along, but squandered it on the criminal cases that stemmed from our fighting instead of bringing my kids back home within a few short weeks or months. Upon my release from jail long afterwards, they truly had no money to fight, and I appeared as a terrible father before the court and an insane son to my parents.

The day I lost custody, the judge clarified that Ethan's allegation was her sole justification. Everything else she said supported continuing unsupervised, shared physical custody of the kids. Minutes before declaring the custody swap, she remarked that I have a suitable relationship and home.

"It appears both parties are bonded with all children—all the children. I have no indication that the two younger children prefer one parent over another."

Two minutes later, she continued. "I believe both of these parents want and desire normalized, healthy relationships with their children."

Before ruling on my loss of custody, she preceded it by saying, "Both residences are proper. That issue doesn't interfere with visitation."

Then she said, "I want this issue about reported abuse to be developed and investigated." Though the BIA never developed or investigated a thing, The Post and I have. Distressingly, I've found extensive investigations such as mine can take several years and the two-year window to defend myself expired before the financial resources to litigate became available. By then, I was facing an uphill battle trying to regain time with my kids, who since expressed they'd rather appease their mother than reestablish a connection with their convict father.

If only they knew what happened in lockup.

Two successive trips from jail to the courthouse were among the strangest scenes encountered.

Upon arriving at the courthouse that dates to the last year of the Civil War, the police van's cordial officer escorted me into the elevator to an upper floor. The officer accompanied me into a small room and stood beside me as I sat with my hands cuffed, preparing to meet the prosecutor. He entered and perched himself across the table, with his graying, buzz-cut hair and eyeglasses complementing the sleazy smugness of his face. Near him hovered a second cop I never met before.

The prosecutor was slimy, continuously averting his gaze as he deflected my questions and made false accusations. Knowing my world was different, I thought it my place to confront his inconsistencies, which appeared to agitate the cop looming behind him by the second. The prosecutor and I exchanged unpleasantries for a few minutes when I asked, "Why won't you look me in the eye? You're lying and you know it."

That cop burst forward, yanked my yellow jumpsuit, and threw me against the wall. The officer that accompanied me from jail remained silent and unnerved, two feet from the fuming cop. Moments later he cooly said, "Settle down." The cop did.

Both the crazed cop and the sane officer brought me back to jail. In the secure little holding area between the outside door and the arrivals/departures cell block featuring eight cells around a desk, the seething cop and I resumed arguing.

"Why'd you throw me against the wall? You know I'm a victim."

"You're no victim!" His finger trembled in fierce anger as he gunned it toward my face.

"I can't believe they let you become a cop," I said. "Look how your trigger finger is shaking." I raised my steady appendage toward him. "That's what a finger should look like."

Jail guards arrived and brought me inside.

One week later, I returned to the courthouse, again not knowing what to expect. As I entered the same room, I saw the same prosecutor seated alone with his eyeglasses resting on the table.

The week before, he silently watched that raging cop shove me against the wall. This time, the prosecutor's demeanor completely changed. Instead of treating me with flippant insolence, he leaned forward and looked me square in the eye, without the obstructing glare of his glasses.

"You healed me," he said in the calmest, kindest voice. "Thank you."

That was it. He stood and walked out one door as the officer led me out the other. On my way back to jail, they cranked more rock and pop music off my hacked *YouTube Music* playlist. I was no ordinary criminal.

23

WITNESSES

I LIKE TO THINK I WAS no ordinary dad, either.

One of the last things I did with Colin and Lucy was make a trip of Colin's summer science project on erosion. As a kid, I had the same assignment, so I roamed the creek that twisted through the woods behind my house. The muddy stream was a five-foot gouge eroded into the landscape. I snapped photos and added lackluster words to the very memorable experience.

Less than a half-mile from our Hagerstown home, the closest body of water to me now is Antietam Creek, a dozen miles upstream from the bloodiest day in American history. The 1862 Battle of Antietam along its banks caused over 22,000 casualties. The Civil War engagement stirred Abraham Lincoln to compose the Emancipation Proclamation five days later, insisting slaves become free.

For two days, Lucy tagged along as Colin and I toured the 40-mile creek from beginning to end, stopping at famed Civil War sites along the way. We splashed in rocky water, got stuck in muddy water, honored the water under Burnside Bridge on the battlefield, and startled a few kids fishing under a Pennsylvania bridge as we noted and discussed the effects of erosion.

As the creek reached its Potomac River end, it passed under a 190-year-old stone aqueduct once used by the Chesapeake & Ohio Canal. Down by the river, Colin and Lucy leaped on rocks at the shoreline as I snagged the final photos of our excursion. With the aqueduct in the background, the optical illusion of Colin propping his sister on her rock was my favorite. I wanted to add it to Colin's posterboard, but he refused. And thank God he did. Because the posterboard was returned to his mom's house, I never saw it again. But that photo watches over me every night from my nightstand.

Colin's class loved the erosion stream table we built best, complete with water pumps circulating a three-foot-long river that eroded the sand as it flowed past. He showed it off to his cousin, who mentioned it in his witness letter on my behalf. When my 18-year-old nephew said, "I'll be a witness," this is part of what he wrote:

> "Brian eagerly showed me a summer project he was helping his youngest son with. He did his very best to help and nurture his son. In the backyard, they set up a contraption to illustrate the process of erosion. Brian took his son to Antietam Creek to further his son's understanding of the topic. Brian went above and beyond the call of duty with his son's best interest in mind.
>
> "This is just one of many examples of Brian's character. That being said, the very idea that my uncle is abusive towards his own children is completely and utterly preposterous. The false and wicked allegations that have tainted his name must be withdrawn immediately."

My nephew's letter was one of three that reached the school, Mental Health Association and The Post. The mothers of Colin's two closest friends wrote the other two. Sadly, because of the kids' disappearance plus the entrance of The Post, I haven't spoken to the families since. After seeing what The Post forced my visitation supervisor to do, I assumed it best to leave them be.

Wonderful parents in their own rights, they provided me with more hope than I could've ever imagined.

One wrote about my time spent interacting with kids:

> "Colin seems genuinely happy when he has spoken of his father. Through the interactions I have had with Brian, he always seems positive and has never had any negative things to say. My mother often goes on field trips with my child, and she has spoken of Colin's dad being on many of those field trips. There has not been one negative experience my mother has seen.
>
> "I am a very cautious mother and have not allowed my child to spend the night with any friends; I have only allowed them to have friends over. Recently, Colin had a birthday party at his father's house and my child wanted to spend the night. Based on the discussions I had with my mother and the way Brian interacted with the children on the field trips, I did allow my child to spend the night.
>
> "When I picked my child up the following day, my child had nothing but great things to say about the experience. My child said Colin's dad took a lot of extra time setting up games and buying laser guns so the kids could all play together and have a great time. My child truly enjoyed the sleepover and did not see or hear anything negative during the time spent at Brian's house."

Aside from supposedly telling friends, the judge said Ethan accused me of specifically targeting people on *Skype*. I didn't use *Skype* and Colin had one *Skype* friend, another classmate, with whom he often spent all day hamming it up online. They shared countless hours goofing around, and little did I know, an older child and their mom were listening. In part, here is the third letter:

> "I have overheard many of the *Skype* conversations between Colin and my child since they became classmates and friends in

the fall of 2015. Usually, I have only heard Mr. Kotler say a greeting and nothing more. One recent *Skype* call where I heard Mr. Kotler talking at length to my child (no more than two minutes) was clearly regarding school and an upcoming field trip.

"I ask to keep the door open so that I can listen to interactions to be sure that my child is having safe and age-appropriate computer time. During the numerous *Skype* interactions that have occurred over the past 2½ years, I have never heard any inappropriate conversations, especially any involving Mr. Kotler. My older child has been present in the room during many of the *Skype* sessions involving Colin and cannot recall any inappropriate interactions. As a senior in high school, my older child has received numerous school guidance sessions (and parent talks) on digital citizenship and inappropriate relationships between adults and children and has never brought to my attention any concerns about the verbal interactions witnessed.

"I found Mr. Kotler to be an outgoing and friendly person and did not feel uneasy or wary of him in any way. Even taking into consideration the recent allegations of Mr. Kotler, I do not feel the need to monitor any interactions between my child, Colin, or Mr. Kotler any more than I have in the past.

"In my limited observations of Mr. Kotler, I have only found him to be an engaged, present, and active parent and would not hesitate to have him be near or interact with my children."

I concealed the letters from the BIA for over a year, thinking they were best left in the hands of the school, mental health professionals, and newspaper. When I revealed them to the BIA in May 2019, they frazzled her, but she did nothing. The kids continued to fail school without their father. Six months later, in November 2019, I sent this email to the BIA:

"Colin's report card for his very first quarter in middle school just came back, and it was terrible. He failed both his Magnet Science and Math classes (remember Colin is a STEM magnet student, S stands for Science, M stands for Math). Now he has failed both while also receiving a D in Merit Social Studies. For three of his main classes, his teachers commented he 'needs to exert more effort' while his fourth says 'failure to exert any effort'.

"As you should recall, there was trial evidence that Colin preferred to do his homework with me. It was evidence that called you out for profiting off this case on the first page of several pages of texts on Trial Day 4. You even asked the judge, 'Did you read this?' She giggled and said, 'Yes.' So you certainly should remember this vividly, yet you removed him from his father permanently, ignoring what Colin wanted all along, for the sole reason of siding with his mother and her attorney who pocketed you $25,000 for this case. Why don't you use that money to get my son the tutoring he immediately needs?

"Because of your handling of this case as Best Interest Attorney, I can't help Colin adequately one hour a week (yes, it's still just one hour because there are no openings for two hours) supervised splitting my time with my daughter where we also eat dinner and play games. He obviously is not getting the help he needs from his mother and the man you allow to play the role of his father.

"West's Annotated Code of Maryland, Maryland Attorneys' Rules of Professional Conduct, Rule 19-301.1 [13] states, 'Attorneys play a vital role in the preservation of society.' Preserve Colin's future in our society by getting him tutoring (you've got the cash for it from this case) or have his sudden and obviously explicable failure remain on your conscience."

That email was sent early in the school year, but the kids' grades plummeted throughout the 2019-20 year. The $25,000 refers to the amount that my ex-wife had paid her, and doesn't include the amount that I've refused to pay.

In May 2020, I emailed the BIA again and attached their report cards. The email, found in Chapter 13, highlighted Ethan failing 5 of 6 classes, Lucy failing all 6 of hers, and Colin failing 4 of his 5 core subjects. The BIA billed me $70 and ignored the important role I played in the kids' lives.

Meanwhile, the kids inherently learned something must be so wrong with mental health daddy that they should keep their distance. The same treacherous alienation that provoked Ethan to lie to the court within months of our estrangement had taken hold for years with Colin and Lucy—and theirs was court-backed.

Once money to reopen the case appeared in 2022, I successfully earned that emergency hearing. After the first court appearance, the BIA, whose hair since grew so homely and long that I didn't recognize her, spoke to me outside the courtroom. "You should've done schoolwork with them during your visits instead of playing games."

In disgusted disbelief, I said, "I had one hour a week with them. They each miss over 20 assignments every week. How can I possibly catch up on what they've learned, help them understand it, and complete 40 assignments in one hour?"

"Well, don't blame me," she said. "It's your fault you don't have your kids."

I ignored her outrageous comment and continued. "There's barely enough time to eat dinner and play a game or two, and I'm supposed to be their only school parent? Why did you take custody from me?" My exasperated voice echoed through the building, causing a police officer to scramble upstairs and separate us.

That summer, about two months later, Colin and Lucy spoke to the magistrate who later deemed their futures "sad". The kids were reticent and, particularly Colin, said little.

The magistrate asked Lucy about me. "Did you guys have a good relationship?"

"It was fine," Lucy said. She offered one complaint that she heard me speak to my parents about the court case, but nothing to suggest I was constantly bombarding them and their friends with allegations of abuse. "He'd take us to parks, concerts, and stuff. I don't know. It was fine."

"So there are some good memories out there," said the magistrate.

"Yeah."

Lucy acknowledged positive experiences and was "fine" living with me.

Then the magistrate turned to Colin. "You too? Have any good memories out there?"

"Yeah."

"What are some of your favorite memories of things you did with your dad?"

"I was," he said, pausing as he got a little choked up. "Well, I was pretty close with him, so we hung out and that was fun."

"So, you guys had a pretty good relationship?"

"Yeah. I think so. But I don't want to keep that or anything right now."

That's alienation in a nutshell—refusing a loving parent with whom you've spent tons of quality time without presenting a valid reason. Though Lucy offered one mild complaint, Colin never did. Lucy later said she'd live with me again if Colin wanted to, but his answer, inexplicably, was no.

"I don't really feel uncomfortable living with him or having contact with him," Lucy said. "I feel like the only reason why I would possibly want to is if Colin did. I don't like the relationship that we've had so far. I don't enjoy hanging out with him like I used to."

Five years of supervised visitation had taken their toll. Lucy said she used to enjoy hanging out with me unsupervised, but I guess an hour or two in a mental health facility isn't as fun as making slime and roasting s'mores with her friends and dad. Her days of taking the reins of a Pennsylvanian Amish horse and buggy with an Amish family and dad had faded into a distant memory.

Why were they done living with me and in need of supervision?

Two weeks later, at the hearing I missed because my lawyer failed to notify me of the time change, the clueless court magistrate was angry I asked her to speak to the kids.

"Pushing this is only making it worse for him," the magistrate said to my lawyer. "It made it no better for your client. I don't know why he pushed somebody talking to them. It seemed like it was all for naught. Satisfaction, curiosity more than anything else."

I'm sorry that I didn't trust the BIA's reporting, which dates to before the original trial. A while after Ethan smacked me, the BIA stopped by my house.

"Are Colin and Lucy here?" she asked.

"Yes, but Colin's taking a nap."

"Can I see Lucy?"

I asked Lucy to come downstairs, and the BIA walked with her down the street. Days later, my lawyer called me to discuss their conversation. "The BIA claims Lucy told her she wasn't there when Ethan slapped you."

"What? That makes no sense. Child Protective Services (CPS) was here last week, and I overheard Lucy speak to the woman. Lucy said, 'I saw Ethan hit my dad. But I don't know how hard because he didn't fall down.' Lucy was standing two feet away when he smacked me."

I later asked Lucy if she told the BIA the same story she gave CPS. She said, "Yes." The CPS report confirmed my story, not the BIA's.

I submitted questions to the magistrate prior to her speaking with Colin and Lucy, requesting that she ask them about the specific allegations that cost me custody since nobody ever had. She didn't. Instead, she chastised me to the lawyers.

"I just wish he would take a look at what the kids are going through as a result of all this. I would love to work on the school issue, as opposed to the direction those questions really indicated to me in terms of where he's going with this. I would love to move our focus to that."

School issues are a symptom of a greater problem, not the only problem. If the cause is never addressed, school concerns will never be resolved. Unfortunately, that continues to be the case. The kids' grades were great during the first quarter after having the fear of court stir them, which is also when the boyfriend left, but they spiraled throughout the year as Colin failed five fourth-quarter classes.

Colin and Lucy met the magistrate in June 2022, two months after police notified my ex-wife she'd have to appear for an emergency hearing. That same night was our last supervised visit together, where an unfortunate confrontation broke out that April evening.

24

DADDY DAUGHTER DONE

W E WERE HIS FAVORITE FAMILY to supervise. He told us so every week with a smile. "You're so easy. It's wonderful hearing your laughter and seeing how much fun you have playing games together. Most families rely on electronics, but not you. I love watching you."

This new supervisor took over for the Mental Health Association after Covid shut down our visits for over a year. My ex-wife and I agreed to this privately run visitation center in Hagerstown, saving each of us the hourlong trek to and from Frederick.

Close to home, my dad accompanied each of these visits, and clearly the kids were having a good time. But these two hours confined in a room with a couch, chair, coffee table, rug, and TV weren't home. It was a far cry from freely exploring Maryland's Renaissance Festival, where we rode an elephant amidst a thousand actors replicating an English village during Henry VIII's 16th century reign.

It was April 2022, two months after we resumed visitation at this new place. Lucy celebrated her 17th birthday with cake, games, and gifts of makeup, manga, and her favorite BTS trinkets.

"How do you know about Rare Beauty?" she asked. When a non-existent dad learns his daughter wants to be a makeup artist, he does his research.

With a pending emergency hearing, my lawyer said the kids were old enough to decide where to live. He recommended we coax them back by buying them out. As the two hours accelerated toward their close, we activated my lawyer's plan.

"Lucy, if you could take a trip, where would you want to go?"

"South Korea and Japan."

"Anywhere in the United States?" I asked, knowing I couldn't take her abroad without my ex-wife's permission.

"No."

"Do you want to go to Hawaii? It's beautiful, and it's halfway there."

"I'll get myself to Japan and Korea."

"Colin, what about you?"

"I don't want to go anywhere," he said. "I don't like traveling."

Disappointed by their answers, I had my own, "Oh well, that didn't work," frown.

Next, we offered Lucy her own car and Colin a new computer, further sweetening the deal with new furniture and wardrobes. The kids smiled with interest.

Then I made the mistake of bringing up school grades.

"When we did schoolwork together, you used to have great grades. I'd love to help you again."

"All you ever do is try to get custody of us," Lucy said, her tone growing louder by the second. "I'm depressed! That's why I get bad grades!"

She never voiced depression before, but years without me led her down a dark road.

When I mentioned grades, she cited custody. Earlier that day, I later learned, police served my ex-wife a summons to appear for an emergency hearing. After not having to deal with the court for three years, it threw her for a loop, and she must've informed the kids.

I showed Lucy her report card from our last year together. "Look how good your grades were."

She snatched the paper, crumpled it into a ball and tossed it. "I don't care. I want to see you supervised."

Hearing that set me off. Because I never told the kids why the court ruled for supervision, they only knew whatever outrageous story my ex-wife concocted. Thus, I thought it was time.

"Do you want to know why I'm supervised?" I asked Lucy. She said, "No." But Colin said, "I want to know."

So, I grabbed my phone and played a 30-second audio clip of the judge. They heard the judge say that Ethan accused me of telling them and their friends about abuse. Colin's face puckered as the supervisor asked if they wanted to go.

Then I played a second half-minute clip of the judge stating the falsely alleged abuse was her reason for ordering supervised visitation. The supervisor encouraged an end to our two-hour birthday visit 15 minutes early. I don't know how much the kids heard of the second clip over the commotion.

On their way out the door, I said, "I'm supervised because I supposedly tell you and your friends about abuse. You know it's not true. What would your friends say?"

After that incident, with our freshly reopened case and a looming emergency hearing, my ex-wife stopped bringing them to visitation. The BIA claimed Colin and Lucy no longer wished to see me. Other than a few brief, surprise visits at school and the bus stop for Hanukkah and birthdays, they didn't for a year.

The only light from having supervised visitation halted was the massive financial savings, because it cost a fortune to visit them. About 20% of my monthly income went to visitation centers for one hour together, which doubled once they upped us to two hours. And the BIA wondered why she wasn't getting paid, not that she deserved to.

My credit score was almost 800, but one of my red flags said, "Your largest credit limit on revolving accounts is too low." I tried to increase it, but because the BIA has $40,000 in judgments against me—and counting thanks to interest—I couldn't even get a credit card with a $300 limit.

At least I haven't been threatened with jail for not paying her, the way many others have. I'm familiar with living absent a cushion of funds, but not because a thief and kidnapper insists on payment for wrecking my family.

Before the BIA cost me my kids, our day at the Renaissance Festival left my bank account empty, but spending its final few dollars to calm Colin during a stuffy crisis was worth its weight in gold.

Near the end of the long day immersed in jolly Olde England where royalty, magicians, and jesters broke into spontaneous street acts, we chanced upon a rock-climbing wall. With the scent of fish and chips floating through the air, Lucy couldn't wait to give it a go. Neither could Colin until he realized sad-looking stuffed dragons were anchored to the top by a bell meant for ringing.

"Daddy, the stuffies are tied up there. Get them down."

"I can't. They're happy up there. Why don't you climb up and say hi?"

"No. Get them down. They're miserable." He cried the whole time Lucy scaled the wall and wanted to leave. Our amazing day was coming to an awful end. Nothing I said comforted him.

But thanks to merry Maryland merchants, we didn't have to wander far before discovering a shop—one of hundreds at the festival—that sold stuffed animals. Colin was obsessed with his stuffies, so when I offered to buy him two stuffed dragons he could rescue instead of the ones high atop the rock wall, he lit up. Their cost emptied my wallet, but it was so worth it. Invigorated with renewed cheer, he wanted to stay so his new stuffies could watch the jousting tournament.

Though he loved small stuffies like his Renaissance Festival dragons, he lived for his Colin-sized stuffy collection that began with a three-foot brown monkey named Jumbo. Ruby, a girl rabbit, soon followed. Then a giraffe, a pink dog, and a brown bear arrived as "You're a good kid" presents. When I want a good cry, I go into his room and hug them. Thank God my dad didn't trash them like everything else.

For Hanukkah one year, a chunky blob of stuffy-shaped wrapping paper as big as Colin sat by the fireplace. It was Colin's pick for his first-night gift. "I think there's a stuffy in there!" The cream-colored bear with green-and-blue plaid winter hat didn't have to wait long to meet his new best friend. A year later, Colin burst into my room, excited as ever.

"Daddy! Daddy! Shmeep has ears!"

"Really?" His hat covered his entire head, with no sign of ears.

"Yeah. Look." Giggling, he reached into a narrow slit of the hat and pulled out an ear. "And there's another one!" From that day on, Shmeep could hear.

Years earlier, while still happily married, Lucy ran downstairs in our old townhome, almost as animated as Colin. "Mommy! Daddy! Look what Ethan did." Smiling, she showed off lots of missing hair. What once were golden-brown locks so flowing, we pinned them out of her eyes with hair clips, became a surprisingly even rice-bowl hairdo several inches shorter.

"I see what Ethan did," my ex-wife said.

"Do you like it mommy?"

"Suuure.?."

Ethan strutted down next, scissors still in hand. "I gave Lucy a haircut. Do you like it?"

"It's actually not too bad," we said. "But don't ever do that again."

Her hair regrew long before our first Daddy Daughter Dance. I was divorced almost a year by the time she turned four, old enough to get her first ticket.

Scheduled around Valentine's Day, a snowstorm took aim at us. Always up for a monstrous snow event, this is the first time I prayed away snow, so we wouldn't miss the dance. One Snowmageddon later, the dance was rescheduled for May, making it our only nice-weather Daddy Daughter Dance.

The annual tradition became our highlight. Every year, in the days leading up to the dance, Lucy and I shopped for her new dress, tights, shoes, jewelry, and hair clips. Some years I did her hair while others were professionally done. I even got her a flower corsage.

We pulled into the Fairgrounds parking lot, commented about how cold it was outside, then checked our winter coats just inside the door. I felt somewhat underdressed. My button-down shirt and tie looked understated next to Lucy. And the quarter of dads wearing tuxes made it worse.

For two hours each year, the dance treated us to an array of Valentine's themed arts and crafts, an unending buffet featuring two chocolate fondue fountains, a DJ, and a dance floor. Little Lucy's chicken dance video is a treasure.

The moment hundreds of balloons dropped from the ceiling brought the most excitement. Lucy and I played balloon volleyball the rest of the night.

Lines formed to get a professional Daddy Daughter photo, printed and framed within minutes. I owned eight of them, one from each year featuring Lucy and her adorable new outfits. They were so precious, my lawyer presented them as evidence during the custody trial. Months later, they found the city dump thanks to my oblivious dad's massive purge.

During the 2017 trial, I thought I revealed more than enough about my warm character. Along with the Daddy Daughter Dance photos, we included team-photo plaques of several of the kids' soccer teams I coached.

Meantime, my ex-wife's indifference was on full display.

After my mom testified, she asked, "Did you see your ex-wife sleeping with her head in her hands on the table?"

"No," I said. "But I saw her falling out of her chair while I was on the witness stand." Leaning sideways with her eyes closed, she slumped over the chair's armrest, almost scraping her knuckles on the courtroom carpet. My ex-wife was completely disinterested in the proceedings.

Perched a dozen feet away, the judge must have noticed I took pages and pages of notes while others testified, and she was barely alive.

Shouldn't that have benefited me?

25

MOM NEVER LIES,
EXCEPT TO HERSELF

M Y OVERLY HONEST MOM CREPT to the witness stand with her walker and settled in on the last day of trial. She answered my lawyer's questions, seated a few feet below the judge who surveyed the proceedings from her lofty pedestal. Upon finishing, as opposing counsel prepared to harass her, the judge said, "I love grandmothers."

Seconds later, my ex-wife's lawyer commenced his cross-exam. "Could you describe your son's demeanor when he gets angry?"

God saw an oncoming bus and told my mom to push me in front. "He yells," she said, as my attorney scribbled on a piece of paper, "That's not good."

"He yells?" asked my ex-wife's lawyer. "Raises his voice?"

"Yes. He takes after his mother." The judge laughed. "It's a gene thing."

"And does he yell inside the house?"

"He does."

"How often does he yell?"

"Depending upon the circumstances, sometimes he's extremely quiet all day. And other times, he's upset about something, he'll really yell. He yells at the situation."

"Does he yell at the children sometimes?"

"Never." That was her most emphatic response in 15 minutes of being crossed.

"Never?"

"Never." The second-most emphatic response was met by my lawyer scribbling, "That's not so bad."

My mom spoke further. "He has never raised his voice to these children. And when Ethan slapped him that night, he didn't raise his voice—and I was right there. And he grabbed Ethan by the wrists, and he said, 'You have got to leave.' Just like that."

As if the lawyer lost his mojo or hit a pothole on a bicycle, his voice cracked two octaves higher when he asked, "Does he raise his voice to you?"

"Sometimes, we'll get into political debates."

"So, he raises his voice to you only about politics?"

"Basically, that's all we fight about." Gee, I wonder why. Look where things led in two months' time. "There's nothing else to fight about," she said. "I agree with him how he raises the children. There's nothing else that we have a confrontation about."

The judge jumped in. "You're like the rest of the world. That's all anybody fights about."

After pausing, my mom said, "He'll come and tell me some things and I listen to him."

"I have to ask," said my ex-wife's lawyer, "because when I asked you the first question about 'Does your son get angry?' You said, 'Yes. He raises his voice.'"

"Right."

"But now you say it's only about politics?"

"That's the only thing. I'm downstairs watching something, and he'll come down, and it's always about Donald Trump. That's what we fight about. And I'll say to him, 'We have gotten through a Civil War; and we've gotten through World War II; we've gotten through Vietnam; I've lived through the protests of the '60s;, I'm a product of the

'60s; I saw the Vietnam War on TV. Trust me Brian, we will survive this.' And that's basically what we fight about. I don't fight with him about the children because I agree with him about how he handles them. We'll discuss it. He'll come into me, and I'll tell him what I think he should do. He listens, and sometimes he doesn't listen. But that's it."

"Who else does he yell to or at?" the lawyer asked.

"It's my husband, about politics. That's it."

"Do you see him yell at other people ever?"

"No, I never have seen him yell at anybody else."

It's a good thing my mom wasn't at my kid's soccer game where I did nothing wrong shouting at half the sideline, my jail cell where I scared the guy in the adjacent cell for being too noisy, or the supermarket bread aisle where the little old lady dropped her shopping list.

Well, the latter isn't true, but three months after my mom's testimony and a month after I contacted The Post, something strange occurred while I was paying for a few items at my nearby grocery store.

Minutes before closing, as the clerk scanned my food, a blond man in his 20s with a doped-up skater look rushed to the register holding a hypodermic needle. "Someone overdosed in the bathroom! He's lying on the floor, and I found this beside him."

The clerk and I darted to the back of the store. Because she didn't want to enter the men's room, I found the guy sprawled on the tile outside the stall taking shallow breaths. As she phoned 911, I noticed a tattoo with a couple names on the guy's wrist, so I read their names aloud. "They love you and they want to see you again. Everything will be fine." Paramedics soon arrived and filled him with Narcan, so everything was.

Amidst all the other daily oddities, I told my parents. They shook their heads and rolled their eyes, assuming I hallucinated the whole incident. I yelled about that.

Shouting at that soccer sideline is true, too, and the lawyer asked my mom about that next, though she wasn't there and didn't remember much of my story.

When the kids began playing soccer, I watched Lucy's practices, thinking she'd have more fun if I coached. And she did.

Before her recent growth spurt that propelled her to an almost-average height like her mom, Lucy was tired of being the shortest kid in her class, something I experienced too. So, she was quick to befriend the one girl on her soccer team who was even shorter. Her parents were both referees, with her dad becoming head ref and present league commissioner. They never would've let their daughter sleep over had I been guilty of Ethan's allegations.

According to Ethan's testimony, the number of kids that would've heard something over five seasons of coaching is considerable. My kids played with many of their same friends year after year, plus plenty of new ones, and they all know nothing alleged was ever said. Though Colin and Lucy only played on rec teams, Ethan played both rec and travel, so his friends were even more numerous.

After one season playing for the highest-level travel team the league offered, it disbanded and was regrouped to include players from a nearby suburb, then rebranded with a new club name. Ethan tried out for goalkeeper as a late walk-on and shined. He joined the team as its first-string keeper, and I discussed helping as the team's third coach.

The two preexisting coaches, whom I did not know previously, were from the suburb. We had a half-dozen preseason practices. Of the three of us coaches, only two ever showed up to practice—me and one of them. Either the head coach or the assistant always called out, and it seemed I was the only one that took helping the kids seriously.

The preseason went smoothly, the parents were kind, and their kids had fun with me. Ethan was excited as ever for me to be his goalie/defense coach. At the end of our last practice, the assistant coach approached me. "Thanks for helping with preseason, but teams can only have two coaches, so we don't need you from here on." It was a lie because teams were allowed three coaches, not two. Ethan was bummed by the sudden news, so I asked the coach for an explanation.

In a long-lost email, the head coach said, "The parents from our suburb don't want you coaching. They heard of you before and said, 'If we knew he'd be here, I wouldn't have put my son on the team.' You're berating the kids, and they don't like it."

The email couldn't have been further from the truth.

I only knew a couple of families on Ethan's team and their kids, all from our city, not the suburb. And they loved me.

The only people from that suburb I knew were from a soccer team that Lucy played against. Because they were a better team, their coach offered a couple of girls to help us out. We played them several times, and girls from that suburb wanted to play for me. One of them, whose father was both the assistant coach and a league referee, hugged me and insisted she play on my team with Lucy every single time.

For Ethan's new travel coach to claim I had a bad reputation among families from that suburb was ludicrous. So, I wrote a two-page letter to the head coach. At Ethan's next practice, he blustered toward me in front of all the parents he'd known for years. "The nerve of you to write this diatribe!" He went too far. I went to the dictionary to discover the meaning of diatribe.

Ethan still played on his rec team that season, and I still coached it. A few weeks after my bitter, sharply abusive denunciation, attack, and criticism, our rec team was slated for a game involving many of the suburb's players. They were managed by the two coaches who cast me off.

Ethan played lights out, easily his best game ever in goal. Then midway through the second half, the head coach's son was injured. It wasn't serious, and his son approached him on the sideline. "Take a knee," the head coach said. But the kid refused. "Take a knee! Take a knee!" The coach's anger escalated as his son continued limping toward the sideline. "Get down! Get on your knee!"

"Stop berating your player," I said down the sideline, still peeved that he accused me of "berating" kids. With that, his son's injury no longer mattered to him.

He hot-footed over and looked up at me, which doesn't happen often. I'm not tall, but I'm the perfect height for a world leader. Think Angela Merkel in high heels. Or Adolf Hitler in high heels. Sorry, just wanted you to imagine Hitler in high heels, but we are the same height. And so is Millard Fillmore.

The referee tried to intervene as the coach shouted at me inches away. "I'm gonna knock you out!"

"I heard that," said the ref. "It's noted, and I'm informing the league office."

More howling emanated from across the field. On the opposite sideline, the parents who were kind when I coached their children began taunting me. The last time they saw me, mere weeks earlier, they witnessed the head coach lacing into me, so they hollered their own choice words as I jogged across the field.

"You know nothing about me!" I said. "I was good to your kids."

The argument with the parents continued in the parking lot at game's end. Cooler heads prevailed, and we left our separate ways.

Days later, the league commissioner and I spoke. "You did nothing wrong," he said.

I wanted to present a hypothetical. "Let's say I did something wrong."

"You did nothing wrong."

"Well, let's say I did something wrong."

"You did nothing wrong."

"But let's say I did something wrong."

"You did nothing wrong."

"Can I say this?" He shook his head and relented his adamant stance that I was completely in the right.

The commissioner arranged a dinner at a local restaurant involving ten of us, including some league representatives, the head coach, his dad, and the assistant. Seated around a long table, the head coach and I faced each other in the middle. I presented the email I wrote in response to his accusation that I berated children. The coaches grabbed the paper, glanced at it, and said, "This is complete fabrication."

Fuming, I stood to walk out, tired of people calling me a liar. "I'm taking Ethan off the team."

Ethan was spared a winless season. Should I be surprised that team had the worst record among all the new club's age and gender groups?

"If the referee makes an official complaint about the threat," the commissioner later said, "you both would have to be suspended for a season while it's investigated. Or we'll just let bygones be bygones. We'll all drop it. The easiest thing would be to not coach Ethan's last two games. You can continue coaching Lucy and Colin now and resume with Ethan next season."

And so it was.

The following season, Ethan joined his more prestigious new club with his longtime best friend from school. At their first practice, my ex-wife leaned against her van and said, "I met a boyfriend months ago and he moved in last week."

Was that sudden enough?

It's what the BIA meant when she said, "It's very unfortunate that dad didn't know that [the boyfriend] was moving in."

26

MARTIN & ME

THE INJUSTICE PERPETRATED AGAINST MY family reminds me of the civil rights movement. Today's judges and entangled lawyers are flush with power to suppress us parents who can be easily marginalized by the court system. Impotent against the court, there is practically nothing we can do, and they know that. Speaking up, perhaps to our own peril, is about it.

"There comes a time when silence is betrayal," said Martin Luther King, Jr. "Our lives begin to end the day we become silent about things that matter. In the end, we will remember not the words of our enemies, but the silence of our friends."

In his famed "I Have a Dream" speech at the Lincoln Memorial, he said, "Now is the time to make justice a reality for all of God's children. It would be fatal for the nation to overlook the urgency of the moment." Those words ring as true today as they did in 1963.

I turned my four-day visit with my rabbi in Florida into a 16-day road trip featuring numerous civil rights sites across the South. From their demeaning arrival at the slave market in Charleston to the Rosa Parks Museum in Montgomery, at the site where the bold woman refused to give up her bus seat to a white man—opening the case that gave rise to King and the civil rights movement—I charted the course of our country's wicked oppression.

In Atlanta, I stood side-by-side with King at his final resting place. He peacefully lies between his family's church and his childhood home where he should've died twice—either by falling over the second-floor railing two stories into his basement, or from that upper floor's full-length window while imitating the Green Hornet as he careened over the roof, down the front steps onto the concrete below. Overcome, I watched the football field-sized pool rush upon the words, "We will not be satisfied until justice rolls down like water and righteousness like a mighty stream," before settling around his tomb.

I visited the modest homes of his later life in Atlanta and Montgomery, the one which was bombed amid the Montgomery Bus Boycott.

Inside the Rosa Parks Museum, King's immortal prayer was on display. A few nights before the bomb exploded on his front porch, he received a threatening phone call. Late that evening, as his strength and courage waned, he appealed to God at his kitchen table for renewed vigor.

The Lord answered him. "Stand up for truth. Stand up for justice. Stand up for righteousness. I will be at your side forever."

Though my courage hasn't wavered, it's been tough remaining patient all these years, especially as I see my kids' struggles and endure the thorough collapse of our relationships. I thought things would've improved years ago, but I've learned through religion that God's timing is always perfect. History has taught that I'm doing the right thing, and that God is on my side.

Although I'm unable to care for my kids right now, I know God is. I take solace in that.

27

MARRIED LIFE

WITH A RECENT APPROACHING BIRTHDAY, I perused the huge bookstore the kids and I frequented together years earlier. The place sells everything from albums, books, and posters to knickknacks, trading cards, toys, games, anime-themed blankets, stuffed animals, and clothing. It was a cinch to shop for them there.

Years on, finding gifts has become upsetting.

I browsed the aisles twice over, unsure what to get kids I barely see anymore. Their teenage years no longer care about Roblox and Minecraft playsets or the latest Lalaloopsy dolls. I reminisced over toys they adored years ago as my eyes watered, no longer knowing what they want.

"Why am I not crying all the time?" I asked myself, almost aloud. "After what we've been through, I should be constantly drowning in tears."

I've had to detach emotionally to continue about my existence, at the cost of shedding too few tears upon incessantly gazing around my desk at the surrounding photos of my kids and the envelope containing Lucy memorabilia. The envelope bears her first-grade writing: "Lucy Kotler's first fang tooth, Tuse. December 17, 2013". The lack of expressed emotion bothers me.

What also troubles me is how difficult it's been when I do see my kids. The hours before our visits were the most agonizing, nerve-wracking stretches of time I dealt with—worse than a court appearance. I want to impress my kids, but time is so limited.

Have I planned a good dinner?

Will they like this new game?

What should I ask them about school?

Can I try to interest them in something new?

Probably not. I don't see them enough and can't take them places to encourage it.

The kids think less of me because it's well-noted that a parent with primary custody is instinctively viewed as superior, while the other parent is seen as inferior. How much more so when the inferior parent is supervised in a mental health facility with lurking security?

Our time together these past seven years has been anything but natural. Everything feels forced. Our relationship used to be spontaneous, free-flowing, and candid, without giving anything a second thought. I call it the joy of parenting. But it's been so long, and they were quite young, so they barely remember that.

By the time Lucy and Colin grew old enough to decide where to live, years of trauma, alienation, and unwarranted distrust of dad had settled in. The court couldn't care less that they caused it. They'll finally listen to these kids, years after the damage has been done. But seven years ago, when the court recognized that Colin and Lucy expressed no concerns about living with me, they were removed with immediacy and indifference. Those innocent children don't realize they are tormented by the court's contempt—and an atrocious visitation supervisor.

As much as I've raved about two of my visitation supervisors, a third was as bad as the BIA. Almost two years into my supervision at the Mental Health Association, my supervisor who met The Post and wished everything worked out for me was off to greener pastures. So was the site supervisor, my favorite observer, and pretty much everyone else.

With a new cadre of women running the facility, nobody seemed to have knowledge of my predicament. They were supervising my behavior unaware of what they were watching for.

On February 16, 2020, one month before Covid struck, I sent the new supervisor nine emails, including the letters from my nephew and Colin's friends, the emails detailing Colin's refusals to go back to his mom, and the five-page story I sent to The Post. It's all stuff my old supervisor read. They were opened and "read" in three minutes—in other words, she clicked and closed them without reading them. I approached her regarding her disinterest in helping me and my children. "Why didn't you read the emails?"

"Because they don't matter," she arrogantly said. "That's not my job."

"Do you know what I'm accused of that the court said necessitates supervision?"

"No."

"Then shouldn't you read the emails?"

She walked out. For a few weeks, I persisted in asking her to read them, assuming she'd make an important witness. But she refused.

I arrived at visitation in mid-March prepared to celebrate the Jewish holiday of Purim with Colin and Lucy. I wrote a Purim play to enact, printed character masks to decorate and don for the play, and brought some Purim-themed games like Pin the Tail on Haman, the wicked villain who plotted destruction of the Jews.

"Lucy couldn't come," said the supervisor as she settled into the room for my visit with just Colin. "She has her first tennis practice tonight." A second woman joined the supervisor with her own note-taking clipboard.

I pushed back our Purim celebration for another week and huddled on the floor with Colin to play two-player games on the iPad the way we used to for years back home.

Still concerned that this supervisor took no interest in helping, I said, "You have another person in the room to watch us. The emails are in my bag, so you can read them now."

"No," she said from her chair. "I'm not reading them."

"Why not?"

She rose from her chair. "Colin, the visit is over. Come with me."

Enraged that she wanted to end our sad little Lucy-isn't-here-so-we-can't-celebrate-Purim visit after 15 minutes, I stepped between her and my son. "You are not taking Colin out of here." She let our visit continue.

At hour's end, Colin left, and she wanted to speak to me. "You need to know why I'm here," I said. "You're not doing your job if you don't, and you're doing nothing to help my children."

Before our next scheduled visit, the facility shut down for Covid. No visitations were imminent when I received a letter from the Mental Health Association that said they're ending their services for us, based in part on me not appearing while I was incarcerated for over six months.

Two years passed before Covid was in the rearview and I learned we could resume visits at a private place here in Hagerstown. That lasted all of two months before my ex-wife was notified of the 2022 emergency hearing, precipitating the clash at the new visitation center that loved us.

The way my relationship began with my ex-wife should've been a clue that I'd be left heartsick. Days before I knew she was the one, I got stomach sick all over the inside of my car.

Shortly after our life as roommates became boyfriend/girlfriend, I took care of her while she was sick for a few days. Then, on my way home from community college two counties away, I became nauseous. After 45 minutes of I-don't-feel-good driving, only three neighborhood speed bumps separated me from a bathroom. In a rush, I bounced the car over the first hump and it was more than my stomach could handle.

I didn't want to mess up the car, so I held my mouth shut for once. Big mistake. Everything flew from my nose. The putrid smell lasted for days, but it still wasn't as bad as Colorado.

Sick in bed, I dreaded the moment when I'd have to remove the crusted debris from every crevice of the carpet and dashboard. When the illness passed, I stepped outside to clean my car.

It was spotless.

"Did you clean this?" I asked, as she followed me to the driveway. She smiled.

It was a far cry from her perplexed look the day I moved in months earlier. A few days before I joined the residence, I visited her brother, with whom she and her young son lived. I hadn't seen him for years. Little did I know, my mom would get angry at me for going, which led to a fight where she demanded I move out.

So, I spoke to my friend about moving in with him and his sister. He told me it was fine. He told her nothing.

On move-in day, I knocked on the door, holding a blanket and a suitcase, with giant stereo speakers already placed on the porch. She opened it and looked confused. "What are you doing with all this stuff?"

"Moving in."

"What?"

"I've got a lot more in the car."

"What?"

"Can you hold the door as I bring everything in?"

"What are you talking about?"

"I'm moving in. Didn't your brother tell you?"

"No."

"Oh, well, I'm moving in. Do you want to help carry some stuff?"

"Okay."

We wound up becoming best friends and soon began dating. Not long after, we learned we'd be having a baby, then decided to get married.

Before our big day, we laid in bed one morning when the phone rang. My ex-wife answered, and my mom's voice was on the other end. Then I heard some of the worst words my ex-wife ever said. "Oh, I can't tell him that."

Before she handed me the phone, I knew Beasley died. I saw my childhood dog weeks earlier for the last time. With him in the backseat, my ex-wife stopped the car short to avoid an accident. Arthritic and a grayed-face man of old age, he fell off the seat. As he whimpered in pain, I climbed into the back and held him, shedding my own tears, aware that he wouldn't be around much longer. He died at a relative's house while my parents vacationed for the weekend in Colonial Williamsburg. "We never would've gone if we knew," said my mom.

At a recent gravesite visit, I realized I may have killed Beasley before his time. We were best buddies for almost a decade, but when I moved out of my parents' house months before he passed, Beasley stayed behind. He didn't understand why I was gone. I feel like he died of loneliness and a broken heart.

My ex-wife loved animals even more than I did and she lived on Animal Planet. When a pet store hired her, she began adopting fish and geckos, though I put my foot down at the cacophony of parakeets.

Because of her fondness for wildlife, I treated her to a drive-thru safari on our honeymoon in the Blue Ridge Mountains of Virginia.

With the windows down in my brand-new car, we cruised the three-mile gravel road through 180 acres of rolling hills, fields, and forest, grasping our white, plastic food buckets. Deer, llamas, emus, and antelope gently grazed from our handheld food troughs.

Then we moseyed along toward the lesser-fed animals near the end of the drive. An ostrich pecked its way toward a full belly when a couple camels nudged it away. Their giant snouts grabbed mouthfuls of dried kibble until they snatched the buckets, flipped out the remaining food near our feet, then grew annoyed the buckets were empty. As we struggled to crank up the windows without ensnaring a snout, a horned, thousand-pound bison approached. "Sorry, buddy," I said. "There's no more food."

He stomped toward the back of the car as my ex-wife said, "We should go."

"I can't. The ostrich is in front of us." As it smiled through its feathers, the camels came back. Just then, the car jolted sideways.

"What was that?" she asked.

"It's the bison. He's ramming the back of the car."

We reached down and gathered the kibble from the floor mats to toss out the window. With the animals distracted, we ignored the speed limit and made our way out with bison hornprints accompanying us back to our bed & breakfast.

Less than three months after the honeymoon, while still living with her brother, Ethan arrived. We settled on his name because it was Hebrew, meaning "firm" or "strong", similar to the very non-Hebrew translation of Brian, defined as "noble" or "power".

Shortly after he was born, we looked for a townhouse in Frederick, about 35 miles north of Washington, D.C. Because of my low credit score at the time and lack of assets, my parents bought one for us, and we made the mortgage payments. Within a day, we loved our new hometown.

"Have you been to the gas station yet?" she asked.

"Yeah."

"They're so nice!"

"I know. Folks at the grocery store are fantastic, too."

We couldn't believe how warm the people were. All over town, people were kinder than the close-to-D.C. suburbs we found familiar.

With 60,000 residents, Frederick was a good-sized, prosperous city surrounded by farmland—a perfect place to raise kids. Of course, that was long before we became entangled in their corrupt courthouse.

Perhaps I should've known our marriage was destined for collapse when *Wife Swap* became one of our favorite TV shows. Two couples exchanged wives for two weeks, and we loved every minute of it. Another go-to was *Kitchen Nightmares*. I liked it because I accomplished the same changes at pizza delivery stores, but friendlier, and she just liked Gordon Ramsey. Whether we lazily stayed at home or toured the world as Toothless by Puck, our Xbox rock band, we had each other's backs.

When 15,000 real-life strangers joined in chorus to boo her, I made them applaud. At the Washington Capitals' arena in downtown D.C., we went to a game with my dad and the kids. In the last row of the lower bowl, I sat on the end holding baby Colin. My ex-stepson, Ethan, and Lucy sat between me and my ex-wife. My dad was beside her on the opposite end. During a break in the action, the KissCam hit the big overhead screen.

After a few uneventful couples publicly displayed affection, my ex-wife and dad appeared—perfectly framed by the bland concrete wall behind them.

She was stoic while my dad offered his infamous head shake. But hockey fans were having none of it. As groans evolved into heartfelt disdain, I had to step in.

Holding Colin, I scuttled across three seats of kids and ducked in. The building erupted in cheers.

The year Joe Gibbs returned to coach football in Washington, my ex-wife and I planted burgundy and gold mums along our front walkway. An orange cat slinked up. As fast as Gibbsy became our cat, he was gone forever.

We went on a ritzy date to an upscale seafood restaurant in Annapolis, right on the water. Seated on a terrace overlooking downtown and the Naval Academy across the harbor, she had the duck, and I made faces wondering why she ordered that. When we finished our classy, candlelit meal, we snatched the bowl of mints by the front door as we ran out.

That was probably the worst crime she committed during our marriage, or perhaps it was snagging the small bottle of sea salt from an Italian restaurant table. Regardless, it was shocking how she treated me after we split. At least God knows I don't steal anymore.

Despite thieving pennies worth of food, she cared about family, and the kids and I adored her.

Our trips to pumpkin patches were always memorable. Taking hayrides past farm animals to pick pumpkins, losing ourselves in corn mazes, and having my ex-stepson question why I asked him to pretend he's whacking Ethan with an ear of corn from behind were yearly traditions for us.

The annual ritual of copacetic religious holidays, however, were rudely interrupted by the evangelical church. And the bungled vasectomy soon after devastated what was left.

28

That Didn't Last Long

MY EX-WIFE BROKE THE NEWS that we were breaking up the Monday before Mother's Day 2009, 11 months after my vasectomy. The month before, I gushed to my parents how lucky I was to be married to my best friend. To say I wasn't expecting the beginnings of divorce weeks later is an understatement.

"The marriage is done," she said with apathy. "My mom is moving me out."

As I cried amidst blubbering, she said, "Stop with the crocodile tears." After several moments that entailed me grasping for air and something worth saying, she realized my tears were sincere. She softened and said, "I'm moving out for a bit. We can get back together and work things out." That never happened.

The next day, I began packing and moved into my childhood Bowie home with my parents by Friday. That began the back-and-forth for the kids. We shared the start of the weekend until their mom picked them up late-morning on Mother's Day. The thought of Mother's Day without my kids and their mother was too much to bear. Peering out the window, I watched her buckle the kids in the van one-by-one, hoping she'd change her mind and turn around.

When the van peeled out of the driveway, I punched the front door. The door won. Bison horns dent metal better than my hand, which ballooned to twice its size throughout the afternoon.

My dad and I took mom out for holiday dinner. As I cut my steak with my Mickey Mouse hand, I wondered how badly I damaged it. Because of the pain meds for my nerve damage, it felt fine.

The following day, my mangled hand's swelling hadn't subsided, so I accompanied my dad to the hospital to get my mom's medical records. "While we're there, I may as well get my hand checked." The nurse saw it and said, "It's broken." The X-ray soon confirmed that.

They referred me to an orthopedist to have the bones set and placed in a cast. "This is going to hurt," he said.

"I don't feel a thing, but please hurry because it's painful sitting like this."

The door thrust my knuckle into my palm, but a couple opioids had it numbed so the knuckle could be yanked back into proper position without any sensation. However, the nerve damage burn cut through narcotics despite me sitting normally upon the exam table.

How bad was the vasectomy pain? Way worse than busting a knuckle on a steel door.

This was the third cast my poor body needed. The first mended the broken ankle that kept me on the bench for basketball season. And the second was thanks to my suckiness on bicycles.

Long before my ex-wife's brother excused me to a random driver for tipping my bicycle off the side of a two-lane wooded road down an embankment at the car's approach, I learned to ride in my grassy Bowie backyard. I was 16. Though my bones survived another high-speed flight over the handlebars down an asphalt hill, they didn't fare as well at one mile-per-hour.

A woman pushing kids in a stroller neared as I biked slowly down the sidewalk in front of my Bowie house. To allow them past, I inched off the sidewalk at the end of our driveway and put my tire into dirt grooves scraped out by our cars. At super-slow speed, my front tire whipped around and threw me off the bike. I broke the bone at the base of my thumb.

More than a decade later, the poorly thrown punch damaged the opposite side of the same hand. The first two casts were white and made a perfect canvas for signing, but this modern era of bone breaks presented color choices. "I'll take pink," I said, as I envisioned having to play a motherly role to my daughter whenever she came over. That pink cast made the news.

I found a group for chronic pain sufferers at a community center. A newspaper journalist from the *Maryland Gazette* snapped photos and wrote notes that first day. Most of us shared our stories. By hour's end, the reporter approached me. "Do you mind if I ask you some questions?"

That week, an article landed in the paper titled, "Support groups created to help chronic pain sufferers regain control." It began:

> "Brian Kotler's life was turned upside down last year after a routine operation left him in constant pain.
>
> "Kotler, a 30-year-old father of three from Frederick, suffered nerve damage during a vasectomy and was left with persistent, intense pain up and down his body. He could no longer work or focus on his studies at Frederick Community College, and he and his wife of seven years recently separated because of the stress, he said.
>
> "'I can't sit through classes. I can't read my books and concentrate through the pain and medication,' Kotler said. '...It's just been pain, pain, pain ever since.'

My words also concluded the article:

> "A year ago, if someone said, 'I'm in pain all the time,' I might have said, 'Sorry, it's a fact of life,'" Kotler said with a shrug. "If you don't have it, you don't understand."

The article included a couple of spot-on insights:

> "Chronic pain can affect nearly every aspect of a patient's life but remains poorly understood, and sufferers often carry the burden in silence.
>
> "The subjective nature of pain can make patients feel isolated and many struggle with misconceptions that their conditions should be visible. Chronic pain can change a person's temperament, strain relationships and lead to feelings of frustration, depression, or guilt, according to the Pain Foundation."

The accompanying newspaper photo exhibited my giant pink cast in the foreground, with the group leader nestled behind it.

Looking back, suffering from chronic pain is surviving, not thriving. At the time, I felt like I was in prison. After having been to jail, I can report they're different. But they both suck.

I tried a few different places in search of emotional support, among them was seeking closeness with God. I returned to synagogue a few times and lit Shabbat candles once. But it didn't last. My wife was changing her name to my ex-wife, my kids were gone half the time—then most of the time, I suffered in constant pain because of that doctor, and I couldn't run my hockey website, work, or attend school like I was accustomed. I lost a lot in 11 months.

Being alone and disabled, I had far too much time to contemplate why I was being divorced. Was it the vasectomy? Had the pain changed me so much, as the article suggested, that I became unlikable? That couldn't have been it.

Did anything precede that? She first discussed divorce the year before the vasectomy thanks to her attending the evangelical church with her mother and the kids. Once the church became involved, it had an incendiary influence on their opinion of me and Jews. Though I harbor no grudge against Southern Baptists, I hope they can better appreciate the value and worth of all people.

I tried rationalizing other causes, but everything stemmed from that. When her resentful mom paid her way out the door of our family home into one of a divorce lawyer, my ex-wife went along for the ride.

Then she claimed we'd file taxes jointly that initial year and split the money, but before we discussed an appointment date with our accountant, she proceeded there with her mom and received the full $5,000 refund. It was spent in one month decorating the trailer home her mom bought for her.

I applied for food stamps on behalf of the kids, but they were denied. Why?

"Because your ex-wife applied first," said the social services woman as she explained their policy. "The early bird gets the worm." They reward the sneaky one.

My ex-wife stopped by before we split and has since received 100% of the kids' food benefits. Why don't food stamps recognize shared custody? I have no idea.

How did my seemingly happy and loving wife suddenly become so vindictive and conniving?

I searched online for examples of antisemitic hatred and was bombarded with my people's past—the most despicable and well-documented example having been perpetrated by Nazi Germany. Isolated from society by chronic pain and depression, I began reading and watching every available film about World War II, the Nazis, and the Holocaust.

My brain was so saturated that I had a dream about Hitler. For someone who almost never dreams, I was fascinated by swooping in, killing the German leader at a rally, and having Nazis in attendance extend their arms in salute, shouting, "Heil Kotler!" Or maybe it was "Kill Kotler!" It was hard to decipher as I woke up.

The way common citizens fell in line with the government's bogus propaganda inciting blind hatred of Jews drew parallels to what I experienced from my ex-wife, her family, and my own kids. I sought to understand how, without any just cause, 99.25% of a population could blame the remaining fraction for all their problems.

So, with a disability lump-sum that would be slowly siphoned as I repaid creditors, I planned a monthlong trip to Germany. I hoped to meet ordinary folks who either sat silent or brutally cooperated as my ancestors were nearly erased from Europe.

Were there similarities to my experience? My own wife and kids turned against me in a week or two, thanks to teachings found in many churches.

My family quickly eroded, much like my superhero façade in that Hitler tale. Things weren't nearly so ceremonious as we strolled past one another under a stone bridge in some German city, and both miraculously survived.

I posted a website and a few social media accounts introducing the book's premise, a project I could maintain at my pace that could free me from the dependency of low-paying disability. The two largest Jewish TV networks at the time began following my story. But as I prepared the trip, divorce court proceedings delayed it.

As months of two-weekends-a-month visits with the kids became years, my focus shifted to seeing them more regularly. So, I never went.

My ex-wife learned of the website and plan to author a book. So, when I finally got the kids back 50/50 in 2013, she stipulated one thing—to remove the website and postpone writing a book regarding our marriage and family until all the kids turned 18. Not knowing a few years later, I'd be in a similar predicament thanks to greedy, corrupt court officials, I agreed.

As The Washington Post became involved in my headaches with the system, they knew I couldn't write a book without being in contempt. The 2013 shared custody agreement specified two things, one immediately after the other. It said:

"Ordered that neither party will disparage or discuss the other parent.

"Ordered that (Brian Kotler) will not publish a book, blog, website, or other communication regarding the children, the parents, the marriage, or the ongoing relationship, until the last child turns 18."

My ex-wife was rewarded custody by a corrupt judge for violating the first order by inducing Ethan to lie to the court, right before it's ordered that I can't publish a book about it.

That original book idea intended to keep interfaith couples and families together. This one includes those from all backgrounds, and that have fallen apart.

My purpose is to reward my kids with living the truth and having a chance of a quality life. If they were honor roll with college and career plans, I wouldn't want to derail them by publishing a book that upsets the apple cart. But they're not.

With failing grades, no plans for further education, and vehement proclamations of depression, they're in the very-high-risk group of fatherless children doomed to lives of poverty. They face extensive health and emotional problems that make them more susceptible to criminal behavior and likelier victims of substance abuse and suicide.

As the agreement's spirit intends, I just want to help my kids—and hopefully millions of other distraught young victims of courts will benefit, too.

29

Mm-hmm

Nearly three weeks passed after I sent my first email to The Post. The new year of 2018 had begun. There were overwhelming, but cryptic, appearances at our supervised visits, and I hadn't heard directly how the process would play out.

In an attempt to expedite things and hearkening back to their website's appeal for info and documents, I sent The Post another email. It said, "Now that you've had some time to gather the big picture, I'd like to provide you with a few more details that should help some things along."

I enumerated the timeline of events, specified the BIA's negligence, proposed her modus operandi, and alleged further wrongdoing by others. The email's last line said, "There's a lot more where this came from."

But as the next few hours passed, I thought, "God, I don't know if that's enough. I have so much, I should show them a bit to give them ideas of what's coming. Then maybe they'll bring me in."

Looking back, the way they hacked my phone, computer, iPad, and *YouTube* accounts, they already had these emails. But I wasn't thinking that at the time.

That evening, I forwarded eight email chains. They included one that documented a meeting with the BIA just over a month after she threatened me with a court hearing if I didn't send the kids back.

The email, which I originally sent to my attorney, discussed the State's Attorney's decision not to prosecute the weed whacker case because she assumed it best to leave to the family court. I quoted the BIA from the meeting.

The BIA said, "'It doesn't make sense, because this is civil. That's criminal. Murder is criminal. They should have pursued it. To say, 'The BIA's gonna handle it in civil court'—no."

She also said, "4-year-olds are used in murder cases." Why did she insist this was a murder case? This wasn't felony murder that the prosecutor turned to the family law court. It was misdemeanor second-degree assault where the key witness was 13 years old.

Throughout the case, the BIA repeatedly accused me of alleging attempted murder, therefore making me sound overdramatic and deceitful. During the custody hearing, a short time after Ethan's false testimony on the last day of trial, she asked one final question to the State's Attorney. "Did you ever consider attempted murder charges?"

"No."

"I have nothing further," the BIA said.

On the stand, I had to clarify why the BIA's repeated accusation that I was wrongly alleging attempted murder was false.

Like I told the court, attempted murder would've entailed him slicing me with the weed whacker, but I didn't die though I could have. Second-degree assault, which was the official police charge, was the threatening action of the boyfriend holding the weed whacker to my face but not slicing me. Did she press the issue to make me appear exaggerated and dishonest?

Later, the BIA essentially admitted during my cross-examination that she didn't fulfill her job which required her to speak to all her child clients. She asked me, "You stated that I did not see Lucy or Colin after that (weed whacker) incident, but you are aware that I personally went to see Ethan at school. Is that correct?"

"That's correct, yes."

"And then from there the recommendation was made that the children go back to their mother and continue to abide by the court order."

"Based on you speaking to one of the three children that you're the attorney for," I said. "Yes."

"Mm-hmm," she said, then switched topics.

That was mid-October 2017. I lost the kids in mid-November and contacted Colin's friends in mid-December. Not yet knowing the judge and BIA shared a law office, I soon sent my five-page story to Colin's friend's mother, explaining my situation. Days later The Post had it in their hands, too. This is the last page:

"A month after trial closed (the middle of last month) we were called back in for the judge's ruling.

"'Neither parent will get what they want,' the judge proclaimed from the off. Within moments, I realized that somebody in that courtroom would. The judge read off every single thing the BIA wanted, word for word, letter for letter.

"The judge never looked at me as she admonished me so harshly. Things she praised me for during trial were suddenly twisted against me, and not a single negative thing was said about the other side. The whole time, the judge sat facing the BIA on the opposite side of the courtroom from me, and not once looked me in the eye. I'll never call her 'Your Honor' again.

"It's clear what happened in the month between trial close in October and the judge's ruling a month later. With so much devastating evidence on the court record against her, the BIA must have appealed to the former chief judge to get his protégé judge to rule with her.

"One year ago last December, at the same time as the winter break tipping point, the judge wasn't even a judge yet. She was installed in a ceremony that very month.

"And according to a Dec. 2016 article on the ceremony in *The Frederick News-Post*, 'The chief judge spoke highly of his former clerk before the investiture.' I'm sure he'd also speak highly of his other former clerk, the BIA. And with so much damaging evidence against her on the court record, you can imagine what must have happened over that month.

"Judges are completely immune, even to corruption and collusion. It was fatal for me.

"As the judge read the ruling against me, the harshest elements ALWAYS referred ONLY to these allegations. Lose custody—allegations. Supervised visitation—allegations. Do it in a mental health facility—allegations.

"I soon realized that the latter of those is exactly what I had been begging for the past 14 months—mental health professionals to speak to the kids.

"And so far, they seem to be siding with me big time. Every request I've made, they've agreed to. They've allowed me to go overtime during my visits (which they never do). In fact, during my intake with the case supervisor, she said, 'Your case is really unique. Well, every case is unique, but yours is *very* unique.'

"I said to the BIA for 14 months that this is a complex case, and someone needs to speak to these kids. Unwittingly, she handed it to me for the first time.

"During intake, I asked the supervisor if she knows the BIA. She said, 'I'm trying to get to know them, but I really don't know too many. What's her name again?' I repeated it. She tucked her chin, genuinely giving it a few seconds of thought. 'No, don't know that name.'

"But she now knows me and my kids extremely well and I'm certain she agrees with everything you wrote, not the BIA and judge. Where I go from here is a whole other question, however. I still need to find objectivity somewhere in the courts down the road, so who the heck knows?

"At least you now see exactly where I am, why this came about so suddenly, why it must have made little sense to you, and why I am so appreciative that you and a couple others are helping, for which I'll be forever grateful to you all."

Her reply was the last time we ever communicated because I got investigators involved and figured I should go off the grid. She wrote:

"Wow, what an incredible ordeal you have been through. I cannot imagine how frustrated you must be with the court system and the outcome. I hope now with new people on your side, you are able to persevere and receive the fairness that you deserve."

30

CELL STORIES

F AIRNESS FELT VERY FAR OFF isolated in jail as a fake criminal, where it's both hard and easy to manufacture ridiculous ways
to entertain oneself. It's hard to do anything when there's nothing to
do. But it's easy to do ridiculous.

A favorite was doing parkour around the cell, insisting on touching
only metal. That meant climbing from bottom bunk to top, jumping to
the bolted-down stool, onto the immovable table, then long jumping to
the sink, and dropping onto the toilet before bouncing off the handicap
handrail to reach the bottom bed. It was done in reverse too, but this
way was easier.

Other days, I incessantly rang the bell to grab the guards' attention. I asked when I'd get out of jail. They laughed and left.

My cell was the only one equipped with a TV mounted on the
wall four feet outside my door. Out of the blue, a guard powered it on
and tuned to a live Capitals playoff hockey game. Minutes later, I asked
another guard to make it louder. He hit the button that changed the
channel and walked away.

I whittled away time stuffing toilet paper into the wall outlet. It
kept me busy for a good ten minutes, until it shocked me a second
time. Apparently, the small initial jolt wasn't enough to dissuade me, so

I needed to be thrown back two feet. It was odd that toilet paper con-ducted electricity, but I was dealing with stuff in there that was impos-sible unless devised for a purpose. Although I haven't tried it at home to compare. Don't think I want to.

Thanks to a guard's instruction, a euphoric few hours greeted me. "You should see what happens when you chew on paper," he said. I'll tell you what happens. The bliss of drugs in a cell happens. For three hours, I re-upped every 10 minutes biting off another scrap. Imagine my disappointment when paper only tasted like paper again.

I felt like a lab rat. Locked in a cage, they continuously bombarded me with unreal situations, as if they wished to note my response. How far can we take this? What will Brian believe? How far will he go?

One day my vent buddy upstairs told me I'd reap a reward if I stuffed my turtle suit in the toilet, then persistently flushed. After occa-sionally getting special goodies interspersed with lousy jail food, like melt-in-my-mouth beef and pancakes with two types of sweet maple syrup straight from Vermont and Quebec, I believed that. It cost me a dry floor, clothes to wear, a working toilet, and access to washing and drinking water for three days.

Successfully living without water made me question science. Why do people theorize life on other planets depends on water? Just because God created our creatures reliant on it doesn't mean they all are. Ha-ven't we developed humanlike robots that never need an ounce of wa-ter? God does that too. Scientists are chasing down mysteries created by God, and the Lord is always infinite steps ahead.

Speaking of steps, I turned my hard-to-walk-in, oversized orange crocs into ice skates by pouring water on the cell's concrete floor. With enough liquid, I could hockey-stop side-to-side like a goalie scraping off ice chips in front of his net. The day I busted my butt, my two favorite guards rushed over within seconds. "Are you okay?" I couldn't believe how fast they came to check on me. "Yes." I was in much better shape than the guy who almost bled out for a half-day across the way after his cellmate cracked his head against the cinderblock wall, though I was in the hospital when it supposedly happened.

I felt famous early on when the guard demanded I yell, "The news made me famous," and I became it a few long months later. "You're a celebrity in here, bro," another inmate told me in Cell Block F after my sixth spray down with pepper and return from the hospital upstate.

My last three sprays were some memorable ones. One was the day everyone in jail was "my brotha". My air vent buddy above me was glad to be my brotha. The cleaning guys were all my brothas. The medicine line up outside my cell door, including the dude that called me a celebrity, were head banging in delirium as I shouted at them brothas. They were happy to see me and seemed happiest to be my brothas.

Then the one black guard—they weren't thrilled with me calling them "guards"—was even less thrilled about being my brotha. I'll give him this: he paused with the bottle shoved through the handcuff hatch and gave me time to turn before he dusted me with spice.

Later, I was in a cell less cool than the last because the clock wasn't visible. Lights were out in the cell block, and the late-night guard was on duty—again not a fan of being called a guard. They prefer being called "CO" because they're Corrections Officers. But they corrected nothing. All they did was guard us by keeping us alive and ensuring we couldn't escape.

Several of the guards were far nicer than one would expect them to be, but I never liked this guy.

With nothing better to do while the cell block slept, he threatened me with a "new fogger". After a few pepper sprays, fog sounded quite nice. Playing hockey as a kid, rinks often filled with fog during the earliest ice times. Sometimes we played at five or six in the morning, when as a goalie, I stood staring off into white. Out of nowhere, someone would appear a few feet from me. What team are they on? Do they have the puck? Do they even know where they are right now?

Picturing going back in time to a delightful, cold winter morning, I said, "Let me have it." That lying vulgarism burned me with the same darn pepper spray they'd been nailing me with all along. And unlike the last guy, he shot it right up my nose as I closed my eyes and inhaled a deep breath of childhood fog.

I thought I won during the last incident. In the arrivals/departures area, I was killing time annoying a new guard who sat behind the centralized desk. The moment I crossed whatever stupid line he had, he reached for his waist as he bounded off his seat. Because he had to scramble around the desk, I had time to duck behind the cement wall. Not one drop of spray hit me. Only the cell's air was dusted with pepper.

"You didn't touch me with your spray and you can't even get me to cough." For 20 minutes, I let him have it. Then I coughed one small cough and lost. I never coughed again, but it was too late. I was already beaten. God had a moment of glory, and so did the coward behind safety glass.

While decomposing in my cell, the vasectomy pain I dealt with since 2008 atrophied too. It culminated a four-year progression.

In 2014, I began noticing something. It didn't hurt as much as a few months prior. Though things weren't copasetic, it became slightly more manageable. A mixture of lying, sitting, standing, and walking was the best medicine. This encouraged me to coach soccer.

Coaching provided an hour of that combo, so I gave it a shot. I felt good for that short period. The long days when I coached all three kids were tough, but being outdoors in fresh air and meeting new people were therapeutic. Distracting the pain helped my body and brain heal after all those sedentary years indoors. Every half-year, the same reoccurring thought crossed my mind. The pain wasn't quite as bad as it was six months ago.

Kicking the pain pills wasn't easy. Withdrawals are brutal, enough to force any sane person to resume their habit. But I discovered a way around them using over-the-counter meds. I empathize with anyone addicted to opioids.

But before that discovery, while suffering hot and cold flashes as my legs kicked relentlessly in an awful bout of restless leg syndrome, I was too sick to change the TV channel. After a soccer game, mixed martial arts came on and I got addicted to that, too. Worried I'd have to fend off occasional weed whacker attacks for the remainder of my kids' childhoods thanks to the BIA, I signed up for a class.

"I need to defend myself against power tools," I said to my trainer.

"Yeah, he wouldn't have gotten away with that if I was there," he said, significantly comforting me. It was an hour or two a week of adrenaline-fueled pain relief.

During the trial, Ethan testified to a symptom of pill-quitting that should've irritated the judge. The county's largest robe heard him complain that I was fat. All 180 pounds of me sat below at least that much of her when she said I looked fine, but that was after shedding fifty pounds.

The day I reached my highest weight, I walked into that mixed martial arts gym. Keeping up with a 17-year-old chick took me to my marriage and trial weight. Six months refusing food in lockup soon after peeled off 40 more pounds to my high school size.

By the time I departed jail in October 2018, the pain eased enough throughout the day to consider returning to work. So, I applied to a few places but learned businesses don't hire felons. I contacted the company my dad works for part-time as a courier, but since he shared details of my incarceration, they wouldn't hire me either.

Because my state's court stole my kids from me, I couldn't land a decent job anymore. Expecting things to break with the news any day, I stopped seeking employment and volunteered my time and energy at our town's synagogue. I'm so glad I did, because I met my rabbi and best of all, I met my God.

While helping the temple over 50 hours a week, I learned to be thankful for my renewed body and health. So, I began hiking, running, yoga, strength training, and playing hockey to stay high-school sized.

A peculiar moment took place on the ice at the end of an hourlong practice session a year after The Post re-gifted me freedom. A few others were shooting around but exited the ice before the hour expired, leaving me to practice skating, stickhandling, and shooting alone.

With no sign of a Zamboni to resurface the ice, I took advantage of the bonus ice time. After 20 minutes of lonesome practice, a uniformed police officer and his K-9 German Shepherd walked from outside through an emergency exit door. They stepped onto the ice and made their way to the center face-off dot.

There they stood still for another 20 minutes, silently gawking at me before leaving. Nobody else, not even a rink employee, was in sight. Odd moments like this were routine, so I knew The Post wasn't done with me.

I discovered that bigger investigations like mine can last five to ten years. So, I made my peace that I was sacrificing myself and my family for a greater purpose.

The Post continued orchestrating impossible scenarios. To end a four-day solo trip to Deep Creek Lake in western Maryland, I meandered through Pennsylvania to the Flight United 93 Memorial. On arrival in the parking lot, a couple dozen visitors milled about every which way. Amidst a very natural scene, tourists bustled to and from the main overlook while others wandered around the visitor's center.

I detoured to the bathroom. The way I spoke aloud regularly, assuming I was communicating with The Post, I must've said I needed to go. Three minutes later, I stepped out to find nobody. Other than parked cars, the lot was empty of pedestrians. I passed the visitor center without a soul in sight as I marched down the deserted quarter-mile trail past a second overlook.

Alone, I reached the bottom of the memorial site where the plane and its passengers made impact. The monument remained empty as I read the names of those who passed and offered a moment of silence before trekking back uphill.

At the top, I traced the flight path to the main overlook. In peace and solitude, I soaked in the tragedy for a few more minutes. I heard and saw no one. The moment I turned to leave, a man approached down the long desolate walkway from a hundred feet away. He was the first person in half an hour. Many others convened in the once-empty parking lot as I left.

Then there were the duct taped cars. Parked on my street and beside my car all over town, vehicles were held together or highlighted with tape of all colors, from silver to black to yellow to blue to red. After ditching my van in the drink, my parents offered me Grandma's 20-year-old Buick. Recognizing all the tape jobs down our street lined with modern middle-class duplex homes, my dad said, "You have the nicest car in the neighborhood."

Taped cars followed me everywhere every day, and they awaited my return home. After being convinced to stop photography the day I found the lotto ticket, the most jacked car of them all sat in front of my local gas station convenience store that afternoon. I wanted to snap a picture, but refrained for my own good.

Years later, it stopped—or I stopped looking. But it was bizarre, and my dad noticed it too.

From all my temple time, I learned Shabbat is a 25-hour day, which begins 18 minutes before sunset Friday and ends 42 minutes after sunset Saturday, when the third visible star fills the night sky.

Late one Shabbat, I put that theory to the test. So, I parked my car in an empty lot and braved the cold breeze to count stars. With whatever radio station was on in the background, I stared upward and waited.

"There's one." Half an hour after sunset, using the *SkyGuide* app on my phone, I confirmed the first evening star. Eight minutes later, another.

Before the third star twinkled into view, a certain song began blasting on the radio. "But baby, I've been, I've been praying hard. Said, 'No more counting dollars, we'll be counting stars.'"

Boosted by the perfectly synced-up music, I counted the third star at exactly 42 minutes after sunset.

One day, while alone in my bedroom recalling a crosswalk's new audible time countdown, I said aloud, "Wouldn't it be funny if the walk signal counted down the time while the stop hand in the other direction said 'Wait,' repeatedly?" The next day, at downtown Hagerstown's main intersection—up the block from the revitalized Maryland Theatre and a prohibition pub—I waited to cross the busy street.

As one direction's timer counted down the time to cross, mine said, "Wait."

"10, Wait, 9, Wait, 8, Wait, 7, Wait, 6, Wait, 5, Wait, 4, Wait..." It was just as funny and even more obnoxious than I imagined, and was back to normal the next day.

While I was living in awe of my newly fabricated world, my kids' downslides worsened. Woefully, the court always ignored my ex-wife's admissions that she had trouble with her kids when they face challenges. During the hearing, and her deposition a month earlier, she spoke of issues regarding my ex-stepson after she broke up with me.

Following years of drawing remarkably close, with me injured as stay-at-home dad, he had just achieved his first perfect marking period of straight As. Then the marriage ended before his next report card.

My ex-wife told the court why he moved to his dad in North Carolina a short time later.

"I was having a lot of discipline issues with him. I think that the divorce situation with Brian and me affected him—impacted him greatly. And I felt like he needed to have his father in his life more."

During deposition, with the BIA seated feet away, she detailed why his grades immediately plummeted to Cs and Ds.

"At school, I think he was goofing around and not cooperating with the teachers. We were having issues at home. He was not doing particularly well at school, and I felt like he needed his dad. He needed to have his father involved in his life.

"At the time, he was uncooperative with me. When I would ask him to go into timeouts, he would tell me, 'no,' and he was bigger than me at that point. So it created a difficult environment for me to discipline him. And I felt like having a man, having his father, would potentially be good for him."

She was right because his grades improved.

But what about me? Why haven't my failing kids needed me all these years? What about the fact that every one of these children immediately does worse without me in their lives? Why doesn't the court acknowledge that I'm a quality dad? Why doesn't the court recognize that I matter?

31

THEY EATS A PIZZA

M Y KIDS HAVE MISSED OUT on a lighthearted, hard-working dad. In my youth, it was suggested I become a comedian. But the pay wasn't good, so I became a pizza delivery driver instead. Not everyone finds me funny, but they all need to eat.

Case in point: I parlayed my delivery success into becoming an assistant manager at a pizza chain, where I had a great driver who never laughed. The guy worked 60 hours a week, and so did I. We both worked hard and enjoyed each other's company, but he took life way more seriously. So, my daily mission was to make him laugh, but it almost never worked.

Everyone else thought it was funny when he opened a pizza delivery bag and found my note inside that said, "Make sure you wash me before you open me." But he shook his head and called me annoying. I could make a pizza, though, and he'd eat it—no problem.

He owned the store's single-day delivery record. On a rainy Sunday the week we were short-staffed, we had no drivers. Though we both already worked 75 hours that week, he insisted on taking his one day off, so I came in and drove for 16 hours.

The next morning, as I was erasing his delivery record from the board and replacing it with mine, angrier than ever, he asked, "What are you doing?"

"Changing the record."

"Stop playing around. Put it back."

"I'm not playing around," I said. "Look at my printout." The several pages that passed through our ancient dot-matrix printer proved that I eclipsed his years-old mark by almost 20 deliveries my first day delivering at the store. Sure, I had to give ten orders away for free, but records don't care if they paid or not. I found every customer to be happy that day. He found reason to work harder and smile less.

Of course, God likes to play pranks, too. Another day at that store, I was helping deliver. I parked my car in back with a few other delivery vehicles and ran into the store. When I returned 15 minutes later, some unknown character looked frazzled climbing out of a car. I did a double-take, and realized it was mine. When I peeked inside, my cellphone was missing.

"You took my phone," I said to the disheveled guy.

"No, I didn't."

"It's not in there. Why were you getting out of my car?"

"I wasn't." Despite me watching the guy, he still denied it.

"Why isn't my phone in there?"

"I don't have it," he said. "I can take my underwear off and prove it to you."

Assuming he was lying, I said, "Go ahead."

The moment I saw his tighty-grayed-with-filth-whities, I turned my head. But no phone clanked on the ground. Guess it must've been in a pocket. He walked away, and I ran inside to dial 911. "Ok, the police are on their way."

I waited out back anxiously, hoping cops were close enough to nab the guy before he fled too far. About five minutes later, a cop turned off the main road onto our side street, then made an immediate left into a sit-down restaurant parking lot across the street. A second and third squad car soon followed, one after the other. All three cops began walking toward the restaurant, so I sprinted 150 feet over.

"I called the police five minutes ago," I said. "Somebody stole my phone from my car, and he went that way."

"We're off duty."

"But the guy's right there," I said pointing to the main drag, which happens to be the longest road on the east coast, stretching from Canada to Key West. Better to catch him fast than let him choose his adventure.

As a fourth police car turned in, the woman cop said to her blue brothers, "Just go inside."

"Can't help you," said the other.

All four officers vanished for their probably free dinner, while I waited half an hour for no other cops to show. Flummoxed, I tramped inside to phone police once more. I'd have used my cellphone, but greasy-underwear man was.

"Sir, somebody will be out to you as soon as possible," the 911 operator said.

"You said that 40 minutes ago."

"They're on their way," she said as the phone clicked.

As I hung the phone on its receiver, our friendly college-campus cop stumbled in to enjoy another one of his free pizzas.

"Hey," I said. "I saw somebody steal my phone from my car 40 minutes ago."

"Your store's out of my jurisdiction. It ends at the start of your shopping center. Besides, he's long gone by now."

"Can you do anything?"

"Nope."

"Can you call the cops?"

"Nope. We're not them."

Why are we giving him free pizza?

Another day, the helpful county cops caused my car's windshield to get bashed in. At our old location up the street, a group of teenagers pulled on the door to enter just after our 10 PM walk-in closing time. After shooing them away like any other after-10 customer as I still took delivery orders over the phone, they came back.

"We're closed. Sorry. You have to call for delivery."

After saying the same thing five more times, a couple cops happened to roll up. While cutting pizzas as they slid out of the oven, the cops slid the kids' hands on their cop cars and frisked them. I never saw them come back.

Once the store closed after midnight, I stepped outside to start my 20-minute commute home. Half the windshield was shattered by baseball bats. I ran back inside and phoned 911.

"Tonight while I was working, some cops showed up and frisked some kids. They must've thought I called you because I was constantly on the phone taking orders. Now my windshield's smashed. You should know who did it."

"Sorry, the officers didn't get their names."

Even still, if courier wasn't my favorite job, it was pizza.

My first delivery job during high school was a New York-style pizza joint blocks from my Bowie house. The first day, they sent me on training.

I hopped in the passenger seat of the guy's Geo Metro and we set off on the slow-speed residential streets of Bowie. After ditching the pizza with the customer, we passed a 25-mph speed limit sign at 70, he pulled his emergency brake, and tire tread scarred the pavement as the car whipped round and round, pulling a 540.

"Man, did I choose the right job!"

Though I never drove that dangerously, I was quick and delivered tons of pizza in Annapolis working five to close just about every night of the week.

Among our duties was cutting hot pizza from the oven.

The cheese baked solid to the edge of our deep-dish pizza, so we wheeled the pizza cutter around the crust to dislodge it from the pan. One day, the cheese was so plastered, the blade slipped off the crust into my index finger's first knuckle. I stared at my hand in disbelief. Seeing nothing but white, I thought, despite the pain, miraculously I didn't cut myself. Then blood seeped across a half-inch wide gap of snow-white bone that I mistook for my skin, illustrating how pale I am.

I clutched my finger and found the manager. "I have to go to the hospital."

"Why?"

"Because we can see my bone."

"Gross. Okay, go."

A few steps toward the door, I turned around. "I'm going to faint."

He waved his hands in front of my face and mocked me. "Oooh, he's going to faint. He's going to faint."

Sprawled on the ground with a ceramic tile pillow, I opened my eyes and peered upwards. "My head hurts. Did I hit my head on the floor?"

"No," he said. "You hit your head on the stainless-steel table, then you hit your head on the floor."

"I told you I was going to faint."

"I didn't believe you."

All that joking came back to haunt me as I stood and gathered myself. "I have to get to the hospital."

"Sit down. We already called 911 and they're sending an ambulance."

I don't know how long I was unconscious, but they were off the phone by the time I came to. Between this and once fainting from a shot at the doctor because I hate needles, can you see why I wanted to be asleep for my vasectomy?

One day a driver said, "Brian, a hypnotist is coming to town. We should go."

"For what?"

"Remember when we talked about wanting to quit smoking?"

"Yeah."

"He'll hypnotize us into quitting."

We bought our tickets to get hypnotized inside a hotel ballroom with a hundred others. Seated in a U around the room, our chairs were on the side against the movable partition separating us from the next room.

The hypnotist began. "Close your eyes. Breathe. In...then out. Listen to my voice. Listen to it calm you. Breathe." That continued for a few minutes.

"Breathe. Feel your body getting heavy. Feel your cares melt away. Listen only to my voice. And your breath. Breathe. Your body's getting heavier. Feel your body getting heavier."

I lurched back in my chair, clashing into the partition. After soothing my way through the next 20 minutes, never quite as heavy as before, I was told to stop smoking.

Afterwards, my buddy said, "Why the heck did you slam into the wall? You screwed it up. I was getting hypnotized and you snapped me out of it."

"But didn't you hear to stop smoking?"

"It doesn't help if you're not hypnotized."

To the hypnotist's credit, I didn't resume smoking until the third day. My buddy only lasted through the morning.

After some failed attempts substituting cigarettes with Dum Dum Pops, I eventually quit thanks to a dire health issue that had nothing to do with smoking.

A line of commercials on TV featured young smokers speaking from holes in their necks. Rare as those circumstances always seemed to me, my almost unprecedented vasectomy issues proved that I, too, could succumb to improbable health scares. I think I quit smoking within a week or two.

I missed out on the biggest tip of my life when I returned to Bowie to deliver for that same company under a new franchise.

A fellow driver brought a $9 pizza to the mansions on the outskirts of town. The Washington Wizards' best player, Chris Webber, opened the door and handed the guy a $100 bill. "Keep the change."

A few years later after moving in with my ex-wife and her brother, I overtipped a guy too. Because I seldom carried bills greater than $20, I reached in my wallet and pulled two bills on the darkened porch. The order was $25 so I figured the driver would be thrilled with a $15 tip. We ordered again that night, the same guy came back and I tipped him $8 more.

I later realized I yanked two $50s allotted for my rent payment instead of $20s, so I begged my ex-wife to drive over the next day to retrieve $60 from him. Sorry guy, I'm no professional athlete.

That new franchise was the world's best. They emphasized hard work, hustle, and customer happiness. After a few months delivering, the store manager coaxed me into becoming a manager-in-training (MIT). Several months into my new position, they fired our regional supervisor just as I was primed to become manager of my own store.

The son of a longtime U.S. Congressman replaced him. He and his dad shared the same name, and papa was in the middle of his 24-year term in the U.S. House.

Almost every day, regional supervisors visited their eight stores. They filled in a two-column chart that hung in the middle of the store.

The columns were labeled: "I like this store because…" and "You need to work on…"

This new hotshot supervisor liked us because "Brian is running a perfect shift." We needed to work on "Nothing." Nobody wrote that nothing needs improvement before, but he did it again the next day. On the third successive day, the "You need to work on…" column said, "I'm going to get in trouble because I have to write something, but there's nothing for you to work on. Great job Brian!"

The next day was a Saturday—the Sabbath. Like usual, I was making pizzas and routing drivers, not attending synagogue or otherwise observing our day of rest. That morning, the store manager said, "Brian, I'm letting you put out coupon door hangers today in the massive apartment complex we were recently assigned. You should have a big day. I'm going to leave so you can run your record shift with one other person tonight."

The orders poured in, and we set our store's record Saturday. Of all the orders we received, three of them were marked late after leaving the store beyond 24 minutes old. They still arrived at the customer in about half an hour. Three lates on a slow day is good, never mind a record day.

The supervisor walked in. "Awesome!" he said. "That's this store's first record in a while. Brian, you're doing great. But why isn't the manager here?"

"She wanted to let me show what I can do."

"That's not right. She should be here because you wouldn't have three lates if she was here."

He jumped on the phone and scolded her. Moments afterward, I confronted him. "Why'd you talk to her like that? She just wanted to help me, and you were happy as could be. You know three lates is nothing. Stores have 10 or 20 every night. You should be pleased that we set a record and handled it, not yelling at the manager who devised it."

With that, my path to getting my own store under this guy evaporated, so I asked to move to a different supervisor's store in another county belonging to the franchise. Our team meeting was soon after. The monthly event hosts company leadership from the president and his staff to the supervisors, managers, and managers-in-training like me. It was early in the year, and we met at a hotel and conference center along the Potomac River just outside D.C.

After the company meeting indoors, we broke outside into separate groups. After meeting with my new region's 20 managers and MITs next to a couple other regions, I encountered my old supervisor for the first time since leaving. Weeks after MITs received $100 shoe store gift certificates as a Christmas bonus, I had yet to see mine. I shuffled across the parking lot and asked him, "Where's my Christmas bonus?"

"I spent it," he said, smiling as he opened the door to his company-provided Jeep Grand Cherokee.

"What do you mean you spent it?"

"I went to the store and used the gift certificate to buy myself shoes." His voice grew louder as he turned up the insults. "I'm a supervisor. I make $100,000 per year and drive a company vehicle. You're just a whiny, pussy MIT!"

I slumped away in stunned silence. Among the dozens who witnessed him shouting, a manager I never met before approached me and said, "I'll be a witness for you." A few others echoed him.

For some naïve reason, I responded by working harder to never get a store rather than seek a lawsuit.

Nearly 200,000 people have viewed my nasty supervisor on a *YouTube* video titled "Congressman's Son Goes Crazy Playing Poker".

At an online table with over $40,000 at stake, he won a hand. "I just won $3,000! Remember when I was in 465th out of 486? Now I'm in 75th place!" He jumped from his chair, screaming like he was in a WWE audition. "That's what I'm talking about, baby! Wooo!!! Oh yeah! Oh baby!" The WWE looked elsewhere.

Moments later, he won another hand and really let his computer screen have it.

"I beat him. I have the nuts. Done! I worked that guy! I worked you! I worked you! I worked you! You thought I was being a wuss, but I had the nuts the whole time! That's what time it is! You got a watch? 'Cause that's what time it is!"

That's the same U.S. Congressman's son who spent my gift certificate and insulted me in front of scores of my peers and superiors. Imagine his elation when he got "First Position!"

32

BAD DAD, WONDERFUL HUSBANDRY

ALTHOUGH I FEEL I'VE BEEN a great dad, every parent wishes they had a redo. Jews are well-known for their avoidance of eating pigs and Lucy's well-known for her love of pigs. Put the two together, and it's obvious I wouldn't have tricked her into eating pigs. Right?

Wrong.

God gave me a slam dunk, and I blew it.

"Daddy, I don't want to eat pigs anymore," said nine-year-old Lucy.

"Okay." I played the role of typical, loving dad.

A few days later, I whipped up breakfast, scrambling a few eggs, adding toast and maple bacon, and plated it.

"Lucy, does that bacon taste good?"

"Yes, daddy."

"You know it's pig," I said, heart cold as a winter day far beyond Pluto.

"No, I didn't."

What the heck was wrong with me? She was short and skinny and was considering eating vegan. Afraid she'd become even smaller, I encouraged her to eat meat. No excuse. There's plenty of meat that isn't her favorite animal and best stuffed little buddy.

I'll never make that mistake again.

I want to shift focus from my awful parenting involving animals to my wonderful husbandry, not involving animals.

After a late night of delivering pizzas until close, some friends decided to make it an even later night playing poker. I never played before, so, assuming the wife was sound asleep, I was game. How does that make me a wonderful husband?

Six of us gathered around a dining room table. My friend from work, a few buddies of his, and one of their wives drew cards with me. I never hit on the wife, thereby completing step one to being a wonderful husband. The non-adultery bit earned me some favor with God, too.

By midnight, I knocked her out of the game, heckling her as I absconded with her $50—money for diapers. Step two complete.

Over two hours later, the last guy and I went back and forth for a good 30 minutes. Then my phone rang.

"Shut up! It's my wife. Don't say a word." I clicked the button to end the sonic irritation, only to discover another.

"Where are you? It's almost three in the morning!" Step three complete—proof I don't stay out all hours of the night on a regular basis.

"Umm."

"You need to get home now!"

"Okay, I will."

I said goodbye and received my cards for the next hand. With a two and a nine of mismatched suits, I went all in. Bluffing worked all game long, but he didn't buy it this time. The ear-shattering screams from the phone must've given me away.

Thus, I missed out on a $300 payday in favor of a serene marriage. Wonderful husbandry complete. Cluck, cluck, cluck.

I had no trouble staying up late, but Colin was another story. As bedtime approached, his voice cracked. "Colin, it's time for bed."

"I'm not tired yet," he said with half the words barely audible.

"Yes, you are. You're losing your voice again."

"Okay, dad. I guess you're right."

One night a year, I insisted the kids survive until midnight. My ex-wife had the Christmas-half of winter break and I had them every New Year's Eve. After the enforced fun of wishing each other a good new year, I was often the first asleep since they were beyond overtired.

The best thing about New Year's Day was sleeping in before resuming the early morning grind of school. I recall my first day of school every year after the holidays.

"What'd you get for Christmas?" kids asked.

"Nothing."

"NOTHING?!!"

My kids got to say, "Nothing from my dad."

Ethan had the most astonishing wake-up ability I'd ever seen. Sound asleep near the end of a long night's rest, I'd nudge him. "Ethan. Time to wake up." He opened his eyes, sat up, and jumped out of bed like it was the middle of the day.

Colin and Lucy, however, were not morning people, much like me. I acted as their snooze buttons after pounding my own a few times.

Because my parents drove me nuts with the same repetitive knock on my door every single day, I mixed it up, drumming different beats on their doors each morning before intentionally burning my daughter's breakfast.

"Burnt food tastes better period," said her Facebook page's tagline. She loved frozen chocolate chip waffles toasted on the highest setting, twice. I made the mistake of nicely browning them once.

"What are these?" she asked.

"Your waffles."

"You didn't burn them."

"Yes, I did. The toaster was on the darkest setting and they're crispy."

"Black, dad. They need to be black."

Lucy also loved macaroni and cheese and her basil plant named Fred, from whom she'd crop leaves for her mozzarella, olive oil, and basil treat. Sadly, Fred got sick, so we adopted Fred Junior. After Lucy was taken by the court, Fred Junior passed on. Fred Junior Junior, Fred Junior Junior Junior, and Fred Junior Junior Junior Junior subsequently joined and departed the family. FJ5 is hanging on by a thread on the same window sill where Fred started it all.

Update: Sadly, FJ5 passed away, but I didn't have the heart to change the story. Since his untimely death, I had to buy FJ6 to make pizza hamantaschen and couscous salad for my Purim party.

Sushi was a favorite of Lucy and Colin. Lucy liked eating it so much, I think she named her mom's bird Sushi. Her futile attempts at teaching Colin and me to use chopsticks turned sushi into finger food, much like Colin's snack packs.

"Can I have a snack pack?" he asked almost every day. So, I filled a plate with random treats like string cheese, yogurt, apples, carrots, and muffins that was always received by a giant smile. "Ooh. Thanks, dad!"

Ethan savored mangoes. None of us ate the fruit but him, so I learned how to pick a good mango online. To him, I never chose a bad one.

We all loved the pizza buffet. The first step was ordering a macaroni and cheese pizza for Lucy if one wasn't ready. While watching *SpongeBob* reruns on their wall-mounted TVs, the kids piled on the cheese sticks and pizza until it was dessert time. That's when brownies, cinnamon rolls, and apple pizza pie took the spotlight.

After a ridiculously well-priced meal, they hit up the arcade in the back of the restaurant. Colin loved it so much, we had his soccer team's end-of-season party there.

Recounting their favorite treats, it's hard to believe it's been only seven years. It feels like another lifetime.

We had our routine, but I'm sorry it didn't include my ex-wife. My parents have been married 55 years, and I know of almost nobody in my sizable extended family who divorced.

While my dad performed magic shows and went on sales calls, my mom booked the appointments as she cooked, cleaned, and drove me to friends' houses, school, and wherever else I needed to be. My dad spent a ton of time raising me, too, whether it was driving me to hockey, losing video games, taking me out to eat, or yelling, "Ow! Darn it!" playing catcher in backyard baseball with his under-padded glove. Thanks to him, I always appreciated the role of a father and prided myself on being an even better one. To my detriment, however, my ex-wife didn't value my contribution as a dad.

I haven't badmouthed her mom much in this book, but she deserves it. Aside from teaching my ex-wife that dads are unimportant, both through speech and by example, she's to blame for wrecking my marriage and destroying my relationship with my kids. She lied in court, so much so that it wouldn't surprise me if she masterminded the fib that cost me custody seven years ago.

When my ex-wife left me, she had no money, no job, and no education. She always refused to involve herself in family finances. I could've bought an elephant, and she'd never have known.

Though she baked and decorated cakes, was caring, funny, pleasant, and patient with the kids, she wasn't motivated by much else. It's unthinkable to imagine her house hunting, filing forms for government giveaways, or even submitting a tax return on her own. How'd she do it? By her mom's urging, insistence, and guidance.

She even passed on her Jew hatred. A short time after moving to Hagerstown, I took the kids to a High Holy Day service at the town's synagogue where I later helped. We left about halfway through the service, after hearing the rabbi wish Christians and Muslims well. In the lobby outside the closed sanctuary doors, I said, "See kids. Us Jews wish everyone well and don't say anything bad about other religions."

Ethan said, "Oh, like Grommy." Of course, Grommy is my ex-mother-in-law who did say bad things about other religions.

My ex-wife told the first BIA 15 years ago that, in our final year together, she returned to school and sought employment in preparation to leave me. In reality, I encouraged her to begin working and to attend my community college, seeking to become a vet assistant. And I helped with her classwork.

When she dropped out of school and quit her part-time job the moment we separated, why did the BIA believe her? She should've seen right through it. But with a background focused on helping needy women, she determined instead, everything I did was wrong.

How could my ex-wife afford to move into a new home when she stopped working and attending school without a personal bank account? Her mom bought it and supported her.

My ex-mother-in-law was never a fan of mine. To her, I had one redeeming quality when my ex-wife and I first united. "At least he pays me the rent on time."

Her husband, my ex-wife's stepdad, whom she called by first name, was not much better. During the salvation period of our marriage, we invited him to the interfaith congregation to meet the reverend and rabbi. His first words to them were sarcastic, distasteful, and embarrassing. "So, what kind of church is this?"

"We're not a church," they said with more grace than he deserved. "We share our Christian and Jewish values and traditions while learning about our heritage." A short time later, my ex-wife stopped attending, and as a result, so did I.

Their disgusting behaviors were exacerbated by the heartless court officials who favored them throughout our 15-year custody case. In what is one small blade of grass of a looming nationwide crisis, Frederick County BIAs and judges continuously gave them what they wanted despite their subterfuge and demonstrable lies.

In spite of everything, I don't think my ex-wife is that bad. The court created her. Why follow court orders when court officials permit noncompliance and further penalize the other parent? Why be truthful when they support falsehoods and she reaps rewards?

The court rouses the worst in people. It's left our guiltless children to become complete shambles—and they're not alone.

33

THERE'S WORSE

I F MY STORY SEEMS APPALLING, I found one that's far worse. Some half-dozen years before Maryland trampled on my family, Connecticut was on full rampage. A multitude of adjoining counties' cases presented similar circumstances, featuring the same judges, lawyers, and doctors involved in ruining the lives of parents and children. From Yale professors to a federally incarcerated corrupt governor, pedophilia was allowed to reign supreme. Among many disturbing cases, one poor boy's barbaric story leaps out.

The child was a tad younger than ten-year-old Colin when we were forced to say our final goodbyes in front of his school. His mother was about my age at the time. What was presumed to be an amicable divorce became anything but when the boy showed worrying symptoms that he was being sexually abused by his father. It was an opportunity for high-powered, court-appointed professionals to profit off the repeated rape and torture of the innocent young kid.

The case began with a longtime judge's handpicked BIA—in Connecticut called Guardian ad Litem (GAL).

The GAL billed the mom more than $80,000 over the span of 15 months, only to ignore the most heartbreaking evidence as she sentenced the boy to a life of hell.

The GAL witnessed the father's obsession with massaging the boy's thighs. So did many doctors. Instead of stepping in, they focused on how they could blame his mother. The young boy began grabbing adults' private parts, singing suicidal songs, and hitting himself in the face. He revealed the "Tickle the Weenie" game his dad played with him while he was undressing one night. The troubled boy frequently urinated on his mother's furniture and drew distressing pictures like a frowning boy being punched in the stomach by a smiling man's giant penis.

His body displayed horrific signs of physical and sexual abuse. He came back from his father's house with a bloody rear end and torn skin tissue. His mom photographed it to present to authorities. Rather than condemn the father and protect the child, the GAL and doctors attacked the mother, saying she took the photos to sexually gratify herself. Meanwhile, the father continued to assault his son, leaving him vacant-eyed, rubbing his butt, and walking bowlegged in pain.

After another visit with his father, the child returned to his mother asking for help cleaning his bleeding rear end. The mother took him to Yale Children's Hospital ER, where a doctor called a social worker, who called police, who called another police department, who dispatched an officer, who called a detective, who referred her to a Special Victims Unit detective.

The SVU detective notified the Department of Children and Families (DCF, Connecticut's version of Maryland's Child Protective Services). She also told the mother to keep the boy away from his father pending a late-week appointment to a sex abuse clinic. To do so, the mother had to keep the boy home from school. DCF, which is headed by the wife of the former Connecticut Chief Judge of Family Matters, charged her with educational neglect, a serious form of child abuse.

That judge's successor made the final ruling against the mother in this case. Like the judges and GAL, the police and DCF turned against the mother and never helped the child.

DCF declined the case, so Yale declined to evaluate the boy.

He evolved to singing songs about electric shocks, which he said is what is done to make him forget the other bad things inflicted upon him. But not all was forgotten as he graphically detailed how an object was forced into his mouth to prop it open, held in place by tape with holes punched in, through which human excrement was forced into his mouth. Moments after he described this to a GAL-appointed doctor, the boy vomited. The doctor blamed his upset stomach on the Chicken McNuggets he ate hours earlier.

Another GAL-appointed physician conducted an evaluation on the parents for $12,000. He determined the father had a mild personality disorder, but the mother was worse. Because the report indicated that the father may have had an issue, the GAL hid it from the mother and her attorney until after the court hearing where the child was taken from mom and forced into supervised visitation with her.

The visitation supervisor was chosen by the GAL and had no training in caring for children or recognizing signs of abuse.

The mother was afforded much more supervised time with the child than I had—upwards of 40 hours a week early on. But she paid for it at $85 an hour, similar to the rate charged me for one or two hours. How much money did the GAL's referral make the visitation supervisor over a 14-month period? $123,000.

During that 14-month stretch, a different doctor was appointed by the court to be the custody evaluator. This doctor billed the mother over $17,000 to recommend the boy live with his father, and the mother should continue her supervised visits.

Why would the custody evaluator turn a blind eye to such blatant evidence of abuse? A decade or two earlier, he directed a program at one of the oldest and most esteemed mental health centers in the United States. Around that time amidst a church scandal, the center catered to hundreds of Catholic clergymen, from New England and beyond, accused of sex crimes against children. After a brief stay and an all-clear, many of those so-called men of God went back to preying on children.

Perhaps the worst offender, with several hundred, if not thousands of victims, was a doctor at a nearby Connecticut Catholic hospital.

The child's mother attempted to bring her own sex abuse expert into the case, but the GAL blocked it. Later, two separate judges made that ruling official, then sealed the case. It cannot be found on Connecticut's Case Look-up system.

In February 2012, one of those judges gave full custody to the father, with no more supervised visits for mom.

Later that month, the GAL was nominated by the governor to become a judge herself. Despite protests regarding this case at her confirmation hearing, a judiciary committee voted 21-16 not to delay the final vote where she was confirmed. She remains a judge to this day.

The judge who handed down the final verdict retired, and like many retired judges, currently runs her own law firm where she mediates, offers consultation services, and performs private judging on all civil matters.

After a distinguished career helping pedophiles elude justice, the custody evaluator retired from being a professor at University of Connecticut and Yale. He still has an address for his medical practice despite being about 90 years old.

Ten years before this boy's case hit the docket, the custody evaluator and the judge who took custody from the mother were appointed to the state's Commission on Custody, Divorce, and Children to study those three issues in Connecticut and make recommendations to improve the system. The governor who appointed them was one of 11 American governors ever to be incarcerated for corruption.

And as of 2015, the child hadn't seen his mother in three years. From what I've discovered online, I'd be surprised if that isn't still the case today.

Many other families have stories too. The more we learn, the better off we'll be. A new book genre should explode onto the scene: "The Court Screwed Me".

34

THEY COULD DO ANYTHING TO ME

T O WIPE THAT OUT, I went through this.

"We're sorry we have to do this, Mr. Kotler." Those words turned an ordinary day in Cell Block F into one I'll never forget.

Before hearing that phrase, I laid alone in my cell doing nothing. I could say I was counting the cinderblocks in a column from the concrete floor to the concrete ceiling, but that would have entailed doing something. I was doing nothing.

Bang! The pounding thud of the handcuff hatch opening was a welcome relief from the monotony of wasting away.

"Stand up and turn around."

I backed up to the hatch and happily received my steel wristwear. It wasn't often I was let out of my cell in the middle of the day—only for a haircut, talking to the social worker, court appearances, and visits from my parents or the lawyer they hired. It amounted to once every few days. Instead, the guard ushered me toward the shower. "Oh! A daytime shower!"

"No," he said before uttering that famous line. "We're sorry we have to do this, Mr. Kotler." We didn't go by "misters" in that place. "Kotler! You've got a visitor." "Kotler! Get down from there." "Kotler! Stop flooding your toilet."

"Have a seat," he said, pointing to a prison-style immovable steel object on wheels. Four glistening shackles accented the litany of thick black straps on the restraint chair. Three other guards convened, each grabbing a limb of mine to ratchet into its manacle. "Tighter than that," one said to another. "Tighter." As the cuffs cranked into my wrists and ankles, they clamped the straps so it was impossible to move.

In stepped the warden. They forced me to spit on his uniform and gently rewarded me a second later with a spit mask—a tied-on, full head covering with mesh to see through.

They wheeled me into the arrivals/departures area containing the eight cells encircling a desk. That day they were empty. As a fifth guard with a thick beard filmed using a small digital camera, they dumped me into one of the cells. After 20 grueling minutes, they freed me from the restraint chair and slammed the door shut behind them.

I had just enough time to untie the spit mask when a guard dropped open the hatch.

He shook a little black canister of pepper spray through the slot. Then he paused so I could read the word "FOXY" on the label, accompanied by a pretty she-fox. "This is different," he said with a wink and a smile.

After all those other pepper sprays, I was convinced this was new. "Yeah, okay," I said with a nod. Then he sprayed me. He was right because this was different—no burn or oxygen-consuming pepper.

Woah! Drugs just kicked in. It was more ecstasy than ecstasy, trippy as LSD, and what was with my voice? I sounded alien.

Bang! The same guard shoved his hand through the hatch and quickly doused me with a non-FOXY bottle of spray like a punk. That bottle burned, but not my skin.

Like glowing charcoal in a grill, my insides were on slow-roasting fire. Waves of euphoria and pain consumed me. That second bottle wasn't pepper either because my skin was fine and I had no coughing fit. But my God, how do I cool off my body?

I rushed to the sink and ran cold water over my head. "I feel amazing! Owww!" I never felt so good and so bad simultaneously. Colorado had nothing on this. I splashed water on my face, chest, arms, and thighs. Guards watched, still filming as the burn increased and I blurted out my social security number and celebrity crush. Was this a truth serum too?

New rules were shouted through the door as the euphoric high dissipated and the burn reached new levels of excruciation. "Dunk your head in the toilet if you want to cool down," a guard said.

While most of my body seared under intense heat, my hands and feet felt fine. Those shackles etched quarter-inch depressions into my wrists and ankles. Though they kind of hurt, the excessive burn failed to ravage my extremities, presumably because the super-snug cuffs were intended to restrict the circulation.

I was soaked head to shin seeking relief from the agony when my cell door popped open. A few guards hurried in with that transport device of terror. As the burning swelled, they bound me to the chair tighter than before. Then they wheeled me through the still-empty arrivals/departures section to a neighboring cell that featured a clear view of the wall clock. The guards departed, and the door slammed shut. Why didn't they unstrap me from the chair this time?

I watched the hands on the clock as I writhed in agony. The more I moved, the more the shackles cut into my wrists.

Time never passed so slowly.

Wait, I've never seen time move so quickly. The minute hand sped up and darted halfway around the clock like a second hand.

Oh no, it stopped moving.

"What are you doing with the clock?" I yelled. "Get me out of here!"

The minute hand moved backwards five minutes, so I shut up.

The more I wanted to move, the more the cuffs dug into my skin. With an unending full-body burn, I struggled to maintain stillness and breathe basic breaths. Thankfully, a fly kept me company inside the cell. I watched her buzz around, helping my mind to ease.

Two guards burst in. They unhooked me from the restraint chair, and I shook my hands to encourage some blood flow. It's good it didn't work. The etchings in my wrists became full-fledged engravings, which helped my fingers and toes because the inferno escalated.

After some harrowing time ranting in my cell, a guard instructed me back to normal. "Run cold water into your eyeballs. Soak a roll of toilet paper in cold water." The instructions grew weirder, but I was in no position to question their effectiveness. "Put your mattress on the floor by the door. Lay on it and keep your eyes closed. Tear off pieces of toilet paper and apply them to the areas that burn most. You can suck water from the toilet paper as a drink to cool off. Whatever you do, don't open your eyes."

I dashed to the sink, flushed my eyes with cold water and doused a roll of toilet paper. On the mattress, I inhaled the cool air that rushed under the cell door as I closed my eyes. The toilet paper tasted like pepper, but the chilly water was refreshing. I ripped shreds off the extra-thick roll to ice down the fieriest areas. As the paper warmed from body heat, I grabbed another piece.

My toughest struggle was keeping my eyes closed. They insisted on fluttering open. I didn't know how long I was supposed to endure, but my wet toilet paper dwindled away.

The slow burn was unbearable and my eyes opened. So, I started over.

The experience, however long that was, proved too intense. To combat my still-searing body, I doused my eyes under water longer and soaked an entire roll of toilet paper, not just the outer layers. Then I settled in for round two.

I squeezed my eyes shut for dear life as I applied toilet paper to minimize the excruciation. The muffled conversation between two guards seated at the centralized desk was too soft to make out the words. Other than that, the silence of the chaotic facility was heavy.

I was the burning bush—ablaze, but unconsumed. Would this ever end?

After months of ordeals with The Post, I wondered if this was the last stand, the final boss if you will. When it's over, will they release me into the welcoming, cool early spring air? Will news cameras and reporters finally unveil my plight and reunite me with my kids?

Time passed. It burned.

Everything burned and burned. And I know living with burn because life ain't so quick and simple. This was different—my whole body was searing.

Why has this entire portion of the jail been so quiet? Why was I alone when I'd always seen 10 or 20 people grouped in these cells? The whole thing couldn't have been more bizarre. And it hurt.

Then something new. The thunderous sound of clapping hands pierced hours of silence. "Am I done?" I asked. The applause continued. "Is that it? It's over?" The ovation intensified. "I'm done. I'm opening my eyes now and standing up."

Within moments, a guard popped the hatch and slid a brown-bag lunch to me. I crunched on my apple as the pain subsided.

I don't know what that was, but those people meant business. They could do anything to me.

The spit mask that kicked everything off followed me whenever they released me from my cell. This included a visit by a court official at a hearing to determine whether to transfer me to the state mental hospital, an overdue reprieve from the insanity of this jail incarceration. That spit mask made psychosis certifiable, and I was off to the crazy farm upstate for months.

The state hospital provided access to TV, board games, magazines, and newspapers. Of course, there was no sign of me in them.

I thought I gave The Post a great story, but as it turns out, they gave it to me. Aware that I went to college for both criminal justice and journalism, they've literally let me write the book on how to get yourself unscrewed by the court.

But the entire time, it's been impossible for my parents to comprehend. They've grown to believe there's no such thing as investigative journalism and have feebly rationalized the events that arose from The Post surfacing into my world.

"I think you were angry about what happened in court," my dad said this past year, alluding to my final arrest. "And you went to that house because you were upset."

I pulled up the *Chambersburg Public Opinion* article on his computer. "Look at the mugshot of me."

"You look happy," he said.

"Because I was. Stop saying I did this stuff because I was so upset."

"But you were upset."

"I was upset with you and mom. The Post was helping me, but I explained hundreds of details that you never believed. Instead, you left me in jail and mental health wards. Two days before I sent everything to The Post, I wrote to my cousin that I was very optimistic, not upset."

"The Washington Post did nothing for you," my dad said.

"They gave me one of the greatest stories ever. The only reason I can claim this is the most unbelievable story anyone's ever read is thanks to them."

"But what did The Post do for you?" His brain just doesn't connect the dots, and it never has.

"People might be much more intrigued reading about being lured into a crime spree and drifting through one bizarre event after another. The story of losing my kids has become far more fascinating. And more readers mean more voices to eradicate the atrocities in our courts. That's what The Post has done for me."

35

My Last Child

LUCY STILL HASN'T COME CALLING for her 18th birthday present. And Ethan seems just fine to have moved on from his dad, not that I know what he's up to these days.

In July 2023, my ex-wife and I settled in mediation with regards to Colin, the last child I had parental rights with. To end litigation, Colin agreed to try reunification therapy, which cost $150 an hour that I was solely responsible for.

In therapy, Colin, wearing his hoodie and long pants on a 98°F summer day, was greeted by the therapist. "Is it cold outside today?" Since he left, I've seen him wear nothing but hooded sweatshirts so he can hide his face.

Later, she asked how he managed not having a dad in his life. "It's hard not having him to bounce ideas off," he said.

A few successful sessions resulted in us seeing one another every two or three weeks in the outside world that we'd been prohibited from for six years. In exchange for Colin's sudden willingness to reunite, I agreed to drop contempt charges against my ex-wife for never informing me of the kids' grades, health matters, or anything else that's enforceable by shared legal custody.

It was never easy seeing him, imagining what could've been had the court not stepped between us. Like he's annoyed with the world—and rightfully so—he always shielded his eyes with long, curly bangs while listening to J. Cole through his customary earbud, sometimes under his hood.

Our relationship defrosted a tad over a game of dreidel in celebration of Hanukkah at a Japanese restaurant that December.

"I'm sure you've noticed a bit of my tooth is missing," I said, tired of trying to limit my smiling. "I got hit in the mouth with a stick playing hockey."

Colin's response surprised me. "Yeah, my teacher always complains about getting injured playing hockey."

"Really? Your teacher plays hockey? We might play against each other."

"He lives half an hour away," Colin said. "So I doubt it."

"We draw players from half an hour away because there aren't other rinks around. What's his name?"

He told me.

"Does he have a ponytail?"

Colin smiled and slowly broke his avoidance of eye contact. "Yeeesss."

The English teacher who emailed me the year before about Lucy testing highest among all his classes despite her failing grade just gave Colin a D. And we play hockey against each other.

Now playing center instead of goalie, I said, "I'll rough him up a bit for that grade."

A month later, opening night rolled around, and God blessed me with a game against his teacher. My first shift of the night, I hit him up high.

"Keep your hands out of my face!" he shouted. He continued yelling at me the rest of the first period as I continued pestering him. Oddly, I never heard another word from him after that period, only from everyone else on his team.

His teammate fired a shot, then thumped my goalie's pads looking for a loose rebound. I thumped his back with a two-handed cross-check, so the ref penalized me. As the ref escorted me to the penalty box, I said, "The guy whacked my goalie."

"I know," said the ref. "But you can't hit him afterward."

"Nobody can whack my goalie."

With the game still scoreless, my penalty expired, and I netted the game's first goal. Their energy sucked right out of them as they murmured. "Why that guy? Anybody but that guy." With them flustered, we scored again a minute later.

Holding onto a late lead, I decked one of their guys in front of our net. The ref tapped my captain on the shoulder. "Watch this," the ref said. "That guy's gonna retaliate and hit Brian back. I'm about to get him for a penalty." As play went the other way seconds later, the guy illegally cross-checked me from behind. The whistle blew, and he went straight to the penalty box.

I later got tangled with their team's best player. He kindly held me so I wouldn't get hurt, then said, "Oh, it's you again." He shoved me.

With the 5-1 game firmly in our grasp and one minute to play, our team's captain said, "Brian, stay on the bench for the last minute. I don't want them giving you any cheap shots."

I guess that's life playing in the top league, the equivalent of the A team I didn't make as a youth goalie. But I'm the second-line center. It's like God's pegged me to play second-string forever.

After the game, both teams lined up to shake hands. I removed my helmet and fist-bumped a few, eagerly awaiting Colin's teacher. When he skated up, I gave him one last paw to the face. "That was for giving my son a D."

He laughed. "You were angering me. Then I saw your name on the back of your jersey and realized I teach your son. That's why I got quiet. You know, I used to teach Lucy too. Colin doesn't talk to me, but Lucy did. She sat in the front right next to me." Maybe now Colin talks too.

Entering our locker room after the game, our goalie said, "Well, Brian is officially the most hated player on the ice."

True, but Colin's teacher now likes me. Anything to help my kids. Am I supposed to call him "Mister"?

Of course hockey's blood rules added insult to injury when I lost some tooth. After taking the next shift off to attend to my brand new smile, I hopped back on the ice.

"You can't play covered in blood," the ref said. "You need to stop the bleeding."

"Didn't I stop it?"

"No."

I missed the last six minutes because dried blood is okay, but wet blood is not.

The entire league gave me a reputation the rest of that season. As playoffs neared with our team in first place, I was stuck with twice as many penalty minutes as the second-place guy.

One of our best players had brain surgery and had to sit out the rest of the season, so another said, "We're going to win the championship for him." Then the captain said, "Agreed, we just need Kotler to start playing with an edge and antagonizing opponents. Getting under their skin and stuff." Will someone throw some skates on the BIA and get her out there?

My Republican-filled team has been ultra-supportive of me since learning I'm Jewish. The way antisemitism has taken hold this past year, I'm much more comfortable discussing Israel with them than I'd be in a room full of Democrats. If only my team knew I'm so progressive.

Colin's crummy grades gifted me a great hockey season, and for Hanukkah that year, I gifted him a new bedroom. I fitted his desk with a brand-new gaming computer and lined some new bookshelves with the games I bought for our supervised visits. The walls were decorated with an *Attack on Titan* poster (his favorite anime show) and a brightly colored *Animal Crossing* framed artwork depicting a dog welcoming him into the Nintendo village from the game I got him post-custody loss. To do it, I used the money I intended for Lucy. She said she'd come back if he did, so it was worth a shot.

Over a cook-your-own-steak lunch, I showed him photos of his computer, his room, and his grandpa playing with his new dog. "She's really cute," Colin said, referring to the dog, not grandpa.

Our sable German Shepherd was a 75th birthday present for my mom. She had German Shepherds growing up, and her favorite was named Mitzi. We discussed getting a dog off and on the past few years, but she said, "I don't want to bury another dog. It's too much heart-ache." Well mom, that ship has sailed. The dog will outlive you.

The day we brought her home from the breeder, my dad preceded us into her bedroom videotaping.

"You scared the hell out of me," she said. I forgot, besides being frightened by tossed balls and feathers, her husband entering a room does it too. Then I followed, holding our new puppy.

"Ahhh! Oh my God! Oh my God! Oh my God!" Her petrified screams quickly became a reluctant grin. "You did it."

"She's yours to name," I said with my own cheery smile. "She doesn't have a name yet."

"She has no name?" my mom said, as she rubbed the puppy's neck while she sniffed her new grandma. "We'll call you No Name." Within seconds, she settled on Mitzi, officially her third German Shepherd named Mitzi.

Disheartened by the dearth of homedog Mandy walks, I've taken Mitzi on plenty of adventures.

Near the stream by the base of rocky Cunningham Falls, the largest cascading waterfall in Maryland, we happened upon a colossal, downed tree. Rather than find a way around the five-foot high obstruction, she leaped onto it and disappeared over the other side as my jaw fell in amazement. All her practice jumping over the couch at home paid dividends.

But she's afraid of actual heights. We took a Shabbat day-trip to Annapolis and parked for free across the creek from downtown near quaint homes, restaurants, and marinas.

Spa Creek Bridge separated us from historic downtown. The post-World War II drawbridge has sidewalks on each side, from which Mitzi enjoyed the view of the water through its metal railing. We approached the top sections of the deck that swung in the air to allow the many sailboats to pass through. Unlike the concrete we'd been walking on, these are see-through metal grating.

She took two steps, then realized she was staring at salty waves 20 feet below. Mitzi froze. I encouraged her to run across the 40-foot span of metal, gleaming in the bright, springlike sunshine. After a second or two, she gave in, and we hustled across.

Downtown bustled that day. Green was everywhere, as partygoers celebrated St. Patrick's Day weekend with a rock concert, curbside meals at outdoor restaurants, plenty of ice cream cones from the popular sundae shops, and a few leprechauns on stilts.

Mitzi and I cruised the waterfront and 300-year-old cobblestone alleys and streets for about four miles of socialized fun. Then we took a break on the hill outside the most historic state capitol building in the country.

Dating to 1772, it's the oldest continually used state house, and once served as our nation's capital. Here, in 1783, the Treaty of Paris was signed, marking the end of the Revolutionary War, and George Washington resigned as commander-in-chief of the Continental Army.

Mitzi and I took a snack break halfway up the hill whereupon the brick Georgian-style building crowned by a gray-and-white timber dome rests.

As I handed her a dried apricot, I realized she was bleeding. Her rear-right paw had a badly broken nail from hanging onto the bridge as I tugged her across. So, instead of making a second loop around town, we headed straight back. Though she seemed fine, I wanted her off her feet.

As we raced back to my vehicle, we found ourselves separated by that same drawbridge. Perhaps if we went full steam, we'd cross in no time, so we started our charge up the bridge.

The metal was shining, as if from a Stephen King horror novel. Mitzi stopped a foot short of the glistening deck. The three-foot-wide skid-resistant bike lane didn't contain the wide see-through holes the sidewalk or most of the roadway possessed, so we stepped off the sidewalk to use it. But to her, it was even shinier metal, so she laid down on the roadway and refused to move.

To guard her tail from getting run over by motorists, I joined her in the street and flagged down a passing police officer. "Can we jump in the back, and you drive her across? She's scared to cross."

"No," he said. "You need to get her out of the road so you don't cause an accident."

Passing pedestrians asked if she was okay. "She's fine," I said. "But she's afraid to cross the grating." In the roadway, we were far enough from the railing so if Mitzi squirmed from my arms, she wouldn't fall 20 feet to the water below. So, I picked up my overweight dog and carried her across. We darted back to the van, bringing smiles to the faces of the concerned passersby from moments before. "Hey, you got her across!"

Back in the SUV, I learned that a broken nail was no reason for an emergency vet visit, so I went forward with my plan to attend a Purim carnival in Baltimore. Dressed as Queen Esther's uncle Mordecai, a shepherd with a Shepherd, we sought to end Shabbat with the holy, candlelit ceremony of Havdalah with a minyan—the sought-after grouping of ten Jews. But Mitzi was sketched to go anywhere near the automated bubble maker outside the synagogue door.

After a different night in silent darkness, she was terrified to go beyond my bedroom door. She's used to spending overnight downstairs with random lights left on and a giant TV blaring all night long. For the longest time, she stopped right at the threshold no matter the time of day or night. After too many failed attempts luring her in with a promise of half my breakfast, I filled a bowl with vanilla ice cream and set it a few feet inside. A couple months' irrational fear disappeared almost as fast as that ice cream.

She's also afraid of fake plastic trees. Anytime I accidentally bumped into one beside our living room couch, she pounced back, startled, and stared at it with worry. One evening, while watching a Capitals game on TV, 14-year-old me resurfaced and got the brilliant idea to scare her. She was upstairs when I grabbed the tree, laid under it pretending to be eaten alive, and called her. "Mitzi! Come here!" I heard her jump off the bed above my head when John Carlson, the best defenseman in our team's history, was bludgeoned by a puck in the side of his.

Concerned that my demented plan may have triggered his skull fracture and near ear-dismemberment, I put the tree back before she saw. Whenever I accidentally graze it, I apologize profusely.

My attack dog, whose tail twirls in circles when she runs downstairs, isn't terrified of everything. We roamed the banks of Antietam Creek and unexpectedly encountered a fisherman wandering through the woods. The hair on her back stood straight, and it took all my strength to hold her as she advanced into a fierce defensive posture, barking viciously. The guy was terrified to move until I told him it was fine a third time.

Another day, on the seldom-traveled road behind our town's community college, we happened upon five deer. Ordinarily, when she spots deer, or squirrels, or rabbits, the chase is on. But not this time.

Head deer and Mitzi launched into an intense stare-down 15 feet apart as the other four deer remained nearby, interrupted from their grazing.

As I watched with curiosity, I thought, "There's only five of them and two of us. We'll be fine."

After a minute, the head deer stomped its foot and Mitzi blazed into action. She snarled and sprinted 26 feet until the leash snapped her back as all five white-tailed deer bounded into the woods, terrorized.

How wonderful it would've been to have Colin, Lucy, and Ethan there, like the Annapolis summer day with their cousins eight years ago.

"We'll see you in downtown at two," my cousin said on their drive from New Jersey.

Thirty minutes later, I called back. "Hey, we got a flat tire on the highway," I said. "But the spare is rusted to the bottom of the van. If you're about to drive past, stop for us. It's hot out here."

"We just pulled into a mechanic outside Baltimore," she said. "Our check engine came on and the car started making noises."

"Unbelievable. So you can't help. Oh good, a highway truck is pulling over. Let me know how things go for you."

As several lanes of traffic crept past, the affable highway guy confirmed I wasn't a cream puff by yanking on the spare. "Yeah, that thing's not going anywhere," he said. "Put your kids in my truck. It's nice and air conditioned in there."

The time it took for the tow truck to fight through the traffic tie-up I caused was enough for my cousin's mechanic to fix their SUV so we could pile in at an Annapolis tire place.

She and her husband bought our boat ride through the harbor, as their kids and mine marveled at the Annapolis waterfront from sea for the first time.

Our shortened day together was sweetened with ice cream cones and souvenir shopping.

"Why don't you guys come back to our hotel?" she said. "They've got a pool for the kids to swim."

The kids and I drove to the massive shopping mall across the street from their hotel for bathing suits, where I'd been going since before I could remember. My old hockey friends often held birthday parties at their awesome arcade in the '80s.

Back at the hotel, all five kids spent hours swimming and diving for coins I kept throwing to the bottom.

"Look how much money I made!" said Colin.

This past year's visits with Colin were missing family. They entailed lunch or dinner out, escaping escape rooms, playing paintball on his birthday, and most recently, throwing axes. His poor memory prevented him from recalling his axe-throwing attempt at the Renaissance Festival weeks before the custody change.

Through the co-parenting app we agreed to use during mediation, I offered to take Colin to shoot pool two weeks after throwing axes. At one of our visits, he asked me about a nine-ball rule while playing a billiards game on his phone. He said he never played the real thing. My ex-wife wrote, "Yes, he would like to try that." Hours before we were supposed to meet, the app alerted me. "Colin is not feeling well today. He would like to reschedule for another time."

After wishing him well, I napped to tend to my onslaught of depression. When I awoke, I sent my ex-wife another message:

> "Hi. Colin and I have been having a lot of fun, but he's still struggling in school. He's failing three classes (two of them badly at 5 and 11 percent). It's a repeat of the first two quarters and he's not progressing. You told the court that you had similar troubles with my ex-stepson and thought it would help if he lived with his dad. And it did.
>
> "Before the custody change, Colin was doing well, and he enjoyed doing schoolwork with me. There's no reason he shouldn't be allowed to come here. He has a beautiful room and his own new computer waiting for him. You've read the letters from his friends that said I provide a safe environment. They conflict with Ethan's false story about discussing abuse, which invoked supervision and custody change in the first place.
>
> "Colin's almost halfway through high school and his future is bleak, not bright. I feel if you discuss with him the potential benefits of having both his parents in his life and encourage him to start

coming here, he'd agree. There's no need for me to bring up the past with him because I only care about his future.

"Kids universally say they prefer having both parents and statistics and studies prove they're better off. I hope you give this serious thought because Colin's running out of time."

Over a week passed without response, so I asked, "Does Colin want to get ice cream and shoot pool one night this week?" No answer.

Two days later, I wrote, "I'm available to take Colin out tonight or tomorrow. We haven't seen each other for almost a month."

Hours later, she finally responded:

"I am sorry for the delay in getting back to you.

"As far as Colin's grades go, I talk to him about schoolwork and his grades daily. He has been on restriction from electronics for several weeks now and isn't allowed to have anything back until he has As and Bs. Colin would like more than anything to get his driver's license and a part-time job so he can start saving up for his first car. Even though he is already scheduled to attend driver's ed in April, I have told him he won't be attending if his grades don't improve and same with getting a job. Unless he has As and Bs and maintains them, he will not be allowed.

"I talked to Colin about living with you or visiting you at your house and I wanted him to be 100% confident in his choice before I responded. Colin doesn't want to live with you and as of right now he doesn't want to visit with you anymore.

"I don't care that you were able to coerce some people who hardly know you to write letters attesting to the safe environment you supposedly provide. I know differently and I saw the marks on Ethan after the last time he was with you."

She concluded her message with a reference to Ethan's injured toe, which was hurt on the opposite side of the door that I closed after he smacked me. I didn't know he was trying to prevent me from shutting it by sticking his bare toe under the door. Police said I did nothing wrong.

Plus, it seems close to impossible to force or threaten two families I hardly know to write praise-filled letters on my behalf. And from Colin's two best friends, no less. But my ex-wife's used to getting away with saying anything. During her deposition, my lawyer asked, "Have you ever lied?"

"Yes," she said, seated a few feet away from the BIA.

"When have you lied?"

"As a kid."

"Oh, you've never lied as an adult?"

"No," she said before squirming, shaking her head, huffing and puffing for the next 37 seconds of silence. Isn't the first sign of a liar someone who said they haven't lied in two decades?

The most honest ex-wife ever also discussed restricting Colin from electronics, something his teachers say is a serious problem with him— and many others. A few schools nationwide have collected kids' cellphones before the school day begins and have witnessed enormous strides. Lunchrooms are filled with the sound of kids interacting with one another instead of the typical hush found when they're glued to their phones. Grades and test scores are up, teachers' stress is alleviated, and bullying is down 40 percent. Parents seem concerned about contacting their kids in an emergency, but they're so rare that happier teachers, improved grades, and lessened depression are magnificent tradeoffs. Maybe schools like Colin's can follow suit.

I replied to my ex-wife two days later:

"Thanks for trying to improve Colin's grades. Instead of taking away things he enjoys, I can provide him things he loves to better his grades. He has a brand-new gaming computer waiting for him and I've helped save money for a car.

"It's understandable that a kid who's been estranged from his father for six years would be reluctant to go back. Insisting he is 100% certain is not a fair standard. If you encourage him to take advantage of my interest and help with his future plans, we can give Colin a better chance of success.

"The numbers indicate this. The Fatherless Generation shares this regarding education.

Children with an involved father are:

40% less likely to repeat a grade,

70% less likely to drop out,

More likely to get As,

More likely to enjoy school and engage in extracurricular activities.

"Various government agencies report other life-altering statistics regarding children from fatherless homes:

90% of homeless and runaway children are fatherless.

63% of youth suicides,

85% of children who exhibit behavioral disorders,

90% of adolescent repeat arsonists,

80% of rapists motivated with displaced anger,

71% of pregnant teenagers,

75% of adolescent patients in chemical abuse centers,

70% of juveniles in state-operated institutions, and

85% of youths in prisons.

Fatherless boys and girls are:

Twice as likely to drop out of high school.

Twice as likely to end up in jail.

Four times more likely to need help for emotional or behavioral problems.

"I propose that Colin come here and split fun and tutoring time. We can arrange one hour to start, and you can wait outside if he wants. I think over the next quarter, he can gradually increase to a few times a week as he feels more comfortable and sees his grades improve. Plus, it would help him from losing out on fun at your house."

Those troubling statistics foreshadow a difficult future for the country and our world because of the sheer number of fatherless children. The U.S. Census Bureau expresses that 21% of all kids are fatherless, a number that exceeds 15 million. It's doubled in the past 50 years. Seeing how 21% of kids account for 70-90% of problem cases should alarm everyone. But not the court, and not my ex-wife.

For days, there was no response. On the one-month anniversary of our last one-hour visit together, I sent one final message:

"It's been a month since I've last seen or spoken to Colin. You say he doesn't want to visit with me anymore, but the week before that, you said he wanted to shoot pool with me. What changed? The only communication with either of you was a letter to you. What did you say to him afterwards that made him change his mind?

"The agreement we reached last July said, 'The parties will permit Colin to have a relationship with Father at Colin's discretion. Mother shall not discourage or dissuade Colin from having a relationship with his Father. Neither party will disparage the other party or the family of the other party in front or within earshot of Colin.'

"Because he wanted to see me before I raised concerns to only you, I did nothing to cause him to change his mind. You did. You said something to discourage or dissuade him from wanting his father in his life.

"I told you, 100% certainty will never get him to reunite with his father. It is an unrealistic expectation. How often have you been 100% certain of anything? Gravity, maybe. What else?

"I've scheduled an appointment with my lawyer in about a month. If Colin doesn't change his tune, I'll file contempt charges at that meeting because you violated the agreement.

"I have no reason to discuss you. I just want a wholesome relationship with my son and to see him succeed. And it wouldn't hurt if Lucy reestablished one too."

There was no response.

Seven months on, Colin's 17th birthday approached. Based on his prior love of fidget spinners and his newfound fondness for drowning out his dad's visits with hip-hop, I bought him a fidget pen and portable speaker. On his birthday morning, I grabbed a cupcake and candle, then entered his school for the first time since Lucy's 18th birthday present went wrong.

After showing ID, I heard a familiar, unwelcome call over the walkie-talkie. "Can an administrator come to the front office?"

"We're sorry," the administrator said. "There's a no-contact order in the system so we can't have Colin come. I know how much you'd like to see him, but all we can do is give him the gifts and cupcake on your behalf."

Back in my car, I pulled the candle from my pocket that I never got to light. It was broken.

Fifteen years in the making, that contempt charge I threatened saw the light of day inside court this January. I hadn't seen Colin since the previous February, but he became part of the most dystopian vision of my life.

Like our last two oddly empty court appearances in Frederick, we again encountered a desolate courthouse at this brand new venue in our hometown half-an-hour up the interstate. That afternoon's docket listed our case and one other, the only case all day without a name. For the few judicial assistants and officers meandering about, we were the featured show a third consecutive occasion.

But unlike every Frederick court appearance and our 2023 mediation, the BIA was absent. My ex-wife didn't have the help of her usual spokesperson, but she wasn't alone.

On a bench outside the main courtroom of the Victorian-era Italianate building, a nightmarish spectacle overwhelmed me. Four others flanked my ex-wife. I couldn't identify a few right away, but is that Colin? And is this blond woman her new lawyer? Is this older guy a new boyfriend? No, I think that's my ex-stepson. And that must be Lucy and Ethan.

Seeing them together for the first time since the KissCam days, I'd hardly recognize them at a family reunion.

Ethan appeared *AnimEmo*, with long, parted hair that screams angsty anxiety filled with the flair of a reliable car.

Meanwhile, Lucy looked more like Al's Pumpkin than mine. She traded the sleek, highlighted honey brown hair she's had since birth for bobbed no-natural-color curls Joe DiMaggio might've married.

Not quite knowing what to say, I asked, "Did you guys get your Hanukkah presents?"

"Yeah," said Lucy, staring intently at her phone.

I was lost for words.

At least I learned the school's front office passed along the cards, dreidel, chocolate coins, gift cards, Colin's Collector's Edition *Percy Jackson* book, and the first three volumes of Lucy's new *Nana* anime. I was so overwhelmed, I didn't even think to ask if they liked them.

Because Colin missed school the day before winter break, they got their gifts with one hour to spare in our eight-day holiday.

During one of our since-canceled outings, Colin said he loved writing fantasy stories and reading *Percy Jackson*. A favorite of young adults, Lucy's gift is the story of a girl Lucy's age who moved to Japan. If Lucy lived in Asia, I thought, I'd see her just as much as I do now.

Having arranged to discuss matters with my attorney beforehand, I found a separate seating area under three decades of portraits featuring our county's Bar Association members. Surrounding me were rows of faces including that lying State's Attorney, a friend from the synagogue, and our county's recently murdered family court judge for whom the courthouse was newly named.

He was shot in his driveway last spring by a distraught father who lost his kids not too dissimilarly from me. The difference is, this dad had anger issues and brought a gun everywhere.

This was our first appearance in our home county, away from the BIA, judge, magistrate and whoever else knew the chief judge so well where we shared married life. Perhaps this would be my first hint of justice. But court only cares about what's happened since that July 2023 agreement. Nothing else.

For 15 years, my ex-wife was steered by a personal lawyer who found new ways screw to me. This time, either Lucy really was her lawyer or she represented herself. Without counsel or the BIA present to design excuses for her, my ex-wife was in over her head at the far end of the 40-foot counsel table. Separated by several empty seats, my lawyer and I listened to the judge.

He asked about the only parties seated in the oversized gallery behind us—our four children. Now 25, my ex-stepson joined Ethan, Lucy, and Colin. "Are there any minors here in the courtroom? Who's under 18?"

"My son Colin," my ex-wife said.

"You're excused from the courtroom, sir. Not an appropriate place for a minor." Apparently it was an appropriate place for my ex-stepson, Ethan, and Lucy, who offered her patented, silent snicker toward her younger brother that said, "Psh! Love you Colin but you gots to go."

He spent the next 50 minutes alone in the deserted lobby outside the courtroom where his mom was being interrogated a few feet in front of his sister, brother, and stepbrother.

After my ex-wife was sworn in, the judge said, "Could you move over one seat so I can see you." Then he asked, "Do you admit or deny that you're in contempt of court?"

"Umm…I am," she said.

"Pardon me?"

"I am in contempt of court."

"She's admitting she's in contempt," the judge said to my attorney. "If she's admitting she's in contempt, there's no reason for you to examine her."

"Of course, but I have no idea what she's going to testify to."

"I understand."

Here's a question: How often do judges rule on cases without hearing an ounce of evidence?

In her defense, my ex-wife said she spoke to Colin. "I asked him…his father wanted him to come to his home to resume visits with him there, weekends or what have you. And did he want to try that and see if that would help with his grades? Because I genuinely did not know what else to do. Colin was upset that his father hadn't really discussed with him his concerns about his grades." (Remember Lucy's reaction at supervised visitation?)

My ex-wife continued and hearsay met one of its stupider moments. "Um, am I allowed to say Colin told me?"

"Don't tell us what Colin said," the judge said. "Colin's available. He's outside. If somebody wishes to call Colin, we can ask Colin. Don't repeat what Colin said."

Why can she testify to his general reaction that he was upset— which she may have incorrectly inferred—but she can't say what he actually said?

Then my ex-wife said, "When Mr. Kotler sent me the message about the concerns about Colin's grades, I'm not sure how else I was supposed to proceed with Colin because I can't just take him and say, 'Okay, you're gonna go spend the weekend at your dad's now so he can work on the grades with you.'"

She can't do that, but the court forced me to tell him, "Okay, you're gonna go live with your mom and you're never coming back."

Now that Colin expresses favoritism toward one parent thanks to alienation the court propagated, they can't say, "You're going to your dad's house for a few hours. You'll be fine."

When the Frederick judge severed our relationship in 2017, she acknowledged Colin and Lucy expressed no preference for either parent. But that's not entirely true.

Shortly before losing custody, Colin was given a couple months to complete a big school project. Every week we were together, he'd come home and tell me stuff so we could work on it together. Then the week it was due, Colin insisted on staying with me. My ex-wife, of course, wanted her week with him.

"But Colin wants to stay so he can finish his project," I said to her. "It's due tomorrow."

"What project?"

For months, he mentioned nothing to her because he wanted to work solely with me. The judge and BIA knew this, yet they still took his dad from him overnight. Colin's past seven years of report cards expose the educational outcome of this mistreatment.

In court for contempt this January, my ex-wife exposed the emotional damage.

Referring to Colin's current refusals to see me, the judge asked her, "Did you encourage him after March?"

"I did not," she said. "I did not because he was emphatic that he was done. That he did not want to see his father because his father was not discussing his grades with him during the visits. He brought it up to me instead, and that's all I have to say, sir." (Again, see Lucy's reaction.)

Later, the judge admitted his ineffectiveness in salvaging our relationship. "The visitation certainly stopped, but it's up to Colin."

Then he said to my ex-wife, "Ma'am, the court is concerned that you had this agreement, that you get kind of these plain, vanilla communications from Colin's father, and then he expresses a valid concern and you stop sending medical updates. The court's further concerned Colin is not seeing his father at all."

He offered a couple save-the-connection suggestions that Colin can easily negate, and based on the past 14 months will for the last six of his youth. Then he said, "I can't lead the horse to water in this situation, you understand."

Courts have all the power to break-up families, but act powerless to fix them.

At least for the first time in the umpteenth court filing, the judge granted me attorney's fees. He said I'd get $1,000, but that's only if she messes up again. I'm sure that'll make Colin like me.

The judge turned to my lawyer and discussed my last few messages to my ex-wife. "I'm not trying to cast any shade on your client at all. I'm truly looking for solutions here. I am impressed by trying to bridge what was a fraught relationship with his adolescent son. But what I didn't see was, 'Hey, could you invite Colin to see me?' It was just kind of preachy, lengthy, you know.'"

"Well," she said. "I think the last message he was inviting him to a Boxcars game."

"Okay, that's great. Thank you for pointing that out. I kind of tuned it out when I started to see the long ones. That's my fault. Thank you for pointing that out."

I thought, "Judge, you need to know this stuff. Those are fatherless kid stats."

My favorite part was the end.

The judge asked my ex-wife, who acted as her own attorney, "Do you mind if I speak to counsel for a second?"

"You, you."

"I just want to speak to your husband's lawyer here for a second."

Then, at the same precise moment, the judge said, "You may come up here if you want," while she said, "Do you want me to leave?"

She stayed seated while my attorney and the judge discussed something behind white noise that the court audio picks up perfectly. He cut the static and said, "Everyone's excused. Thank you."

My ex-stepson wrapped his arm around my ex-wife as Lucy and Ethan led their way out the door to snag Colin and run.

My lawyer turned to me. "Who's the kid with real dark hair?"

"That's Ethan."

"This whole time, he's been staring you down."

"I have a terrible memory," Colin said a short time after we renewed visits in Fall 2023. It was a new complaint that he often repeated, and it's true. Of everything I've been through, this hurts the most.

Colin can't even remember the fun we used to have together. And I'm certain he can't recall pumping his fist in the air and shouting, "Yes!" when I told him in October 2017 that we had at least one more month together. That's the day I learned the judge would make her ruling in November. Sadly, that October excitement gave way to November sobbing. If only the judge could've seen it.

Colin never grumbled about poor recall before the court snatched him, but since our icy reunification, he shared every visit that his memory is awful. It's an all-too-common symptom among abused children.

So is a rotten self-image. If you lost your dad because a judge declared him unworthy, what would your opinion of dad be? What happens to your self-esteem knowing you're half him?

The court exploited Colin and his siblings, and cruelly ousted their father without considering their feelings. Their attorney ignored their opinions, failing grades, inward demeanor, and overall suffering, and should be imprisoned for child abuse.

The world can't fathom how bonded Colin and I were, and no book could possibly portray it. For him to own 20 fleeting memories of our first nine years together is heartbreaking.

I'm in the same boat. Sometimes I push away terrific memories because they're too painful. Imagining our games of hide-and-seek where I scrambled to find him amidst a massive pile of stuffies instantly brings a tear to my eye. But I snap myself out of it before I become overburdened by grief. Does he even remember our frequent games of hide-and-seek?

How does a 99ᵗʰ percenter like Colin, with his razor-sharp mind and lightning-quick logic, know to suppress joyous scenes with his father? Failed memory is common among emotionally abused children, and I've had my own sample as to why.

I had trouble recalling stories about Colin. I can't possibly put in words how close we were, yet I couldn't think of stories. Losing such positive life experiences causes us to suppress memories of them. Otherwise, we'd be in a constant fog of despair reminiscing about the great times we've forfeited.

Still, because I'm middle-aged, I have memories. Colin doesn't.

He was so young when he was forced to subdue his memories of me, that he's left with practically none. The boy who was once so full of exuberance from the pleasure of life and the potential it held has grown cold and distant. He doesn't seem to care much about anything anymore.

The moment I think of the kids, it makes me mad or sad. Rarely do I smile. No parent should feel that way.

When I picture them, I envision who they were seven years ago, not who they are now. The sad fact is, I don't really know them now. They were loving, jubilant, vibrant, and full of hopes and dreams. But I see none of that these days.

During those fleeting six months of since-stopped visits with Colin, his mom never said a word to me during drop-offs and pick-ups. Not one.

Of course, his sister and brother haven't spoken to me either.

How warm could I have expected Colin to be?

36

So Help Me God, Please

ALBERT EINSTEIN HAD HIS CLOCK tower outside his patent office window for inspiration. I have my stately oak tree.

Whereas Einstein was inspired to devise the theory of relativity by imagining time stood still when moving at the speed of light, I'm concerned whether or not I'll live to see another day.

While I sit at my desk, the one whose particle-board cabinet door Colin's foot dismantled while excitedly fending off intruders with his *Skype* friend, I glance out my window. Five massive branches dominate the sky. A thumb juts from the side of the tree's palm, and all four fingers, appropriately sized, are splayed from the top. Stretching from the ground, the tree is an entire forearm narrowing near the top before fanning out in perfect hand shape. The 70-foot tree rests atop a fairly steep four-foot hill.

It's either God's right hand lifting me up the mountain, or God's left hand about to smash me from above. If this is God's hand, I've discovered the easiest method for time travel.

These days, the best I can do to father my kids is to mentally travel back in time. I have recollections of days together on sunny soccer fields and hitting up the Hawaiian ices truck after a hard-fought game. I know I was a good dad, no matter what my kids may think today.

Though I don't have my kids, I thank God. I'm grateful for being blessed with such wonderful children that I miss them dearly. I'm thankful for the cherished memories, and I'm hopeful we'll create new ones someday. I'm in pain, not from the vasectomy anymore, but because God gifted me children. And they really are phenomenal kids.

I absolutely revere my photos and videos of them, but I kick myself every day for having almost none.

Because I was disabled, I was around for everything. We had boatloads of time together and I missed practically nothing. But I didn't record it.

Whenever we went places, be it the moonbounce, Renaissance Festival or their soccer games, I watched other parents with their faces glued to cellphones videotaping. Why are they watching everything through their tiny phone screen instead of sitting back, being present, and absorbing their children at play?

That's what I did, and I'm so sorry I did. Those parents can time travel, and they don't have to hope a giant tree one day does it for them. They can delight at the past, seeing their kids score goals, ride an elephant, or bounce in exuberant laughter as if they're standing right there and it's happening right now.

Meanwhile, I'm stuck with faded glimmers of flashbacks to years long ago, unable to relive little Lucy's adorable pleas for Mandy to stop wagging her happy tail so she could learn to walk. And worst of all, my forgetful children won't regain those memories.

If God ever does give me back my kids, I'm taking lots of video.

And I'm celebrating every holiday.

I missed so many Jewish holidays with my kids, but I've gone all out in recent years on them. Hopefully I can instill the same love and passion for them that I've discovered, much of it through food.

As fellow congregants and friends continuously raved about my cooking and suggested I open a restaurant or food truck, I realized all those years in the pizza business weren't wasted. However, I hate throwing away food. So, the expensive trips to the grocery store to buy large bunches of herbs, only to see them wither and get discarded, motivated me to grow my own.

At a recent study class with my temple, the biblical herb hyssop came up in discussion. "I grow hyssop," I said.

"Brian, can I ask why you grow hyssop?" my rabbi said.

"Well, I started an herb garden last year and wound up with 37 herbs. One of them was hyssop."

Turned out that was too many herbs, so I cut the quantity in half last spring. But I needed more pots because all the vegetables I started growing took up more space.

The Torah, our most precious gift from God that has bound us to our ancestors, not only says that hyssop purifies our souls, it demands that we care for one another equally. More than any other commandment, we're instructed 36 times in these five sacred books of the Hebrew Bible to treat the stranger, the widow, and the fatherless with fairness, dignity, respect, and appreciation. God knows our millions of fatherless kids need our help, and it might just start with parental alienation. It's insidious.

Some 22 million parents report being alienated from at least one kid. At least one. There's only 71 million kids in this country. That's a lot of parents acting up and a lot of kids let down.

Antiquated laws need changing and as my rabbi profoundly professes, behind-the-scenes criminal activity must be made transparent and brought to justice.

Many credit Abraham Lincoln with having said this country will be destroyed from within, not by outside forces. Though Lincoln probably never said that, it's attributed to him because it's so credible and it stands the test of time. Just like Honest Abe himself.

For almost 250 years, judges in this country have profited, both personally and financially, off the suffering of everyday people like you and me. Inside a courtroom, litigants are outnumbered and out-maneuvered. But in the public sphere, judges are.

In state courts, where 99.6% of all court cases are heard, 30,000 judges and their subordinates are tasked with ruling on 100 million cases each year. That translates to 3,333 cases per judge annually.

One at a time, judges can do whatever they want. But turn that number around, and it's time to hold them accountable. Who's guilty? Follow the money.

How incompetent are our judges and system?

A judge with 30+ years of experience was assigned to family law cases without ever having studied or worked in family law. His clerk said she knew more than him because she took one family law class in law school. How many families' entire futures rest in his hands?

Judicial oversight committees rarely investigate complaints of in-experienced judicial decisions, abuse, and corruption. Over 90% of grievances are dismissed without investigation. How many judges are getting away with crimes simply because the oversight committee re-fused to investigate?

Corrupt family court judges don't just work family court. These same people preside over all civil and criminal matters and are en-trusted to implement justice. Their misdeeds hurt all of society.

Donald Trump and I have one thing in common, we both don't trust judges. He has trouble with judges at the top, I have trouble with judges at the bottom.

Although the failed system and judicial immunity have protected judges from countless crimes for hundreds of years, there are rare in-stances where they've faced punishment. So we have hope.

Perhaps the worst offender in American history was Judge Martin Manton of New York. Dubbed "the tenth-ranking judge in the United States," behind only the nine Supreme Court Justices, he corruptly swindled $17 million in today's money. Throughout the Great Depression, the "merchant of justice" profited off all types of cases. Everything from patent infringement, constitutional challenges, and federal criminal prosecutions were fodder. As rumors of his unprecedented corruption circulated, he resigned in 1939. He was disbarred and sentenced to two years in prison, of which he served 17 months. A million a month ain't a bad deal for him.

More recently in 2022, a pair of Pennsylvania judges were ordered to pay $200 million in damages and sentenced to decades behind bars for sending thousands of juvenile offenders as young as eight to for-profit private prisons. The children weren't allowed to establish a defense or say goodbye to their families. What was in it for the judges? The prisons paid them $2.8 million.

From time to time, judges have been imprisoned for much smaller kickbacks, too. In 2019, former Texas judge Rudy Delgado was sentenced to five years for accepting three bribes from an attorney totaling $6,000, then attempting to obstruct justice by contacting the attorney and devising a false story about the payments.

But more often than not, in the few instances an investigation is launched, either nothing happens or judges receive a private reprimand, they remain on the bench, and the public never knows. The system needs upending.

Anti-corruption courts are sprouting in parts of the world where efforts are focused on corruption. These courts are unaffiliated with the rest of the justice system and impartially detect and prosecute cases of corruption. America would benefit from this, because what we have now is akin to organized crime.

I healed a prosecutor. Maybe I can heal some judges, too.

A few months after thanking me for healing him, the prosecutor appeared at my release hearing where he sealed my felony charge without acknowledging me. The Post must've blue-suited him real good to get him in on our secret.

My life as a rock song has seen quite the evolution over the past 15 years, from a band called 30 Seconds to Mars getting me through my break-up to Dishwalla, a one-hit wonder that encapsulated my post-Post existence in "Counting Blue Cars", except for me they were red. Then there's a song by Chevelle (a band that's also car): "Seeing red again. Seeing red again. Seeing red again. Seeing red again."

I wish The Post sat down and spoke to us early on, but they said no Brian, we've got enough to go on and your life's about to become way different.

I had a certain vision when everything kicked off with The Post. First, I was worried my kids couldn't be around other kids at school, so they'd probably have to be home-schooled. I thought moving to Colorado would be fantastic. Once the smell was obliterated, it was beautiful on all fronts. We could live in a mountain home with some horses on a ranch for the kids.

But now that seven years have passed, the plan is different. The kids are older now, and I've discovered that so many other families could use help, too. Jewish values have taught me that the most noble thing someone can do is selflessly help others.

God and Judaism have instilled faith that I know no matter what happens, I'm doing right. I'm not afraid fighting courts because God is on my side. I always believed it's about who you know, not what you know. Well, now I know God. We're taught to fear God, and nothing else. We all should feel that way.

I trust that God wants the world in a better way, and fixing the courts would bring us closer to Heaven's ideal.

What else is Heaven's ideal? I think most would say a long, happy, healthy, wealthy, safe life. How can we help that along? Less fighting and more acknowledgement of facts.

I've shown my parents this chart ranking among all 50 states the conservative ones that voted for Trump in 2024 versus liberal states that backed Kamala Harris:

	Liberal	Conservative
▪ Life Expectancy	Top 11	23 of **Bottom** 24
▪ Happiest States	5 of **Top** 6	10 of **Bottom** 11
▪ Healthiest	11 of **Top** 12	**Bottom** 14
▪ Poverty	6 of **Top** 7	11 of **Bottom** 13
▪ Bachelor's Degrees	7 of **Top** 8	29 of **Bottom** 30
▪ GDP/Capita	8 of **Top** 11	10 of **Bottom** 11
▪ Gun Deaths	**Top** 9	16 of **Bottom** 17
▪ Crime	6 of **Top** 7	13 of **Bottom** 18
▪ Violent Crime	5 of **Top** 6	15 of **Bottom** 19

While cooking spaghetti at the stove recently, my dad looked at the chart. "Who's your source?" he asked.

"Mostly the government," I said.

"Who put that together?"

"Me."

"Let's not get into politics."

My dad finished cooking 20 minutes later, enough time for the chart to sink in. On went his news while he ate, so the chart could sink out. He wants all our states to be mired at the bottom. Not exactly Heaven's ideal.

God made me a statistics guy since birth.

Is baseball's Ty Cobb, whose .367 batting average has been the all-time record for a century, really a worse hitter than Mario Mendoza, the man for whom the Mendoza-line is named to indicate hitters who struggle to bat .200?

Is LeBron James and his record 42,000 points worse than my 6-foot-basket jammin' friends because he averages 1.2 dunks a game while they averaged dozens?

Is Jerry Rice, who caught the most passes in NFL history, a worse receiver than my broken old Sony?

Is Lionel Messi inferior at soccer than me and Ethan because we scored two goals per game with Xbox Messi while real Messi scores only one?

Is my single goaltending win against a pro hockey team more impressive than Martin Brodeur's record 691?

Fox News would suggest it is. But I say I'm only better than Pete Peeters, the NHLer who snagged the loss because Scott Stevens' reputation as the most ruthless hitter in history didn't help him score two.

Two months ago, two months after the spaghetti incident, my dad said, "I trust investigative journalism. I don't trust political journalism."

"All Fox News discusses is politics," I said. "You saw The Washington Post website's investigations page that said, 'If you're aware of corruption, we want to know.' It didn't say, 'If you've got dirt on Republicans, we want to know.' According to your logic, you don't trust Fox News but you do trust The Washington Post."

In order to justify why being ranked at the bottom is better, he's learned from his TV to lie about anything and everything.

"When you were growing up in the '60s and '70s," I asked my dad recently, "were newspapers slanted only toward liberals?"

"Not that I can think of," he said.

"That didn't completely change when Fox News arrived and said they were. To reason why being statistically ranked at the bottom is better, Fox News has to lie to you. And they do. Their primetime anchor makes $40 million a year to tell you your life is better, even when it's not. What does he care if others struggle to earn $40 thousand a year as a result? He and his colleagues are fine."

One positive about dealing with my parents' *mishegoss* for so long is I've learned how to make peace with the other side. Though I'm a registered Independent, we couldn't have more disparate political beliefs. Of course, being Independent, I thought it might be fun to run for President as head of the Pick This One party.

One of our few political agreements regards our elections. The Democratic presidential candidate won Maryland by 13 to 33 percent each of the past nine elections. Nationwide, the difference was under five percent six times.

"My vote doesn't matter," said my dad, referring to my state's almost guaranteed backing of liberals.

"If we used popular vote instead of electoral college, would your vote carry more weight?" I asked.

"It would."

When campaigning, presidential candidates ignore our state in favor of the only five or ten that truly matter. Why do so many Americans have such little say in our next president?

And why do my dad and I have so little in common? But despite our differences, we can make things work. I can bring up politics and instantly start a fight that can last for days. Or I can bring up weather, sports, or *Scrabble* and live in harmony without end.

My rabbi put this into perfect perspective. After the attack on Israel by Hamas in 2023, we discussed how to extend the olive branch to Muslims. "What can I say to them?" he asked.

"It's not easy making others understand your perspective," I said. "That's what I've experienced with my parents. I can show them statistic after statistic and it does no good. How many times do I have to tell them people in liberal states live 5-10 years longer than those in conservative states? They'll never get it."

"So, we need to focus on our commonalities," he said.

"Yeah, I think you're right."

When I see Muslims in religious dress, I smile. It's wonderful when we live side-by-side in peace, holding doors open for one another. Over the years, I've met many Muslims, and they're some of my favorite co-workers. They're hard-working, caring, and love family, just like Jews. Although because cricket was more their speed sportswise, it created confusion. "You don't know about batsmen and wickets?" one asked.

"Vatican tickets? I thought you were Muslim, not Catholic."

Why we live in such distrust of each other, I don't know. I think they're great.

As opposed to my experiences with Muslim folks, my dad and I are on completely opposite sides of the spectrum. His warped idea of immigrants often comes up first if I do mention politics. "Terrorists are flooding across the border," he said. "You won't be happy until someone you know is killed in a terrorist attack."

"Has there been a terrorist attack by a foreigner in 20 years?"

"Well, no."

"Does Fox News show you the businesses that rely on kindhearted, undocumented immigrants to help fuel our economy and food supply?"

"No."

A month later, I can raise politics again.

"Terrorists are flooding across the border. You won't be happy until someone you know is killed in a terrorist attack."

Nothing I ever say sinks in.

My dad used to buy The Washington Post every day, mainly for the Sports section. He trusted their scores and statistics reporting, but apparently nothing else. I grew up trusting them, too, but it went far beyond sports.

Nowadays, we trust *Merriam-Webster*, our go-to *Scrabble* dictionary. Once I learned how to play, he has a hard time winning. My mom just has a hard time playing. When we include her, she mulls over each move for up to a half-hour.

"Mac," my dad said. "Make a move already. We've been waiting 20 minutes."

"Well, if you stop talking, I can."

"We haven't said anything for 20 minutes," I said.

"Well, you are now. How am I supposed to think with you talking?"

Both my dad's head and mine fell into our hands simultaneously.

But between writing a book and demoralizing my dad in *Scrabble*, everything I knew about numbers flew to the verbal side. I have the mental agility of Ethan or Lucy, not Colin.

Despite my cognizance at *Scrabble*, my parents still think I lost my mind. As did my cousin, who I later discovered is hooked on the same news as my parents. Perhaps that's why she believed them and hitched herself to the "Brian's crazy" train, leaving me out to dry. We haven't spoken since that Allentown evening seven years ago.

Because of Fox News, nobody believed that The Washington Post would help. And it made things worse.

My kids and I have been in free fall.

Off to a Sniffspot with Mitzi, we hopped in my dad's SUV. I pressed the ignition and the first words through the stereo were, "Nothing the media says is true."

Since buying his SUV three years ago equipped with SiriusXM, he listens to Fox News wherever he goes. That station is on almost every time I get inside. As someone who has a deep appreciation for journalism and a healthy fear of tyrants like High-Heels Hitler, I love America's Bill of Rights expressing freedom of speech. But it should be illegal to constantly bombard listeners with blatant lies.

The trouble is, people like my parents believe them. They've tricked my parents like those #Lagos book publishing scammers that got hold of my sales maestro dad.

Thanks to those untruths, Colin and Lucy had to endure for years whatever caused him to scream, cry, and hide; and her panic attack and stress-related breathing difficulties.

Whereas my parents have been anything but empathetic these past seven years, the Bible has. God has shown time and again that our cries are heard and God's love and mercy abound. That's how we became a free people thousands of years ago. We're challenged so we become stronger, and we should be thankful for the conflict in our lives. The strength we derive from it draws us closer to the divine.

But hatred does not. We expend too much energy hating and being hated. Could you imagine if God hated us so much?

The New Testament says, "Love is patient, love is kind. It does not envy, it does not boast, it is not proud. It does not dishonor others, it is not self-seeking, it is not easily angered, it keeps no record of wrongs. Love does not delight in evil but rejoices with the truth. It always protects, always trusts, always hopes, always perseveres."

Throughout history, our ancestors have encountered troubles, and when they turn to God, they're pulled through. King David is well-known for his ability to remain faithful, even when his enemies were numerous, powerful, and in pursuit.

Almost half of the Book of Psalms is attributed to him, and many of his writings express his pleas to God for help and mercy. Thanks to his persistent appeals and faithfulness, David was afforded abundant goodness in his lifetime and a special place in Heaven. So much of what he asked God for, I pray for too.

I'm amazed how I can express my sincere supplications for help using only words of the Psalms from David and other psalmists. So many are fitting, it's hard to pick and choose. But using snippets from